Selling: Management and Practice

Peter Allen

BSc (Econ), AMBIM, AMISM, MBIMA, MIEx

Formerly Senior Lecturer in Marketing at the Polytechnic of Wales and
Principal Lecturer in International Marketing at the
Buckinghamshire College of Higher Education

Fourth Edition

THE M & E HANDBOOK SERIES

Pitman Publishing
128 Long Acre, London WC2E 9AN

A Division of Longman Group Limited

First published as *Sales and Sales Management* 1973
Second edition 1979
Third edition published as *Selling: Management and Practice* 1989
Fourth edition 1993
Reprinted 1994 (twice)

© Macdonald & Evans Ltd 1973, 1979
© Longman Group UK Ltd 1989, 1993

British Library Cataloguing in Publication Data
A CIP catalogue record for this book can be obtained from the
British Library.

ISBN 0 7121 0854 8

Founding Editor: P W D Redmond

Typeset by ROM-Data Corporation Ltd, Falmouth, Cornwall
Printed and bound in Singapore

Contents

Preface

In an earlier book I wrote in the preface that 'Selling is a little understood and much maligned aspect of business'. That situation and attitude has now changed and selling is recognised as a fundamental and vital ingredient in the business process. It is, indeed, the powerhouse of all business. The very recognition of the importance of the area has, in turn, created the need for better selling and, in particular, better preparation for selling. Global business competition and the integration of most of western Europe into a fully fledged economic community in 1993 has accelerated this process. Companies in Britain and throughout Europe are increasingly finding themselves engaged in international competition. It is no longer feasible to recognise as competitors only those companies of the same nationality. For example, British companies making kitchen products now compete with firms from France, Germany, Japan and elsewhere as much, probably more, than they do with other British manufacturers. The same situation exists throughout Europe. This dynamic increase in competition is led by the selling process as each firm and organisation fights to obtain its share of an increasingly competitive market and, although the market itself may grow as wealth and opportunities increase, firms cannot simply rely on that expansion to offer them a share of business. Firms must sell more effectively than ever if they are to obtain a secure position in their own fields.

There are many firms in Britain who now recognise that there is no longer room for amateurism in selling — an attitude that was forced on companies in other countries, such as what was West Germany and in Japan in the years of reconstruction after 1945. That we have taken some time to catch up in realising the importance of selling is just one aspect of the problems that have beset British industry in the 1980s and 1990s. The European Community has now opened Britain's doors to internationally-minded companies skilled in selling and marketing. If this country is to win back its share of markets in a whole range of products and services, then its companies have to increase their sales and that means they must become ever more professional and skilful in selling.

This book combines the two important areas of the management and the practice of selling so that they can be recognised as an integral whole: the one cannot be divorced from the other. Both rely on theories of management, economics and sales as well as the practical aspects that are only gained from experience. Every company and every customer will be different and so practices that work for one set of circumstances may have to be modified, changed or revised for another. The salesperson, the sales manager or sales director must have a flexibility of mind and attitude that is rarely called for in other parts of business. Expert sales skills and management can only be obtained by carefully applying sound principles. It is necessary for those involved in selling to have a thorough knowledge of all aspects of the sales function and the ways in which they interconnect with other marketing and business activities.

Selling: Management and Practice examines the entire sales function from the viewpoints of both the sales force and sales management. It will be a valuable source of information and, it is hoped, inspiration for people studying for business and, especially, marketing examinations; those beginning careers in selling, marketing and business generally; and those engaged in the training of company sales forces. For those with experience in business, this book will provide much information and many practical suggestions for extending existing knowledge.

Figure 17.9 was included in my earlier book, *Sales and Sales Management*, and was reproduced from *Principles of Management* by permission of South Western Publishing Co. Inc.

P Allen
September 1992

List of illustrations

1

The selling environment

Introduction

1. What selling is and does

Selling is at the cutting edge of any firm's business operations. It is that part of the company, however big or small, that meets the firm's customers, from whom the business is derived. It doesn't matter how good the firm's technology, its manufacturing ability, its financial structure or its human relations are, it is the quality of the selling activity that determines whether the firm will survive or not.

The people who perform the selling activity meet customers or work with customer information to understand and interpret the material they receive. How the firm reacts to that data and what it does with it is the subject of this book.

2. The firm's environment

It is usual to regard the firm as an assortment of facts, figures and persons going about its tasks on a day to basis. In reality the firm is more analogous to a living organism. The firm, in its own environment, could be described as an *ecosystem* — a term borrowed from the study of ecology, which is concerned with the study of living organisms and their relationships with their surroundings.

In an earlier book, *Marketing Techniques for Analysis and Control*, I suggested that, 'An organism, to survive, has to be capable of adaptation — a process of change by which it modifies itself to a form better suited to the evolving environment'. We can liken firms to organisms inasmuch as they, too, evolve to suit the changing business environment.

3. What is the nature of the selling environment?

Firms must always be capable of modifying their behaviour in response to their environment, in much the same way as animals or other living organisms adapt to theirs. Take, as an example, the species of moth that, in the heavily industrialised regions of its range, has adapted to a melanistic, or, dark form. This adaptation helps it to survive in a habitat where the trees on which it lives have darkened as a result of industrial pollution. A pale-coloured moth is easily seen against a dark background and so light moths are soon eaten by predators. In rural, cleaner, habitats the reverse is true. How is this example paralleled in industry, though? Simply, firms that don't adapt to changing conditions are also 'eaten up' by predators. Small grocery shops in town centres were put out of business in the 1960s and 1970s by the growth of supermarkets, and these, in turn, have been threatened by out-of-town, one stop shopping centres. In the more stringent times of the early 1990s, high unemployment and rising fuel costs are starting to affect the out-of-town shopping centres. Those small stores that have managed to survive, have had to modify their operations (behaviour) to survive. The grocers become specialised delicatessens, for instance. Small decorators' shops too, have been decimated by the rapid growth of huge DIY superstores, but, the serious decline in house sales in the 1990s has, in turn, placed them under threat because the demand for decorators' materials and furnishings has declined as well.

A firm is a living organism that has evolved from lower and generally more simple forms of life that have themselves been successful in the past. It is a continual process of struggle that Charles Darwin described as the survival of the fittest. When the Chancellor of the Exchequer told us in 1991 that, as a result of the recession, the firms that survive will be 'leaner and fitter', he was applying Darwinism to the nth degree.

Consider firms that have changed over long periods of time. Durant, wagon makers to the Old West, became General Motors; Boulton-Paul, aircraft manufacturers, became window and door manufacturers; but what happened to BSA motor cycles or the manufacturers of motor cycle sidecars?

4.   Environmental factors and their relationship to change

As long as the institutions and forces in the business environment remain relatively stable, the system will survive from year to year without major change. However, the rapid changes in technology and politics in the last half-century especially, have rocked that stability. Generally one of three conditions exists:

(a) *Stable environment.* This is one in which the major influences — economic, technological, legal and culture — remain stable over long periods. For example, Britain in the nineteenth century.

(b) *Slowly evolving environment.* This is one in which gradual and recognisable changes take place. The individual firm survives to the extent that it can predict such change and has the time to adapt in preparation for it. The technological and economic changes of the 1950s and 1960s in Britain evolved slowly and so most firms had time to adapt. Nevertheless many industries still did not adapt, trying to retain the status quo.

(c) *Turbulent environment.* This is one in which major and unpredictable changes occur. The war in the Middle East in 1973 had a catastrophic impact on Western economies because of the escalation in energy costs, and indeed, many industries have never recovered from the effects of this.

Although the changes resulting from the 1973 'Oil War' were very damaging to many industries, other industries and firms have arisen as a result. Extracting oil from the North Sea only became viable when oil prices in the Middle East escalated, and whole industries based on energy conservation — from double-glazing to wind-generated electricity stations — have developed in the wake of a realisation that energy sources are finite and will be increasingly expensive. Even the Green movement has arisen from this realisation and has spawned a new generation of environmentally friendly consumer products.

From these examples it can be seen that changes in the ecosystem are not all bad, and that business can benefit from these changes provided management perceives the change and is able to adapt.

5. Environmental factors

Management science has a significant contribution to make in aiding the firm's survival in such a turbulent environment. Firms have an advantage over organisms in the natural world in that they are able to investigate their environment, any likely changes that might occur and predict, to a certain extent, what modifications are necessary.

Businesses exist in order to fulfil the needs of the environmental niche in which they operate at a particular *time* and *place*. They can no longer be static enterprises. For example, a West Midlands firm has been making wire rope for generations. When interviewed, the Managing Director declared that the grandfathers of many of his present employees had worked there and that, if they were to return today, they would not see much change. He went on to say, though, that of course their traditional market upon which they relied, coal mining, was in drastic decline and that they would have to search elsewhere for new markets. Given the apparent traditions and complacency one wonders how well equipped that firm is to change, and why, in 1992, eight years after the prolonged coal strike of 1984 and the subsequent decline in mining, they are only now recognising that they *may* have to look for new markets.

Such examples show us that, without a doubt, firms in the tough, competitive conditions of the 1990s must be dynamic, resembling living organisms in their technique for survival, which is to react to their environment, and the sooner the need for change is perceived the more likely the firm is to be able to adapt successfully.

The early 1990s has been a time of recession for Britain and most Western countries and there are many causes of it. However, how much of the recession is the result of the so-called 'peace dividend'? As far back as the mid 1970s, economists were predicting that if the United States disengaged from the war in Vietnam, it would create mass-unemployment. The sudden collapse of the Warsaw Pact and the removal of the hitherto perceived threat of conflict has brought about major cuts in arms production, throwing thousands out of work. There is a call for the defence industry to adapt to 'peaceful' conditions and produce consumer goods instead, but how can that be done in the short term? In 1945, military equipment was still, by today's standards, relatively simple — aircraft were still largely made of wood and/or sheet aluminium. A firm like Boulton-Paul, mentioned earlier, could change to woodworking-based industries, or Saunders Roe to making road tankers, but a company making high-technology radar and missile electronics can't change that quickly. What is it to do? Use its electronics skills to make televisions, microwave ovens or home videos? The markets for such products are already saturated. So, in today's environment, there is a need to identify change much earlier because, for many firms, their specialisms cannot be adapted in the short term.

What is needed is a rapid reaction to the stimuli that signify the need for change. The stimuli, which we term 'environmental factors', include:

(a) changes in technology;
(b) changes in market conditions;
(c) changes in legal requirements or restrictions;
(d) changes in competition;
(e) changes in economic influences;
(f) changes in the political environment; and
(g) changes in the culture patterns.

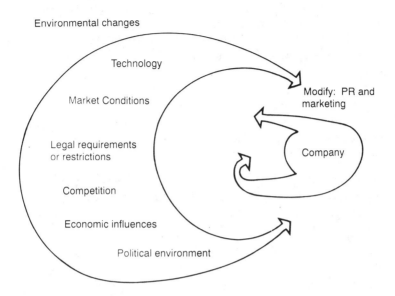

Environmental changes

Figure 1.1 *The environment and the factors of change*

As we have seen, if it is to survive, a firm must respond to any adverse or favourable changes in the environment as soon as possible. Let us look at a few examples of such changes.

European Community legislation increasingly affects business throughout Europe. The imposition of a ban on tobacco advertising will be a legal change that will adversely affect tobacco sales and, as a side-effect, maybe those sporting events sponsored by tobacco firms. Doesn't this just open up opportunities for tobacco companies and to other sponsors though? Earlier restrictions on tobacco advertising show that it does. Tobacco giants moved into supermarket operations and one firm branched into potato crisps. The result was a growth in that market from around £11m in the early 1970s to around £400m by the early 1990s.

EC legislation and the Single Market that began in 1993 offer both threats and opportunities for firms that recognise the need for change and can adapt.

We have looked at defence and tobacco industry changes, but there are, of course, many others. Changes in technology occur constantly. The development of the microchip has fundamentally altered many products, while plastic has long taken the place of metal for a wide range of goods. Better communications and satellite TV have created a smaller world as communications are almost immediate, with huge implications for exporters.

All these *environmental changes* have altered the conditions under which firms operate, for better or worse. What can a firm do about them?

6.   The company's response to change

Figure 1.1 shows the environmental factors as they impose change on a company. If it is to survive, the company must respond in one of two ways — possibly both:

(a) it will modify its own environment by altering its communications, sales force, advertising, public relations and other marketing activities; or

(b) it will make its own adaptations, undertaken as a reaction to an identifiable need for change.

Between the stimuli and the reaction will be the decision process, which will have determined the nature of the response.

The initial response to change will be a reconstruction of the organisation's structure so that it is able to deal with the new situation. As will be seen in Chapter 18, most organisation is a process of *reorganisation* in response to changing needs. The organisation's sales manager has a particular responsibility to ensure that the sales function is suitable to the task.

It is the interplay between the environmental factors (including the competition) and the company's response that creates the 'market'.

7.   The marketing concept

The marketing concept is an approach to business that sees the customer as the most important element to its entire operation. This concept is a major step forward for many companies that, in the past have been product-, or production-orientated, that is, seeing the *product* as being the most important factor in its business. Major companies, such as the American chemicals giant, Dupont, now train everybody in the organisation, (in their case something like 17 000 employees), to see the customer as paramount.

A simple way to express this change in emphasis is to say that:

(a) in production-orientated firms, profit is seen as a product of sales volume, whereas;

(b) in companies that have adopted the marketing concept, profit is seen as emanating from customer satisfaction.

A company that adopts the marketing concept *integrates* all its operations with the aim of maximising customer satisfaction, and this clearly has great implications for sales management and the sales force. This is because, instead of having to persuade customers to buy what the company makes even if they do not entirely match what the customer *needs*, in a truly marketing-based company, the sales force should be able to provide what the customer *wants* to ensure customer satisfaction and, hence, repeat business. This theme is developed further at 17:**33**.

8. The market

'Market' is an all-embracing term for the assortment of buyers and competitors for particular products who are in close enough contact with one another to ensure that the same general price level will tend to operate in all sections for similar products. To this we could also add the various market forces operating in the environment that affect market conditions. Markets may be categorised in different ways, including:

(a) by geography, such as the French market; or
(b) by product, e.g. the tyre market.

In whatever way a market is defined, however, it must be measurable — that is, have parameters that define it. This is vital for sales management because effective management requires objectives, and these, in turn, must be measurable. For example, a company operating in the highly competitive and volatile computer software market must have as precise an estimate as possible of the size of the market, both currently and in the short-term future, say five years, if it is to successfully develop new products and obtain the maximum market share of that market in the most cost-effective way. It would be possible to define the extent of the market for a particular segment of it, such as, home computers/word processors, by expressing it in measurable terms. The figures might be:

Total UK market	250 000 per year
Consisting of:	
market for new computers	45 000
replacement market	32 000
imported computers	65 000
Total	392 000
Less exports	20 000

These raw figures would need to be considered in the light of the compatability of its own software and perhaps examine particular segments, such as the small business market, the home study market, the school/college market, the games market. It is these kinds of calculations and considerations that enable management to plan for production and for sales management, in particular, to plan for the right level of market penetration and share, making forecasts to answer the questions:

(a) How many software packages can we sell each year?

(b) How many should we manufacture each year?

(c) On the basis of these figures, what will they cost to produce?

(d) On these figures, what is the economical price at which we can sell, and how will that compare with the prices of competitors' products?

(e) If the price comparison is unfavourable, what sales strategy should we pursue to make our product more attractive to consumers than the rival products?

9.   Creating markets

Any sales plan has to be based on a realistic assessment of whether a worthwhile market exists for a product. If a firm develops or invents a product, will it be able to sell it? The answer to this question often lies in the nature of the market itself. The nature of the sales environment is characterised by the *heterogeneous market*.

10. Heterogeneous markets

A heterogeneous market is one in which there is a precise match between differentiated segments of demand and differentiated units of supply. Such markets rarely exist, however, except in exceptional circumstances.

One such circumstance occurred in Britain between approximately 1939 and 1953, when rationing was imposed on a variety of goods. Cheese was one such product. Each person was allocated a certain amount of cheese that could only be bought in exchange for money accompanied by a ration coupon; when the coupons were used up, no more cheese could be bought. This system meant that the government's Ministry of Food could estimate how much cheese was available and, knowing the size of the population, could calculate how much could be allocated to each person. In other words, there was a heterogeneous market in which supply and demand were equal.

The important point for sales management, and marketing in general, however, is that, under those conditions, there is virtually no possibility of competition between different makes of cheese or any other rationed product. There is no point in giving a product, such as cheese, a recognisable *brand* name that people could ask for, because consumers could only get a predetermined quantity anyway, — demand being controlled by rationing. Therefore, there could not be competition between suppliers.

In today's markets, firms are free to *create* demand for their products and they do so by *differentiating* them from those of competitors. Although the population as a whole may demand a type of item, individual firms can create differences for their products that will persuade consumers to ask for their brand in preference to another. This is seen in the sales of many variations of a product, e.g. cheese or butter. By developing a brand image to give their product a separate and recognisable identity, firms can advertise and promote it on the basis that it is unique. When someone buys a brand of butter, say Lurpak or Anchor, they do so in the belief that they are buying something different to other butters and which they prefer. Such brand identification is essential to building a market for a product, whether it is butter, cheese, motor tyres or display systems.

11. The search for market homogeneities

In promoting a company's products, sales management seeks partial homogeneities with the wider market. It works like this: a company, selling any product, aims to find partial homogeneities among customers who have enough characteristics in common to form groups. Larger segments of the market may be formed around these groups by the influence of marketing and sales communications. This phenomenon is illustrated in Figure 1.2.

(a) homogeneity in teenage market for records:
    (i) first segment;
    (ii) extension of segment — younger;
    (iii) extension of segment — older;
(b) homogeneity in same teenage market:
    (i) segment 1 — male teenage market, e.g. football wear;
    (ii) segment 2 — young married female market, e.g. baby wear.

In each case we are dealing with a group of people that divide into several different markets. Young people buy fast foods, clothes, records and cars, watch television and have young children. They don't all buy the same products though and, in a sense, each company endeavouring to sell to these people 'borrows' them for particular products. A manufacturer of proprietary baby medicines sells to much

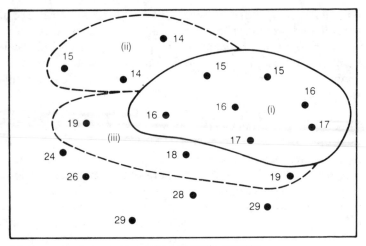

(a) Homogeneity in young people's market for records:
   (i) first segment
   (ii) extension of segment – younger;
   (iii) extension of segment – older.

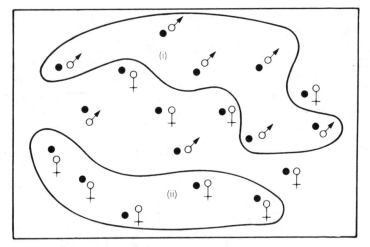

(b) Homogeneity in same young people's market:
   (i) Segment 1 – male teenage market, i.e. football wear;
   (ii) Segment 2 – young married female market,
      i.e. baby goods.

Figure 1.2 *Homogeneity in the young people's market*

the same people as a manufacturer of furniture. They may not all be selling to them at the same time and people may fit into different groups for different products. For example, a family may buy modern furniture but prefer traditional cough remedies. The same phenomenon also occurs in industry where, e.g. a steel works may buy cars, paint, stationery, office cleaning services and a vast range of other products. The seller aims to identify and select particular groups to buy his or her products. These identifiable groups are termed *market segments*.

12. Discrepancies in markets — opportunities for selling

Markets that are defined as heterogeneous must also be regarded as differing from each other. At any time consumers may demand products that are not available. Equally, suppliers may endeavour to sell goods for which no demand exists.

Example————————————————————————————————

My own company patented an entirely new form of mobile exhibition stand, called *Trailerbition*, which unfolded from a small trailer that could be towed behind any car. It could be put into an exhibition hall and unfolded to give an instant exhibition stand 4.5 metres long by 1.5 metres wide. There was no comparable product on the market and, therefore, no demand for the product. We had to *create* a demand by means of advertising, press releases and personal selling. By hiring out the stand to firms that were interested, but initially not attracted enough to buy one, we were able to get the product into exhibitions and used by a number of well-known companies. In due course, those firms became convinced enough of the benefits of the product to buy their own Trailerbitions and, after some months, a more general demand was created as other firms saw the stand.

————————————————————————————————

Any new product is in the 'no existing demand' category and an important aspect of selling and promotion is to bring together the two sides of the discrepant market.

In such discrepant markets, it is possible for the discrepancy to be removed by one of two forms of innovation:

(a) if customers demand a product not currently available, it can be provided by innovation in product — a great deal of new computer software is in this category;
(b) if a new product is created for which no market exists, demand can be created by innovation in marketing and selling, especially promotional activities.

Market imperfections growing from discrepancy create a dynamic and radical situation arising from demanded products without supply and current products without demand. This characteristic of market behaviour takes four forms:

(a) creativity in product innovation;
(b) creativity in sales innovation;
(c) its dynamic impact on the business environment; and
(d) its influence on selling and marketing in general, which stimulates changes in functional behaviour.

13. The search for differential advantage

The search for differential advantage may be seen as the selection of strategies to achieve a desired market position. For example, many products that at first glance are very similar can be distinguished by promotional claims, such as, 'with fluoride', 'with ignition control additive', 'with polyunsaturates' etc. All these differences are on the marketing/selling side of the equation. This search for promotional/brand image/differential advantage stemmed from the realisation that heterogeneity existed in demand as well as supply and was not just a customer response to promotional activities by suppliers. In other words, there is a major advantage to be gained from identifying

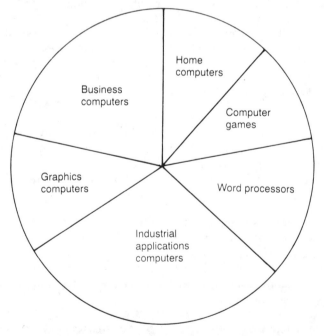

Figure 1.3 *Segments in the computer market*

special characteristics required by customers and stating that the product satisfies them.

14. Market segmentation

Market segmentation derives from concentrating differential advantage on the demand side. This is possible because markets are made up of identifiable segments that each demand different characteristics of the product. For example, the market for computers may be divided into several segments, as shown in Figure 1.3.

Market segmentation involves dividing the whole, heterogeneous market into smaller, homogeneous segments in order to be able to identify opportunities and needs and match them with precisely created products. For example, look at the following simplified segments of the industrial surface coatings market:

	Local authorities	Steel works	Warehousing
Waterproof external coatings	×		×
Acid resistant coatings		×	
Floor coatings	×		×
(a) medium durability			
(b) long-term durability		×	

Identification of groups of individuals with common characteristics does not necessarily make a market segment. It is only when these characteristics relate to their behaviour as buyers and consumers that a segment exists. For example, a group of schoolchildren may have many characteristics in common — age, outlook, appearance, preference in clothing or fast foods — but none of these may be relevant to the publisher of school textbooks.

True market segmentation exists when a product relates strongly to certain customers, but not to others. For example, the exhibition equipment can be used by many companies in almost all types of industry, but segmentation only exists when groups of companies have a common interest in exhibiting; many companies don't exhibit.

15. Sales and segmentation

The analysis of market segments is fundamental to sales strategy. All managers should use the concept of segmentation when making sales plans with the aims of achieving optimum profits and minimum costs. Sound segmentation makes it easier to target customers, both actual and potential. There are two main concepts involved:

(a) the selection of sales objectives requires an ability to measure opportunities in different segments effectively;
(b) the ability to assess the needs of different segments and apply the information to the selection of appropriate marketing-mix decisions (these are explained in Chapter 3).

Segmenting markets begins with identifying customers' needs and interests and then subdividing a market into homogeneous sub-sets of customers that can be reached with a specific marketing mix. In intensely competitive markets, individual manufacturers may achieve their sales objectives by choosing a segment of the total market the needs of which are not entirely satisfied by the mass suppliers and concentrating on that. For example, the paint market is dominated by industrial giants like ICI, although there are around 3000 other companies in Britain producing paint. Many of these companies are selling to segments either too technically specialised for the giants or too small, such as a local market.

16. Sales policies and objectives
Market segmentation and the way a company sees itself in a particular market has a major impact on its sales policies. Market segmentation will influence:

(a) the company's decision about what products to make;
(b) the prices the company will charge for its products;
(c) decisions on how the company distributes its products; and
(d) determine the sales organisation structure needed to sell the products.

All these factors come together in a sales policy that must match the way the company perceives its market position. For example, a company manufacturing electrical switches might analyse its market and decide to tackle particular segments as illustrated in Figure 1.4.

Market segmentation and its effect on a sales organisation

17. Some examples of market segmentation
In the above example, the manufacturer may well employ different salespeople to sell to each major outlet and may also introduce the

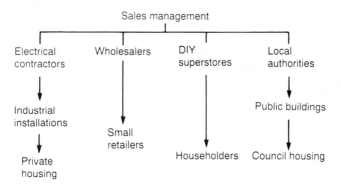

Figure 1.4 *Sales management*

products to the users lower down the channel of distribution. Other manufacturers may actually alter the product for different sectors of the market. Here are some examples:

(a) clothing manufacturers make goods for:
    (i) different levels of the trade in price terms;
   (ii) different age groups;
  (iii) seasons;
  (iv) foreign markets;
(b) tyre manufacturers produce goods for:
    (i) earth-moving equipment;
   (ii) lorries;
  (iii) family cars;
  (iv) fleet cars.

18. Benefits of market segmentation

Sales management will only undertake segmentation policies if it can be shown that the company will benefit. The company may gain by being able to:

(a) identify sales opportunities more quickly and, by a process of comparison and evaluation, select those policies that will benefit it for the longest period;
(b) plan more effectively by concentrating its research, planning and sales communications in limited segments, thereby allocating its resources more effectively;
(c) direct its promotional activities more accurately at the characteristics of each segment;
(d) undertake longer term product and sales planning by concentrat-

ing on product/market segments of which it has greater experience; and

(e) with a continual market segmentation policy, measure and monitor current competition activity as a gauge for its own activities.

In carrying out a policy of market segmentation, sales management has to be aware of its limitations and the difficulties that may be encountered. The problem is to determine which buyers' characteristics are likely to create the correct segmentation within a particular market. In selecting these characteristics, three criteria must be applied:

(a) *measurability*: the degree to which the company is able to collect information of a measurable nature;

(b) *accessibility*: the degree to which a company can apply its sales effort to a selected segment — how far the existing sales communications offer access to the segment;

(c) *substantiality*: whether or not the selected segment is large or profitable enough to merit consideration as a separate segment (as a guide, the segment should be the smallest unit for which justification can be made for a separate sales programme).

19. Product life cycles

One of the most important and fundamental concepts in sales management and marketing is that of the *product life cycle*. This is an historical record of the life of a product, showing the stage in its life the product has reached at a particular time. By identifying the stage that a product is in or may be heading towards, companies can formulate better marketing plans.

All products have 'lives' inasmuch as they are created, sell with varying profitability over a certain period of time and then become obsolete and are replaced or simply no longer produced. A product's sales position and profitability can be expected to change over time and so, at each successive stage in the product's cycle, sales management will need to adopt different tactics. The product life cycle concept seeks to explain and illustrate this process.

Figure 1.5 is a simplified product life cycle, showing two main features. However, before examining these, it is important to bear in mind that this is only a graphic presentation of a life cycle and its parameters are those of the page. Such a diagram inevitably portrays a cycle with equi-distant columns that represent different stages in the cycle and suggest that the time periods covered by them are the same. In reality, however, the width of the columns will vary enormously

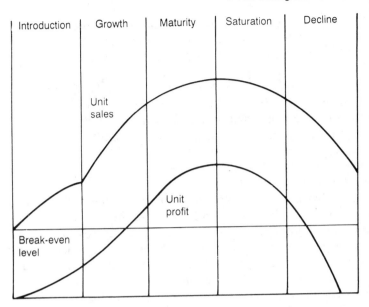

Figure 1.5 *Simplified product life cycle*

depending on the type of product. For example, a pop record may have a total life of only a few weeks, while many consumer products last years. Guinness, e.g. has been sold for 200 years and if it is now in the maturity stage the column would be extremely wide! Other products, such as the Sinclair C5 electric vehicle lasted only months and *never* reached a 'maturity' stage.

20. The curves on the product life cycle graph
The two main features of the product life cycle are:

(a) the unit sales curve; and,
(b) the unit profit curve.

The unit sales curve of a consumer product typically jumps on introduction, as a response to heavy advertising and promotion as customers buy the product experimentally. This is generally followed by a levelling off while it is evaluated — the length of this period depending on the use to which the product is put. Once initial purchases have been evaluated, the unit sales curve rises steadily through the growth phase to the maturity phase, when the product is widely accepted, and so on to saturation level. By this time a new product will have attracted competition and, from this point, all additional sales have to be won by increasing the sales effort; it is a phase when selling pressures become important. Eventually, the product's sales decline as later versions come on to the market or competition is too strong.

In retrospect, most firms know what happened to their products from launch to withdrawal. They can compile this information from the records of unit sales. Unfortunately, unit sales are not the complete story as it is *unit profit* that is the important guide, although this is not always recorded accurately. It is this figure that sales management has to monitor, though, to ensure an effective marketing strategy and to produce effective profits.

At launch, the product is costed accurately on the basis of production costs plus selling costs. Initially these are not likely to vary significantly, but, when the product is proving successful, competitors enter the market. For example, Pot Noodle was a new product concept (so-called kettle cooking) when it was introduced and was so successful that quickly other versions were launched by competitors. Such competitive 'copy-cat' products are sometimes, though not always, cheaper. With a competitor in the field, the original firm has to respond, using various combinations of the marketing mix (*see* 3) in order to maintain its market position. It can create more advertising, run special sales promotions, improve deliveries, make more frequent sales calls and so on. The extra expenditures are costs that are not all accurately attributable to the product and the result is that, long before unit sales are noticeably falling, unit profit has already fallen. The falls and rises of these selling costs are shown against falling production costs in Figure 1.6.

Product life cycles illustrate the unpredictability of sales strategies, no matter how well conceived they were at the outset. For example, when Unilever introduced *Radion* washing powder, its strategy was to penetrate a market dominated by *Daz*. Because *Radion* would have, initially at least, a small share of the biological washing powder market in which *Daz* was the market leader, Unilever attempted to *segment* the market by introducing a powder aimed at people it believed were concerned with residual odours in their finished wash.

In theory, that should have enabled Unilever to gain a market lead in that segment and their product would grow rapidly in sales while the competition (Proctor & Gamble, the manufacturers of *Daz*) took time to develop their own versions. In practice, Proctor & Gamble short-circuited the process by quickly creating an advertising campaign that derided the idea that clothes still smelt after washing, using

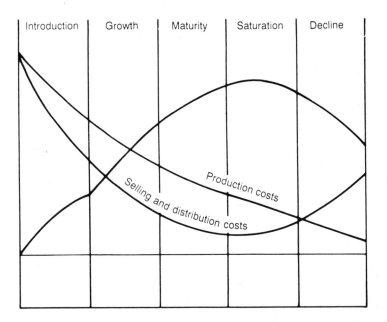

Figure 1.6 *Changing costs through the life cycle*

the slogan *'Odours? No, I use DAZ.'*

In an unexpected situation of rapid retaliatory competition such as this, the product's life cycle would show up as a slowing down of growth in unit sales and a failure of growth in unit profit because of the need to counter the competitor's advertising campaign with an enhanced one of its own.

21. Plotting the sales curve

The product life cycle, then, presents an historical picture of what happened in the product's 'lifetime', so how can this be used as a current, ongoing aid to management decision making?

Every sales manager has a chart on which the progress of sales is plotted and this can be used as a guide to the stage of development each product is currently in, which is vital to successful sales strategy. Of course, the current sales chart doesn't have lines indicating the stages through which the product will pass, but then, as was said in 1:19, these will vary greatly for each product. An essential management skill is being able to interpret sales results *and draw in the stages as they occur*. Deciding where each stage begins and ends is, however, rather arbitrary. Usually the stages are based on where the rate of sales

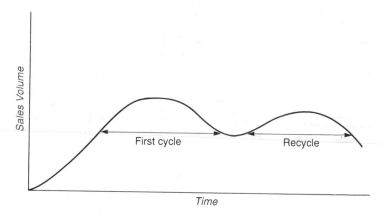

Figure 1.7 *The cycle–recycle pattern*

growth or decline becomes pronounced. Researchers Polli and Cook proposed that an operational measure be based on a normal distribution of percentage changes in real sales from year to year.

Not all products produce the typical S-shaped product life cycle chart. Some products show a rapid growth from the very beginning, thus skipping the slow sales start of the introduction stage. Other products, instead of going through a rapid growth stage, go directly from introduction to maturity. Some products move from maturity to a second period of rapid growth. Another researcher, Cox, studied the product life cycles of 754 ethical drug products and found that they divided into 6 different patterns. The most typical form was the cycle–recycle pattern (*see* Figure 1.7).

Cox explained that the second 'hump' in sales was being caused by the traditional promotional push in the decline stage. It is also possible to continually regenerate sales growth by discovering some new characteristics that can be exploited. The cleaning powder Flash, for example, started its life as a washing powder and was unsuccessful; it was later successfully relaunched with a changed formulation as a floor cleaner. Products may, therefore, be recycled on the basis of new usages, or new markets. For example, a range of golfers' trousers was produced with gimmicks such as special pockets to hold golf balls, a 'cartridge' belt to hold tees etc. When the first enthusiasm had died down, the product was re-launched *without* the gimmicks in overseas markets as lightweight, showerproof trousers and this strategy was very successful.

Plotting the product's position in its life cycle is a matter of noting significant percentage changes in the rate of sales, usually unit sales. For example, if a new product climbs slowly but steadily on introduction and then takes off, producing significant and sustained growth, say 5 per cent more than previous sales, then it may be judged to have entered the growth stage. Alert sales managers would then be ready to adjust the marketing mix accordingly (*see* 3: **2**). When sales begin to slow down as the market matures and new customers are harder to find, then there will, again, be a significant change in sales, perhaps a decline in growth to a steady 2–3 per cent rise. At saturation there will be many competitors in the field and this is when most segmentation takes place; this will probably be marked by a neutralisation of growth, say a steady 2 per cent rise or fall. When the product becomes old-fashioned, outdated or superseded by a newer product, sales will follow a sustained decline, marked by falling sales of, perhaps, a steady 5 per cent fall.

By plotting these changes, sales management is aware of the development of the product and able to respond with the appropriate strategy, even to the point of preparing for a product's successor.

Studies by Buzzell of grocery food products and Polli and Cook of various consumer non-durables showed the product life cycle concept to hold up well for many product categories. Those planning to use this concept, however, must investigate the extent to which it holds up for the products in *their* industry. There needs to be a normal sequence of stages and that these have an average duration. Cox's research findings, mentioned above, indicated that most ethical drugs followed the normal product life cycle, with an introductory stage of 1 month, a growth stage of 6 months, a maturity stage of 15 months and a decline stage that was generally greater than total of the previous 3 stages — mainly because of the reluctance of manufacturers to drop drugs from the product mix too soon.

22. The product life cycle and cost recovery

There is ample evidence that product life cycles generally have been shortening. This has been due to increasing competition and a consumer readiness to buy new products, hastening the saturation stage. However, a serious recession, such as that of 1991–2, will have a profound effect on consumer spending behaviour as money becomes tight and this, in turn, will be reflected in industrial buying and investment. Paradoxically, both high consumer spending power *and* a serious recession both mean that products make profits for shorter periods and this has serious implications for the profitability of that particular product as well as for the company as a whole.

23. Product life cycles and sales management

Product life cycles are important to marketing strategy and segmentation policy generally because, as the phases of the cycle change,
so the product becomes suited to a different segment of the market
and to differing strategies:

(a) *Introduction*. An essential management skill is to be able to develop the market and product *together*. A new product launched on
an unprepared market will take a long time to succeed; equally, a
prepared market for which the product is not readily available represents a waste of resources and may be harmful to future plans. Early
products often perform poorly and are replaced as better quality items
take over (often those of competitors that have learned from the
originator's experience, e.g. Polaroid v. Kodak or, on a much wider
scale, the philosophy of many Japanese companies in the 1960s, which
was to copy and develop Western products as an instant way of
acquiring technology).

(b) *Growth*. Management must aim for growth, which will lower
production costs. If these savings can be passed on to the customer in
lower prices it will encourage further buying and strengthen the
company against competition. The strategy for achieving volume in
sales will include advertising consumer goods and intensive personal
selling of industrial goods.

(c) *Maturity*. Here, the first signs of segmentation often appear as
competition becomes stronger and some companies attempt to pull
in the price-sensitive segments of the market by lowering prices. The
original company will ensure that customers recognise its products
and understand their benefits by implementing strategies of aggressive, informative advertising to consumers and vigorous selling to
the industry.

(d) *Saturation*. When there are many suppliers in the market, it becomes saturated. Management will try to increase product differentiation in an attempt to win a share of a segment that is possibly
undersatisfied by existing suppliers. Often this leads to gimmicks, e.g.
the supply of industrial adhesives in useful buckets or giveaway
offers in sales promotions to consumers — often seen in petrol sales.

(e) *Decline*. Demand eventually falls away, there are diminishing returns for promotional efforts and aggregate competition. Cost pressures
rise steeply and the company seeks ways to save. It is the phase of price
wars when quality drops and worn out equipment is not replaced.

Each phase of the product life cycle presents sales management
with a number of choices for segmentation and strategy. The basic

need is to get the most out of the existing market, which may mean encouraging increasing use of the product by existing customers or developing entirely new markets, perhaps in other countries.

Progress test 1

1. Can you define what is meant by the term *ecosystem*? (**2**)

2. List seven factors that make up the business environment. (**5**)

3. Market imperfection arises from discrepancies in supply and demand. What are the four forms which this market characteristic takes? (**12**)

4. What are the five benefits offered by market segmentation? (**18**)

2

Customer creation

Identifying the customer

1. Who is the customer?

A salesperson or sales manager frequently finds it difficult to identify the real customer. This is not as strange as it might at first appear. Consider the following situations:

(a) a mother buys shoes for her young son;
(b) the works buyer places an order for a machine 'ool at the request of the works manager;
(c) a local-authority purchasing department orders school-books;
(d) one government department orders exhibition equipment for another.

In each of these cases the person placing the order is not the customer, if we accept that the customer is the person who actually *wants* or *uses* the product. On the other hand, it is also true that many people who *want* a product may not be able to pay for it.

2. What is meant by 'customer'?

There are various types of customers, from individual people buying products for personal use in shops, to groups of people involved in industrial purchasing decisions. Although companies selling products normally have actual, existing customers in mind, it is equally important that they should consider future or potential customers for their products. In general terms, 'customers' are the individuals or groups the firm identifies as existing or potential purchasers of its products or services.

There are various types of customers:

(a) *Buyers*. This term is normally used in the organisational or industrial context. For example, factories have buyers and so do department stores and supermarkets (they may also be termed 'purchasing officer'). In some organisations there may be several people involved in an industrial buying decision, forming a decision-making unit (DMU).
(b) *Consumers*. These are usually private individuals who buy for

their own satisfaction. They may literally be consumers, e.g. of food and drink, or they may 'consume' in the sense that they buy more durable products for use over a long period.

(c) *End users*. This term generally means organisations or people in organisations buying products in a finished form for use in their own operation, such as tools, computers, trucks etc., rather than for incorporation into finished products. For example, a manufacturer of motor car equipment may buy lamps to incorporate into its own products but is an end user of computer printer ribbons.

3. Purchase influences

As mentioned above, many purchases are made at the request of other people, who are termed purchase influencers. This is often seen in relation to products for children. For example, in 1988 Clarks advertised their shoes using a little girl in a 'fairy story' situation, which was no doubt meant to persuade other children to want Clarks' shoes because of the fairy-story implication. Many breakfast cereals and foodstuffs are specifically aimed at children in the hope that they will persuade, or *influence* their mothers to buy them. In the organisational situation, however, the purchase influencer can be a powerful ally in selling a product to a buyer.

4. Decision-making units (DMUs)

A DMU is usually a team of decision makers involved in an industrial purchase. Such a unit may, in fact, consist of only one person if the product is routine or low-value, such as office supplies. However, an expensive, one-off purchase may well involve a number of people. For example, the purchase of an expensive, computer-controlled machine tool costing many thousands of pounds may involve the works engineer, works manager, financial expert and even representatives from the board of directors. It is important for sales management to discover at the outset just who is involved in such major purchases.

5. Sales myopia

The *real* customer may well be hidden behind a fog of intervening stages of distribution. For example, the sales manager of a menswear manufacturer believes the other customers to be the buyers on the staff of specialist shops, department stores or mail-order catalogues, but may not readily identify as a customer, say, the woman in the family who influences her husband's choice. It was this myopia, or, short sightedness, that led to the demise of many established menswear firms when they failed to recognise the move away from formal suits towards more casual wear.

In a similar way, a company making electric motors regards its customers as being firms that buy electric motors to power the domestic appliances and electrical tools they manufacture. It may not occur to the firm that its real customers are the buyers of the domestic appliances and the users of the power tools, nor that the market may be influenced by the level of house purchases or the number of young people getting married and setting up a home. In determining sales potential, the firm should be studying the needs of its ultimate consumers, not solely the requirements of a certain manufacturer who is an intermediary. When faced with a choice of developing sales to a company making tools or to one making appliances, it should be looking at the economic prospects of both consumer and construction markets.

Table 2.1 is an example of market forecasting by identifying the end use, in this case for china clay, which is used as a finish for

Table 2.1 *Forecast consumption of coated printing papers in 1974 by end use*

End use	1968 (000 tonnes)	1974 (000 tonnes)	% Increase 1968–74	Per annum
Publishing				
Trade and technical journals	66	88	33.3	5.0
Consumer magazines	33	38	18.2	3.0
Part publications	8	23	187.5	19.0
Books and directories	20	27	35.0	5.0
Total	127	176	39.4	5.7
Advertising				
Mail-order catalogues	23	33	43.5	6.5
Direct mail and trade catalogues	20	35	75.0	10.0
Holiday and travel literature	14	22	57.1	7.5
Other advertising literature	55	73	32.7	5.0
Total	112	163	45.5	6.5
Labels and wrappers	40	54	35.0	5.0
All other users	18	26	44.4	6.0
Total	297	419	41.4	5.9

(*Source: The United Kingdom Market for Coated Paper, 1968–74, English China Clays Sales Company Limited*).

high-quality paper. In this example, English China Clays analysed the end users of its products, the publishers of holiday brochures and mail-order catalogues, firms that produced glossy advertising materials, not the intermediaries that produced the paper, because demand is generated at the point of *consumption*, not in the channel of *distribution*. (this point is enlarged on in Chapter 3).

6. Reaching the customer

The decision as to who is the real customer, then, is a significant one. The manufacturer who identifies the ultimate consumer at the end of a complex distribution chain will have an advantage over competitors. The manufacturer of industrial chemicals that gives its salespeople a brief introduction to the product, a collection of leaflets and a bag and then sends them out to sell, is not doing anybody much good. Salespeople will waste their time in endless cold calls on the basis that 'if you make ten calls a day, someone will buy', but will be incurring excessive costs in wasted resources.

Success in selling is often generated by the ability to see or to reason beyond the immediate buyer or placer of orders. If a salesperson can identify the real buyer of industrial goods as the person with the problem, that is the engineer, supervisor, designer, then he or she is well on the way to selling the company's products successfully. Having sought and won the approval of the person with the problem, the salesperson will then have an introduction and talking point with the actual buyer.

7. Relating products to customers

Once manufacturers succeed in identifying the real customers, they are able to match product opportunities to customer expectations.

The whole marketing process begins with conglomerate raw materials of all kinds and extends to collections of finished goods in the hand of consumers, each representing a market segment. Simple deductions can be made about the types of customers for ranges of products. The customers for tights and lipsticks are mostly women, whereas razors and shaving cream are mostly used by men. In an industrial context, the buyers of paint may be found in local authorities, shipbuilding, contracting, baking and many other industries and commercial undertakings.

8. The role of the manufacturer

After discovering how products are related to customers, manufacturers should recognise that the needs and expectations of a particular market segment must be fulfilled and that they have a role to play in this process. If manufacturers undertake this role successfully and identify the needs of their customers clearly, they are then in a position to define precise objectives for selling their products.

Salespeople can be armed with the knowledge of:

(a) who their customers are;
(b) where they are to be found; and
(c) the nature of their needs.

Salespeople then have a starting point from which they can attempt to answer the questions:

(a) What can be sold?
(b) What quantities can be sold?
(c) At what prices can they be sold?
(d) Where can they be sold?
(e) How can they be sold?
(f) When can they be sold?

Manufacturers must always keep in mind the needs of their customers as social conditions and fashions are constantly changing. Many industries find themselves falling between two stools — too big to appeal to the purely local population out of loyalty and too small to have a national reputation.

An example of changing conditions may be shown by the way in which alcohol is bought. Traditionally, drink bought for home consumption was purchased at an off-licence, but in recent years the growth of supermarkets has produced a great change in customer buying behaviour. Breweries that failed to recognise this change early enough found their off-licence sales falling. In one case a brewery's market research showed that 80 per cent of purchases of alcoholic drinks were made by women who preferred the convenience and ease of buying alcohol at a supermarket with the weekly shopping. One way the brewery countered the problem was to redesign its remaining off-licences to make them self-service and more appealing to women.

9.   Profitable advertising

To be effective, advertising must attempt to reach the individual customer, both existing and potential. A knowledge of the market segments concerned and a clear objective will help in this aim, but more than just reaching a customer, advertising messages should be selective for the advertiser's products. In other words, they should make the reader or viewer want that *particular* product, not that *kind* of product. For example, if you placed an advertisement for a foreign package holiday, it will *not* have succeeded if it has raised general interest in holidays abroad but not induced the customer to buy your particular package.

So advertising, like selling, must be specific and motivate customers to relate their needs to our particular products and develop a loyalty to our brand or make. This may be based on quite trivial considerations, but such loyalty can be extremely powerful.

Example

When lecturing, I have frequently asked the audience whether they have loyalty to a particular brand of petrol. In most cases people will say that they favour one brand more than another; some always buy Shell, others BP or Esso etc. When asked *why* they favour that brand, they frequently say that their car performs better or they feel it protects the engine better. It is a trick question really because, when visiting refineries, I have often seen petrol tankers from many *different* companies filling up at a refinery belonging to a *particular* company, e.g. a BP refinery. In Spring 1988, there were questions raised in the House of Commons about the practice of petrol companies selling each other's brands of petrol while advertising and promoting the special benefits of their own brand. It was admitted that, in most cases, tankers do refill at the nearest refinery. The point is that customers develop brand loyalties and then justify them by a belief that particular brands have certain qualities not possessed by other brands. In reality, as all petrol is produced in accordance with British Standards, it shouldn't vary within a grade of petrol.

That advertising and promotion is successful in establishing brand loyalties is obvious from the above examples and tests of consumer loyalty to specific cigarette brands have produced similar results. The continuing growth in advertising expenditure also indicates the faith that manufacturers place in advertising.

10. Identifying the correct advertising medium

Precise identification of the customers of a product is essential to the avoidance of wasteful advertising. The high cost of this, however, is a growing problem, especially with so many publications appearing and promising results. The questions of 'who' and 'where' the customers are must must be answered accurately.

Example

There are many magazines claiming to reach exhibition designers and exhibitors. They will often promise advertisers a free write-up if they buy advertising space. In most cases, the magazine has an extremely limited readership and usually generates only enquiries from people wanting to sell to the advertiser — and rarely is the promised free write-up forthcoming.

11. Deciding what appeals to customers

Different types of customers may require entirely different kinds of information about the same product. The motor oil manufacturer may be required to sell its products to several types of customer:

(a) users of the product, such as industrial or fleet users;
(b) re-sellers of the products, such as distributors, retailers or garages; and
(c) ultimate consumers, the motorists, for example.

Successful salespeople will recognise differences in the needs of their customers and, by a process of product analysis, will answer two fundamental questions:

(a) What do customers want from my product?
(b) What can my product do for customers?

For example, a paint salesman might consider selling a 20 litre drum of paint used for the exterior of buildings to 3 types of customers: distributors or contractors, householders and industrial users.

12. The distributor or contractor

Distributors and contractors have different needs to those of the users of a product, because, while the latter are seeking its benefits, distributors and contractors are seeking profit and, if possible, increasing their profits over and above those they make from their current products.

This increase in profits may come from a higher profit margin per unit sold or from an increased turnover. High profit alone is not an inducement if the product is little known and stays on the distributor's shelf too long, tying up capital. Contractors are also seeking to enhance their reputation by doing a good job of work.

13. Householders

The householder is a consumer and is more likely to be motivated by durability and finish and the wish not to have to do the job again for as long as possible. Salespeople may decide that, in many instances, it is the woman of the house who is the purchase influencer, in which case she will probably be interested in:

(a) a good colour range;
(b) clean, bright and new appearance;
(c) non-flaking surface;
(d) non-toxicity;
(e) a good brand name; and
(f) the social value of a freshly painted house.

Price will be important, too, and must accord with the customer's expectation, and ability to pay, as well as offering quality within a price range.

14. Industrial users

Salespeople must understand the needs of industrial users and decide on the advantages and benefits their products offer them. The following list could be made for the drum of paint being sold:

(a) seals and waterproofs surfaces;
(b) needs only a single coat application — low labour cost;
(c) is resistant to atmospheric pollution or weathering;
(d) has durability — low recurring maintenance costs; and
(e) is non-toxic — safety factor.

At this point, no mention is made of the price per unit, although it is a good idea to relate the price to the overall cost of the work involved to show the customer that there are savings over a period of time. Industrial users are concerned with solving problems that either threaten or are already damaging the business operations. Cost is considered as an opportunity cost — the cost of *not* repainting is the possible damage that might occur by neglecting to do the work.

Industrial buyers are always seeking some benefits that they are not currently obtaining. These may be:

(a) economy of time and money;
(b) savings in labour costs;
(c) increased productivity;
(d) simplified operations;
(e) improved safety;
(f) improved value of their own products;
(g) enhanced selling power of their own products;
(h) better product performance;
(i) increased product reliability;
(j) lower maintenance and service requirements; and
(k) ways to enhance their reputations as buyers.

15. The oblique approach

Example
A manufacturer of shopfittings discovered customers by offering a survey of design problems and shop layout. The campaign produced a high response rate and salespeople were given the names of interested firms. They carried out a detailed survey of problems, made sound, practical recommendations and produced draft designs of new layouts. From the initial surveys, 20 per

cent of reports produced immediate business. A further 15 per cent produced business within 6 months.

The scheme was successful in several ways. It:

(a) introduced the supplier to many buyers;
(b) enhanced the reputation of the suppliers for technical efficiency;
(c) substantially reduced selling costs; and
(d) firmly established the supplier on the market.

The surveys and draft designs were sent to proprietors, buyers and managers, which enabled them to support their own recommendations to purchase new shop layouts.

This method of contacting customers is known as the oblique approach.

Example

A company took over the distribution of a range of surface coatings. The manufacturer did not advertise and was unknown in that area when the distributor was appointed. The problem was that, although a great potential existed among the major industrial users in the area, most of the work was placed through appointed contractors, who had agreed prices, making it virtually impossible to sell the new products. The price structure did not allow the distributor any kind of discount sufficient to induce a contractor to use the new products.

To overcome these problems, the distributor offered a consultancy service to the contractors. They undertook survey work for a particular contractor; this was generally of a hazardous nature that made most available coatings unsuitable. However, the distributor was then able to offer the contractor extra work that he could not otherwise have done. The contractor found the relationship enabled him to expand his work beyond its former range. They made a joint approach to the works involved and, between them, won extensive contracts. *Each traded on the reputation and skill of the other*.

By this unorthodox, oblique approach, which recognised that the prime needs of the works were to solve problems with minimum risk to the buyer, many sales were achieved.

Progress test 2

1. What is meant by the term 'customer'? **(2)**

2. What is the term used for a team of decision makers involved in an industrial purchase? **(4)**

3. How will knowledge of the market segments help to improve the effectiveness of advertising? **(9)**

4. 'Industrial buyers are always seeking some benefits they are not currently receiving.' See how many you can list. **(14)**

3

Achieving the Sales Objective

Investment alternatives

All industries and professions have developed their own methods, tools, systems, customs or implements which will be pertinent to their practice and will be deeply involved in their success.

Business is no exception to this rule and, within its overall framework, the sales/marketing function has developed such 'tools', or 'elements', commonly referred to as the marketing-mix variables. It is important to remember, though, that the elements are used to achieve particular ends but are not ends in themselves. Although this book is primarily about the sales function it must be realised that in modern, fully integrated business operations, no function operates in isolation.

During the last decade we have also seen the realisation by many non-business organisations — public administration, political parties, charities, health organisations, etc. — that they, too, have to 'sell' their services, or communicate their messages much more effectively, so that the use of the marketing mix elements are now applied more rigorously to their efforts as well.

Whether in business or non-profit operations managers of the selling/promotional function take decisions on how to allocate the available resources on a cost-effective basis to achieve determined strategies. Sales managers must, in directing and controlling their operations, take into account two sets of variables:

(a) *independent variables* — i.e. the factors which make up the business environment and over which the firm and its management has only marginal control, (*see* Chapter 1) and,
(b) *controllable variables* — i.e. the elements of the marketing mix.

These interrelating factors are illustrated in Figure 3.1, although here we are concerned primarily with (b).

1. **What do we include in the controlled variables — the marketing-mix elements?**
The controllable variables constitute a set of elements which management can apply to particular strategies or problems in discreet amounts according to the objectives. They are controlled variables in

terms of the degree to which they may be individually applied.

The concept of the marketing mix is usually credited to Professor Neil Borden of the Harvard Business School, although what he did was to formalise and define what many business people had been doing for a long time. Because the mix has existed a long time and in many forms, its formulation is something of a matter of choice and the number of elements varies a great deal according to the views of different experts. Some have suggested an extended list containing as many as thirty variables while another, J. E. McCarthy, has suggested a convenient way of referring to them as the '4 P's'

- product
- price
- promotion
- place (distribution)

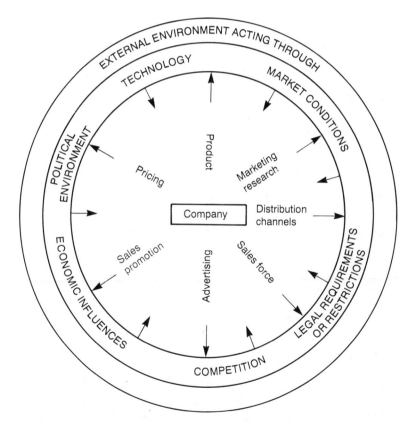

Figure 3.1 *The independent and the dependent variables*

Within this simple framework McCarthy grouped various other factors according to their general derivation, e.g. credit under price. However, this scheme is too simplistic and is perhaps best regarded as an *aide memoire*, especially as it groups under promotion — advertising, sales promotion, selling, and public relations — which as we shall see are very real *alternative* strategies among themselves and should be considered separately. Another failing is its total exclusion of market research which has to be used to provide data upon which all other sales decisions can be taken.

I favour a larger but simple structure that includes the essential and distinctive elements that are alternatives in most marketing strategies:

(a) product;
(b) marketing research;
(c) channels of distribution;
(d) sales force;
(e) advertising;
(f) sales promotion;
(g) pricing.

Different organisations may include other elements according to their particular needs, for example, packaging may be of major importance, or warehousing, but it is convenient to use these seven as a basic model.

The use of the different elements not only varies according to their purpose and techniques, i.e. advertising, marketing research, sales force, etc., but also in the *role* they fulfil in the overall sales strategy. This can be expressed as a spectrum, one end being concerned with *strategic* aspects, and the other end concerned with *tactical* aspects. Look at it this way; in a war situation, the field marshal determines *where* the battle will be fought, which was Napoleon's great skill, and subordinate commanders will decide *how* it will be fought. Put in the context of competitive markets, decisions have to be made on strategic issues, such as:

(a) the kind of product to be offered;
(b) the market or segment to be targetted.

Then, tactical decisions have to be made on:

(c) how that market is to be reached, say, by advertising;
(d) what kind of sales approach will be used;
(e) when will sales promotion be employed; and
(f) how will pricing be used to stimulate sales, or resist competition.

Using the simple seven element approach listed above, then it can be allocated to the spectrum according to its role.

Strategic decisions: *Set objectives*	*Tactical decisions:* *Meet objectives*
Marketing research	Channels of distribution
Product	Sales force
Pricing	Advertising
	Sales promotion
	Pricing

Pricing has been put in twice because:

(a) it can play a *strategic* role in *deciding* the market segment to be targetted. For example, a cosmetic manufacturer may produce two products in two distinct price ranges; one for the teenage market, priced low for experimental and frequent buying in bright 'young' packaging to be sold in multiple stores such as Woolworths; and another version for the older women's market priced higher, for people with higher purchasing power, and packaged for more sophisticated taste, to be sold in department stores and specialist shops. (It is claimed that 90 per cent of the price of a cosmetic is the package!)

(b) it can play a *tactical* role in price cutting to create a larger market share, e.g. petrol price wars, or to limit competitor activity, e.g. a company with a major share of a market that perceives a threat from competitors entering the market with new products could slash its prices to the point where a competitor would be deterred by the low profit margins.

These concepts of strategic and tactical roles are important because they underline the roles of the sales force, advertising, et al, to meet objectives that have been determined by higher management. For example, a sales team must sell a certain volume if the firm is to be cost effective and advertising has to reach an identified target market if it is to meet sales objectives.

2. Deciding on the mix

Deciding how the money is allocated is a function of the marketing/sales budget and decisions on where to allocate the money will depend upon the objectives. The separate elements can rarely be used in isolation and their combination to suit particular strategies requires a blending in appropriate proportions, *see* Figure 3.2. For example,

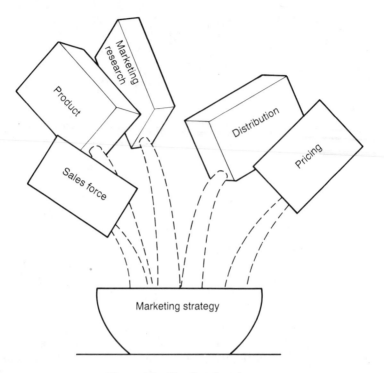

Figure 3.2 *Blending the mix*

different blends of advertising, product modification, pricing and sales promotion can direct versions of the same product to different market segments, as well as to different markets.

One may emphasise *consumer effective variables* — or marketing elements — such as tv advertising, resulting in a consumer-directed strategy, or emphasise *industrial effective variables*, such as a highly trained sales force or informative press releases, resulting in an industrial-directed strategy. This might be applied to a cleaning product for the home directed to consumers by tv advertising, or a janitorial product for industry, advertised in trade journals, combined with sales support.

This need to 'blend' or combine different elements to achieve a sales objective is born out by various researchers and it generally increases the effectiveness of a sales strategy. For example, if advertising is used in conjunction with selling of industrial products it can increase sales by around 20% and substantially contributes to the reduction of the total costs/total sales ratio, because advertising

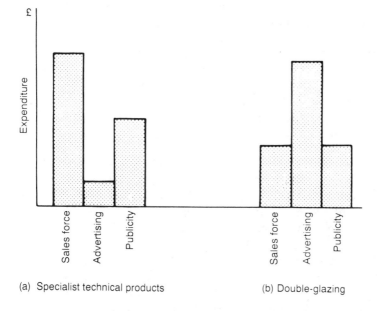

Figure 3.3 *Alternative investment decisions*

prepares the market in advance and makes customers aware of the product and its problem-solving potentials.

Freeman (1962), Levitt (1965), Lilien (1976, 1979) all suggested that advertising is particularly effective when combined with personal selling. However, it should be remembered that measuring the effectiveness of advertising alone is almost impossible. Therefore, it must appear more effective if measured in combination with a measurable element such as personal selling.

Each of these variables, then, can be combined in almost infinite sets or mixes to generate a wide range of customer need-satisfying products and services. The way these variables are combined result from, but also are part of, the construction of sales strategies. The changing use of the mix depends upon the firm's perception of its market position. This is developed further at 14:**15**.

The amount that is spent on each sales tool can be considered as a measure of *investment* and the basic criteria apply to whatever range of tools is under consideration.

Figure 3.3 is a simple example of two alternative investment decisions.

Alternative (a) is the way a company making specialist technical products, perhaps for the medical profession, and heavily dependent on a highly trained sales force, might choose to allocate its expenditure. It allocates a large part of the money to the sales force itself, perhaps in training and keeping them up to date with the latest technical developments. Less is allocated to advertising because the company probably only advertises occasionally in specialist medical journals. On the other hand, it allocates a larger amount to publicity, which could include public relations exercises such as special functions and exhibitions that help the sales force to meet and get to know its specialist customers.

Alternative (b) is for a company selling in a larger and more general market, say double glazing. They will be heavily dependent on advertising to create a demand and make customers aware of the product before they actually meet a sales person. Accordingly, less is spent on the sales force itself with many consumer products, like groceries, 'selling' may play a minor role to advertising. These are general examples and clearly between the two is a whole spectrum of choices, each determined according to sales policy. How to allocate the budget is a major decision for any new company or, indeed, any company venturing into a new product or a new market. Like all investment decisions, the choice of sales tools will be subject to:

(a) understanding of the proposition;
(b) realistic forecasting of results; and
(c) evaluation of alternative solutions.

3.   Decision making

In all business management there is a prime responsibility to allocate resources, whether to decide between alternative sales tools or to choose between launching new products or revamping and extending the lives of existing ones. In deciding how to allocate resources to alternative tools, sales management will try to assess the likely outcome of spending money on each of the alternatives and will then choose the 'best'. 'Best', however, is never certain, because we can never be absolutely sure of the outcome of a course of action — there are too many variables. For example, all the evidence and calculations may suggest to you that advertising will be the 'best' course, then, unexpectedly, along comes a major competitor with much larger resources able to swamp the media with a vast campaign that quite overshadows your own and switches buyers to *their* brand. If you had known in advance of the competition's intentions, you might have decided to go for sales promotion and price reduction instead.

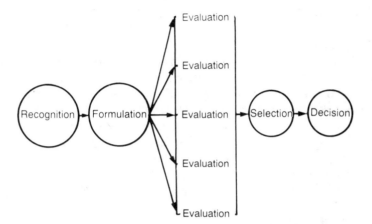

Figure 3.4 *The decision-making process*

Sales management is responsible for applying judgement decisions to difficult situations with imperfect knowledge.

4. Strategic decision making

There are four steps in strategic decision making:

(a) recognition of the need to make a decision;
(b) formulation of alternatives;
(c) evaluation of alternatives; and
(d) selection of alternatives for decision.

This process is shown in Figure 3.4. *Recognition* is the need to decide in which tool to invest resources. *Formulation* is a written statement of the objective that is to be achieved. This is an important step because it forces managers to think clearly and identify the objective, rather than having a woolly notion of what is needed. *Evaluation* is the process of calculating the effect of spending money in different ways, e.g. for an investment of £X000 in the sales force, what will be the likely, predicted return? The same exercise is repeated for advertising, sales promotion and so on. *Selection* and the final *decision* will then be based on calculated predictions that may still only be the 'best' estimates, but they will have been arrived at by the 'best' method. If necessary they can be revised in the light of experience.

The product

5.   Purpose of sales

The product, or the service, is an element of marketing which can be used to change the firm's strategy or competitive position, especially in response to environmental changes, such as technology. More recently recognition of pressures on the world's physical environment has led to the introduction of many, so-called 'green' products. Some of those have been existing products 'greened' by claims of being made from re-cyclable materials, e.g. packaging, while others such as aerosols, have had their chemical formulations changed and carry labels testifying to their being 'ozone friendly'.

6.   What is a product?

When we think of a product, we usually visualize a tangible object with physical properties, e.g. the well-known image of a *Mars bar*, or a Black and Decker power tool. But a product is more than its physical properties and in considering one, we may well ascribe intangible attributes to it. When you describe a microwave as convenient, a chocolate bar as satisfying, or a computer as 'user friendly', you are citing performance characteristics that describe the product's ability to satisfy consumer needs. Equally, an industrial buyer may be more interested in the efficiency of a power tool than its colour or shape.

The Armstrong-Kotler model of a product shows that there are three components or sets of attributes to a product, illustrated as follows:

(a) the *core* attributes = the benefits it conveys, i.e. a chocolate satisfies hunger;
(b) the *tangible* attributes = its physical attributes, i.e. its characteristic taste; and,
(c) the *augmented* attributes = its support services, i.e. a bar that is available when you want it.

These three components are important for sales people to recognise, because when customers, whether consumers or industrial buyers, buy products they are initially concerned with the *benefits* of the product, i.e. those characteristics consumers see as potentially meeting their demands. In industrial selling this is especially important because buyers are looking for *solutions to problems* and so sales people must identify the appropriate, key benefits, of their products to particular situations.

The other attributes, the tangible, and the augmented, will only become important to customers when they have understood the benefits. The tangible attributes might mean good design features, or efficiency of handling, and the augmented attributes might include servicing, guarantees, good delivery, etc.

7. Product differentiation
This is the process of building into a product characteristics which make it different to those of competitors. It may be attained by artfully blending the marketing mix variables resulting in a new marketing mix, e.g. physical characteristics, advertising, labelling, branding, or producing different versions of the product such as varieties of potato crisps. It is important to distinguish between product differentiation and marketing segmentation. Basically the former aims to make the distinction on the *product* side and the latter on the *customer* side, for example:

(a) Product differentiation. Heinz spaghetti and spaghetti hoops
(b) Market segmentation. Heinz beans versus Cross & Blackwell 'Weight watchers' beans.

In the second example, the product has been altered to meet the needs of a distinctive segment of the market. In any sales strategy, management must look at the advantages to be gained from each of the above.

The sales force

As this book is primarily concerned with selling skills, it follows that the treatment of the sales force under the sales 'tool' will be short. In this we shall be concerned with the sales force as an investment alternative to the other tools.

8. Role of the sales force
The role of the sales force has changed over the years from being the sole, or at least major, influence due to developments such as:

(a) widespread use of advertising by means of:
    (i) television;
    (ii) newspapers, magazines and journals;
    (iii) poster advertising; and
    (iv) mailed 'special offer' promotions;
(b) higher investment in 'brand' names and the resultant high promotional activity;

(c) development of better communications, leading to greater ease of travel and distribution has reduced the number of salespeople;
(d) growth of telephone selling; and
(e) a combination of all the above, usually termed 'merchandising'.

These trends have been developing over a number of years and should be seen as flexible responses to changing environmental situations. For example, after about 1959 when small cars like the Mini became available, it was economical to have numerous sales personnel travelling around the country, a trend that developed further as motorways expanded and communications between major cities were vastly improved. However, after the inflation and fuel price rises of the early 1970s, the cost of motoring rapidly increased, putting pressure on salespeople to sell more to cover rising costs. Then telephone selling and the use of the telephone as a substitute for sales calls began to develop. The development of the sales force is, nevertheless, still an area where considerable competitive advantages may be achieved through good sales and product training and sound planning.

9.   The need for professional selling

A highly trained and well-motivated sales force is absolutely vital when selling industrial and commercial goods, and in exporting, because companies in those sectors cannot be motivated to buy by persuasive appeals alone. Tell engineers that your paint comes in a variety of pretty colours or in convenient-sized cans and they will be unlikely to be interested. What they want to know is, 'Will your product resist acid contamination or steam and how long will it last … ?' The distributor, both at home and in export markets, will want to know about quality and also about the level of profitability and the return on investment in stocks.

Perhaps it is not too extreme to say that some of the failures of Britain to export successfully in past years have derived from a lack of understanding of the need for top-class professional salespeople in these markets. The traditional attitude of British industry towards exports has all too frequently been: '… plan for the home market and hope overseas customers will like them …'

Business people who compete in export markets know that their companies are up against the toughest and best competition in the world. British salespeople are out-classed by their foreign rivals if they:

(a) are less well-trained;
(b) have not been given enough information or authority to deal on the spot with queries and negotiations;

(c) do not have the very best information, samples or prices; and
(d) worst of all, British salespeople are at a profound disadvantage if they are undervalued by their own company.

10. Need for improved sales force
In industrial and export selling there has been a growth in the need for better selling skills, that is:

(a) greater technical proficiency;
(b) greater personal skill; and
(c) an ability to identify product opportunities.

This means the sales force is a key factor in the increasingly competitive world and it calls for greater efforts from both sales management and the sales force. It also necessitates a higher level of training, both in selling and in product knowledge and market awareness. Management must realise that the skills of the sales force are as important as those of all other functional personnel in the organisation. In some highly competitive sectors, such as exporting, they are vital to the company's success.

11. Management's task
To obtain the right calibre of sales personnel, management must pay greater attention to:

(a) remuneration — higher basic salary and less 'incentive' in the form of commission;
(b) a greater realisation of and respect for the skill of sales personnel — less of the 'carrot and stick' approach;
(c) greater leadership from management, which will motivate the sales force to higher aspirations; and
(d) delegation of responsibility, creating more job satisfaction and more job prospects.

The important aspects of leadership will be dealt with fully in Chapter 15 on sales management. The other vital areas of management of the sales force will also be explained in subsequent chapters.

Channels of distribution

12. Reaching the consumer or user
The channel of distribution is a tool that explains and clarifies the methods by which products are able to reach the final consumer or

user. The final consumers are the person (or persons) who are the ultimate consumers of the product, e.g. the people who wear the shoes or drive the motor cars. Users are similar but the term is more appropriate to industrial selling, being, e.g. the person using the tools in the workshop. They are both important to the manufacturer as it is only by accomplishing a sale that the business purpose is fulfilled:

Business purpose = profit
Profit achieved by making a sale
Making a sale implies a customer
This must be a satisfied customer.

The sale of goods by a manufacturer to a wholesaler, factor, contractor or retailer, or from a wholesaler to a retailer, are only steps in the distribution chain. They do not represent final competition. This is best illustrated by goods in a shop. If groceries are sold up to a supermarket, they then have to be sold to consumers, otherwise there will not be repeat orders. It is only consumers (or users) who 'destroy' goods — by eating them, drinking them or simply wearing them out.

If it is true that demand is satisfied only by the consumer or user, then it is reasonable to assume that the services of all those involved up to the point where the consumer or user is able to obtain them are part of the process of supply.

13. Flow of supplies
The equalising of supply and demand is at the root of sales and the accomplishment of this balance is the purpose of the channels of distribution. They must be so conceived as to maintain an efficient flow of supply at all times and it is important for all concerned with sales to understand how vital the channels of distribution are to efficient selling.

Channels of distribution will vary according to the needs and circumstances of the market as will the pattern of concentration and dispersion. Surmounting all considerations will be the need to meet the demand in terms of *time* and *place*. As an aspect of the sales process it provides for:

(a) storage of current supplies against future demand;
(b) storage of supplies at a place where demand is expected to occur; and
(c) transforming the product by sorting, grading or processing.

The addition of time utility and place utility will be the purpose of distribution at all times. Translated into selling terms, one sells the

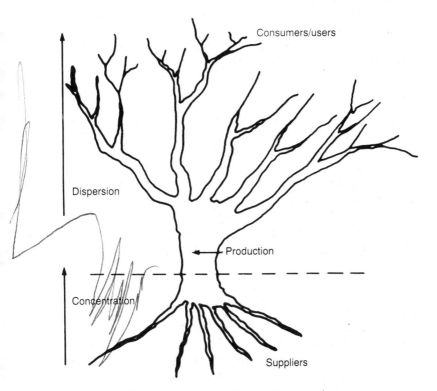

Figure 3.5 *The total distribution process*

benefits underlying these utilities, that is *time utility* is the convenience of being able to supply or deliver when the consumer wants it; *place utility* is the ability to have the product where it can be obtained, whether that is in the supermarket or delivered to the factory where it is wanted. Conversely, it is also the ability of the consumer/user to *obtain* the product when it is wanted. For example, a replacement printer for a computer has little utility for the consumer if it cannot be obtained fairly locally within a reasonable time of the need for it arising.

14. The logistics of distribution

There are two important elements making up the working of distribution:

(a) concentration; and
(b) dispersion

It is possible to compare these elements, at opposite ends of the process, to a tree. At one end there is a system of roots, reaching out to obtain supply, which is moved through the trunk and dispersed through the multiple branches, as illustrated in Figure 3.5.

15. Concentration

This is the collection of the output of diverse suppliers and its concentration by retailers, wholesalers or manufacturers, with the objective of sorting, grading, assembly, further processing and, ultimately, sale. It is important both when the product is to be consumed in its original form and when it is to be further processed. The process for marketing complicated manufactured goods involves considerable concentrations of parts, both from within the company and from other manufacturers. Computers, telecommunications, aircraft and cars all result from assembling enormous numbers of component parts made by various suppliers.

16. Dispersion

This is the part of the distribution process occuring after the concentration of production. From each concentration there follows a dispersion, leading to the final distribution to the ultimate consumer or user. Dispersion occurs in several forms:

(a) to *retailers* and then to final consumers/users;
(b) to *manufacturers* for further processing;
(c) to *wholesalers* for distribution to retailers; or
(d) in *exporting*, it may be through *importers* who will behave in some cases like wholesalers and in others like retailers, according to local practice.

The pattern of concentration and dispersion differs considerably between commodities. The distributive pattern for industrial items differs generally from that of consumer goods in that the users of industrial goods are themselves producers. As the goods are often of high individual value, they are frequently sold direct to the user:

(a) *direct to the ultimate customer;*
    (i) through 'tied' outlets, such as flour millers who own bakery shops; breweries selling through their own hotels or pubs; petroleum companies selling through their own service stations; or
    (ii) direct to the user or to the door, e.g. industrial cleaning materials; tools suppliers; double glazing;

(b) *to the retailer via the wholesaler;* or
(c) *direct to the retailer.*

Distribution offers competitive advantages to firms that find ways of moving themselves closer to the ultimate customer. For example, Avon Cosmetics has traditionally sought the buyers (housewives) at home with its well-known jingle, '*Avon calling!*'. Recently, however, the trend towards more wives' working away from home, has led Avon to develop the practice of selling to them at their workplace. Another example of seeking competitive advantages is in the high-tech world of computer technology. Dell Computers was set up to sell computers to university students. In the face of competition from the giants — IBM, Honeywell, etc. — the firm sold direct to its customers. It provided a 'tailor-made' service that could not be handled by the conventional retail stockist and also passed on the retailers' discount to the consumer.

17. The transvection concept
Individual sales are termed transactions, and the entire chain of stages in a channel of distribution is termed a *transvection*, a useful way of describing a system. (*See* Figure 3.6.)

For sales managers the transvection concept is an important way of understanding how their production reaches eventual customers. Decisions have to be taken on the evaluation of each stage in the process and on whether greater efficiency would result from modifying the distribution channel. The method of doing this would be the same as is outlined in 3:**2**.

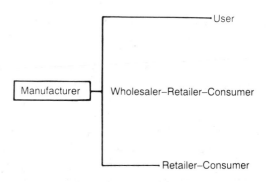

Figure 3.6 *Transvections*

18. Cost and efficiency

The concentration of industry into larger production units during the 1960s and 1970s put greater emphasis on the need to influence mass consumer markets, which, in turn, increased selling and marketing costs. For example, the decline of corner shops and the proliferation of supermarkets, and now superstores, have concentrated buying power for a wide range of consumer products. This put pressure on manufacturers to offer more competitive prices for larger volumes that, in turn, dictated larger concentration of production to turn out the products at lower unit costs and also necessitated increased advertising to create sufficient demand — a cycle of demand creation, lower prices, greater volume and more demand creation. The greater demand from customers with a higher disposable income has led to an increase in the costs of advertising, packaging and promotion. Mass production has done much to offset the additional costs.

In the 1980s, however, we saw the growth of small businesses once more, many the result of redundant workers being displaced from large organisations. This growth in the plethora of small firms tested the ingenuity of sales management to cover all the activities of these small businesses at an acceptable cost. It is in these circumstances that analysis of distribution channels becomes a vital part of sales planning.

Careful analysis of the existing distribution channels and creative innovation in streamlining or otherwise modifying the transvection are increasingly important tasks of sales management.

Marketing research

19. The links between sales and marketing

We know that sales and marketing are closely interwoven and in Chapter 17, on organisation, we shall see which factors determine where the emphasis should be put. Marketing is, strictly speaking, the 'strategic' end of the the sales and marketing spectrum and sales the 'tactical' end. That is to say, in a large organisation with distinctive marketing and sales functions, marketing will *identify* goals and sales will *meet* them. This is a generalisation but it helps to explain their roles, especially in relation to *marketing* research and *market* research, the one primarily concerned with identifying product opportunities and the other, with specific markets. Nevertheless, there are many large and successful companies, both consumer and industrial, that are 'sales-led' and use marketing research.

20. Different types of marketing research

Marketing research is a generic title embracing a wide number of different kinds of research. They are:

(a) marketing;
(b) market;
(c) consumer;
(d) advertising;
(e) industrial; and
(f) economic research.

21. Marketing research

In this study, the term is used to embrace all those research activities that are intended to aid sales or marketing management in the strategic decision making. The objective of such research is to provide data to help in solving marketing problems. It can be defined as the application of scientific methods to the solution of marketing problems. Marketing research endeavours to provide information such as:

(a) whether a market exists;
(b) the possibility of creating a market;
(c) a comparison of quality and price with competitive products;
(d) the extent to which demand is satisfied by existing suppliers;
(e) the opportunities for advantage over competitors;
(f) an examination of competitors' sales techniques; and
(g) an evaluation of alternative methods of distribution.

For any progressive sales organisation marketing research must be a continuous process, as economic and political changes, both at home and abroad, keep situations fluid and market conditions may change rapidly. Competitors may break into the field and gain an advantage with an unsuspected product innovation. For example, Amstrad with its personal word processor. All these factors mean that amendments to marketing plans may be necessary at short notice.

In very large organisations, even the different types of research may be important and large enough to develop into full-scale departments. Here, however, we shall take the view that marketing research is concerned with such areas as identifying marketing opportunities, product planning and the deeper issues of consumer behaviour.

22. Research as an aid to decision making

Management's task is to take decisions on planning, coordinating and controlling. Ways must be found in which to lower the degree of uncertainty and risk in making decisions such as

(a) what must be done;
(b) specifying the personnel to do the work;
(c) seeing that the work is done; and
(d) evaluating how well it was done.

Managers, therefore, are receivers of data that help them to take better decisions. Their effectiveness in carrying out these tasks will depend on the sensible use of the data collected. Their ability to take decisions will also be determined, to a large degree by the quantity, quality and relevance of the data collected. Improvements will originate in the systematic

(a) selection,
(b) collection,
(c) processing,
(d) analysis, and
(e) communication

of relevant information and in the capacity to make sound assumptions for accurate forecasting and planning decisions.

23. Market research

An investigation for a particular product leads to an appraisal of the market. If a company was thinking about selling a new product or selling its existing products in a new market, say the Netherlands, it would need to find out as much as possible about conditions for the sale of its products. The company would need to collect data that would help it plan the correct approach. For example, what competition is there, what prices are appropriate, what selling approach must be adopted? As an example, we may take a brand of car polish. A number of pertinent questions will help to reveal the market:

(a) When is the car polish used?
(b) In what quantities?
(c) Where is it bought?
(d) Who buys the product?
(e) What special problems must it overcome?
(f) What price range would it be expected to fit into?

The replies will reveal much about the car polish we should be producing and how we should sell it. We could then take the investigation a stage further and consider the competition we are likely to encounter. It then becomes relevant to ask; 'How does the polish compare with competitive products for brilliance, long-lasting shine, quality, price, packaging etc.'

In reality, any sales plan constructed from this type of information alone fails to take account of all the forces that will be ranged against the product.

24. The process of market research
Market research arranges its tasks in three ways:

(a) collecting information about the market;
(b) analysing the data;
(c) communicating its findings to management.

Information may be collected in three ways:

(a) *simple*: by personal observation of customers, noting their buying habits and trends;
(b) *desk research*: by the use of official publications and statistics; this is also known as *secondary research*; and by
(c) *original research*: by undertaking sample surveys, designed to reveal new information in answer to specific questions; this is also known as *primary research* and is much more expensive.

It is possible to collect marketing research data without commissioning specific marketing research; many exporting companies, and industrial companies generally, gather marketing data as a continuous process. The methods of gathering such data may include:

(a) sales force or agents' reports;
(b) trade fairs and exhibitions;
(c) personal visits to export markets;
(d) press reports and media coverage;
(e) trade associations;
(f) current or existing government reports and surveys.

Virtually all marketing research is conducted to better understand the marketplace, to find out why a strategy failed, or to reduce uncertainty in the management decision-making process.

The cost and technical nature of the research rises from (a), which is cheapest and can be undertaken by any sensible business-person, to (c), which can incur high cost and is usually undertaken by specialist firms.

25. Sources of information

Information needs will depend on the nature of the problem; the following are some usual sources:

(a) internal sales data (invoices, records);
(b) published information (government statistics, economic data, market surveys);
(c) data available on request but not generally published (information from government sources or trade organisations); and
(d) new data collected by sample survey methods.

26. Wider implications of competition

All products compete with obviously similar products, but it should also be realised that products often compete with dissimilar products. For example, if we were selling household paint we would have to understand that it has to compete with other protective measures that could be employed, including any of the following:

(a) other paints;
(b) liquid plastics;
(c) timber preservatives;
(d) fungicidal treatments;
(e) plastic laminates;
(f) formica;
(g) galvanising; and
(h) methods of construction.

This brings into question the concept that we are working in the 'paint market' — in reality *we are working in the coatings/protection market in which paint is only one alternative.* Thus,

(a) a paint for treating domestic window frames is connected with the building and timber markets;
(b) a paint for coating steelwork may be in the corrosion market or the structural market or the chemical market or the fabrication market.

Whatever markets the products are really concerned with, they will all operate within the complexities of that market. We will be competing not only with other paints that will do the job equally well, but also with other forms of treatment.

If this is valid, then the company has to make out a case that is far more comprehensive than a statement of quality, colour, durability etc. It has to give evidence that it can save buyers money and enable them to allocate further money to other requirements at another time.

27. Advertising research

This is a more specialised aspect of consumer research and is concerned with understanding consumer motivations and predicting the effects of advertising messages.

Its role in developing a 'brand image' has long been one of its more important aspects, but, in recent years, it has sought to identify underlying reasons for consumers' loyalty to or dislike of particular propositions. Advertising research has turned to psychology in an endeavour to understand the deep-rooted feelings consumers may have towards certain products. This application of 'depth-research' into such apparently straightforward propositions as instant coffee, hair shampoo, toothpastes and cosmetics, has thrown new light on consumer buying behaviour. When this knowledge is accurately and sensibly applied, it becomes a powerful tool for marketing. For sales management, the results of advertising research can be powerful aids to selling by providing information on how customers regard certain propositions or view the relative strengths of certain benefits.

Advertising

28. Informing customers

The whole process of selling products or services to the market is intimately concerned with understanding customers' needs, motivating the sale of the product or service and distributing it to customers — whether private consumers or industrial buyers and users. Advertising is that part of the process that is concerned with informing customers of the existence of the product or service. If your company invents and produces a product, no matter how excellent and desirable it is, it will not sell until people know about it.

Promotion of a product can take one or more of three main forms:

(a) *non-personal*: advertising;
(b) *semi-personal*: sales promotion; or
(c) *personal*: selling skills.

Whatever kind of promotion is employed at a particular time, it will have as its objective several aims:

(a) *to build goodwill* for the company;
(b) *to maintain continuing customer satisfaction*; and
(c) *to keep the volume of sales at a profitable level*.

Advertising and sales promotion are identified as two distinctive sales tools, fulfilling different purposes. In this they offer management a choice for investment.

(a) advertising — non-personal, long-term communication;
(b) sales promotion — semi-personal, short-term motivation.

29. Deciding where to spend the money, advertising or sales promotion

Deciding which to use or, as is more often the case, how much of each to use, is another investment decision and would employ the process already described. In reality, of course, the decision is intricately involved with the sales objective and the question must be asked, 'Which is likely to help attain the sales objective most effectively?' The answer will vary according to the objective and also the different kinds of companies.

A large brewery intending to launch another brand of canned beer will need to spend heavily on consumer-targeted advertising, possibly on television. It will probably support this with a sales promotion campaign, perhaps selling the new beer at a specially low price in its own pubs to encourage people to try it. This two-pronged campaign will ensure that:

(a) *by advertising*, large numbers of the targeted audience, that is beer-drinking consumers, will be made aware of the new brand and recognise it when they see the product;
(b) *by using sales promotion*, people will be encouraged to try the product when they have the opportunity, in the pub or a supermarket's off-licence section, say.

A different company, for instance one making tools for the garage trade, will launch its new product by a sales promotion campaign, perhaps a cash discount on the new model or even a sales competition among its own sales force to encourage them to sell the new product. This may be backed by a limited advertising campaign or a mail-shot to all likely users, such as the garage trade.

30. Objectives of advertising

The importance of advertising was recognised as early as the nineteenth century by Lord Macaulay, who said, 'Advertising is to business what steam is to machinery — the great propelling power'.

Advertising may be defined as 'any paid form of non-personal

presentation and promotion of ideas, goods or services by an identified sponsor'.

Companies using modern production methods, which generally
involve heavy financial investment in plant and machinery, need to
be sure of a continuous market for the products being made —
whether they are cars, computers or baked beans — in order to recover
that investment. At the time of writing it has been announced that
British Aerospace have secured an order from the Australian freight
airline, TNT, for 75 of the BAe 146 airliners at a cost of some £900
million. It sounds a stupendous amount until one realises that BAe
need to sell about 150 aircraft just to break even! For small companies
making their own products, the sums may be just as important, if
considerably smaller.

Advertising's task has become central to the modern economy in
a capitalist society; this results from its role in the communication
system. The need for information about a vast range of ideas, products
and concepts has arisen from the advertising process. Manufacturers,
and to a lesser extent distributors, have been able to create and sustain
the mass market by constantly seeking and achieving reduced costs.
This, however, has only been made possible by effective advertising
in conjunction with an efficient distribution system, at the heart of
which must be skilled selling. After all, whichever way you look at
the process, at some point somebody has to buy the product and the
corollary must be that somebody else is selling.

31. The role of advertising

Because advertising as a concept has become fundamental to
industrialised society, its role in creating markets has become an
important aid to individual manufacturers and businesses of every
kind. Its essential role may be determined as follows:

(a) to aid the creation and maintenance of sales;
(b) to persuade consumers/users to become *actual* consumers/users;
(c) to inform consumers and create demand;
(d) to increase demand for a product or service.

32. The communications gap

Buyers, whether consumers or users, are faced with a wide range
of choice in satisfying their needs. Many products, although not
identical, can be substitutes for one another. Advertising is a means
of bridging a communications gap and accelerating the satisfaction of
consumer wants. It does this by communicating:

(a) that products or services exist;
(b) what they are like;
(c) what their benefits are; and
(d) their price.

Once it has been decided to market a range of products and the mechanics of production and distribution have been worked out, it is the role of advertising to bring the products to the attention of the targeted customers and present them in attractive ways to generate interest and desire for further information. Then it is the task of the sales force to convert customer interest into sales.

Brand names and advertising are closely linked and, while trade names may acquire significance as a result of advertising, the real role of advertising is to quicken the process of acceptance of a brand image by consumers. During the mid 1980s, perhaps this was best exemplified by the promotion of hitherto unknown Australian beers in the British market.

33. Limitations of advertising

It should be remembered that advertising is only one of many causes of customer purchases, others include:

(a) price;
(b) presentation and packaging;
(c) ability of the sales force; and
(d) the quality of the product.

Advertising is a medium of communication and does not, of itself, sell products — it creates interest and needs:

(a) advertising will not sell products that are not wanted by customers;
(b) advertising will not sell products by itself, it requires the cooperation of all the sales and marketing processes;
(c) to succeed in motivating customers, advertising has to be used continuously;
(d) advertising may motivate customers to buy without establishing a brand (or a type) loyalty.

Example

Mr Jones sits watching television on a warm summer evening. An advertisement appears exhorting him to buy 'Dingo', a new Australian lager. Unable to resist temptation any longer, Mr Jones leaves home intent on buying a glass of 'Dingo'. The first bar he reaches sells only that well-known Yorkshire beer, 'Pennine', but Mr Jones, motivated to settle his thirst by purchasing 'beer' buys a glass of 'Pennine' brand, thereby benefitting the advertiser's competitor.

Similar situations arise with other products. For example, petrol brands. In both beer and petrol sales, the manufacturers' tactics are to control as many sales outlets as possible, so breweries buy pubs and petrol companies buy service stations. In this way they assure themselves of a specific market share in a particular area.

34. Problems of advertising

Deciding how much to invest in advertising as a tool of sales management is difficult, because it is hard to quantify both in terms of predicting and measuring results.

£X000 invested in a campaign results in sales of Y000 units of a product. For sales managers the question becomes one of determining the relationship between the amount invested in a campaign and the level of sales achieved. The decision maker has to be able to equate a given sales objective to a planned level of advertising. The decision on advertising then can be reduced to a few major questions:

(a) Should we advertise at all? If the answer is yes, then;
(b) How much money to invest?
(c) Where to advertise?
(d) How to organise the advertising campaign?

To a large extent, the fundamental decision depends on the sector of business in which a company operates. If a company is making fast-moving consumer products, like cosmetics or household products, then the need for mass consumption to absorb the mass production (as was explained above) will necessitate advertising in an appropriate medium, probably television. If, on the other hand, the company is making a specialist product for industry or for organisational buyers like hospitals, then the selling task will demand personal selling to explain product attributes and benefits and to give advice. In these circumstances, advertising's role is much reduced. So, although the decision on whether to advertise or not remains, it becomes simplified to some degree and sales managers have definite guidelines to help in their decision making.

Once the decision to advertise has been made, however, there is still a problem in quantifying the results. There may well be difficulty in determining whether the level of sales owes anything to the advertising or would have been more or less if no campaign had been mounted. This is the more difficult decision.

35. General considerations

Among the general considerations affecting the amount to be invested in the advertising appropriation will be the following:

(a) whether the product or service being advertised is new, established or declining;
(b) the nature of the product or service;
(c) competitor activity.

36. A product life cycle

As we saw in Chapter 1, it is a useful exercise to relate products to life cycles. To recap briefly, all products are new at some time and thereafter they 'age' and eventually decline and die off. What varies is the time that the cycle takes to complete. For example, a product like Guinness has had a life cycle so far of more than two hundred years, albeit during that time the product will have been modified, improved or upgraded, although the name has remained the same. At the other end of the scale, a pop record may have a life of just a few weeks, or even days.

During the course of the product's life it will be necessary to promote it in different ways, as shown in Figure 3.7. As you will see, for most consumer products this means heavy advertising when the product is launched to make it well-known as quickly as possible. As the product matures competition will increase and it will be more appropriate to fight off the rivals by using sales promotion tactics. For

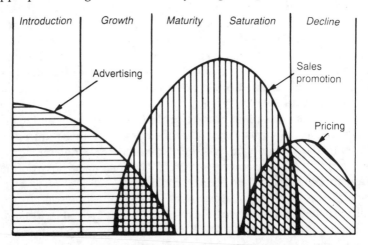

Figure 3.7 *The product life cycle and marketing mix decisions*

example, a firm launches a completely new product at £5. Initially there is no competition, but if the product is successful other firms will produce their own versions: this happens with food products, e.g. pot noodles. At that point the makers of the original product can either use pricing to retain brand loyalty, or alternatively, and depending upon how the firms see the market developing, it will more likely use sales promotions to retain brand loyalty at the original price but possibly offering money-off coupons or some other attraction. Later again, when the product has peaked and begins to decline as newer products take its place, it may become appropriate then to use pricing as a means of 'buying' sales and under-cutting rivals. By then any more expenditure on the product will eat into any remaining profitability and the company will not wish to re-launch it, especially if a replacement product is imminent.

Sales promotion

37. Promotional activities.
Promotion can be defined as any activity that promotes sales; in this sense the concept can include:

(a) advertising;
(b) sales force; and
(c) pricing.

38. Sales promotion
Here we are concerned with sales promotion as set out in 3:**28** a semi-personal short-term motivation. We can imagine advertising as a broad 'scythe' and sales promotion as a 'rapier'. It is a precise tool of sales management that can be used to stimulate sales for particular purposes:

(a) product innovation and launch;
(b) new territory exploitation;
(c) to stimulate sales at particular periods; and
(d) to encourage personnel to sell certain products.

39. Methods of promotion
In the widest context, sales management will use promotions in a great variety of circumstances and will utilise many methods, which may include the following:

(a) pricing;
(b) trade offers;
(c) consumer offers;
(d) sales aids;
(e) packaging and presentation;
(f) exhibitions;
(g) in-store promotions;
(h) special occasion promotions; and
(i) public relations.

40. Product innovation and launch.

The purpose of sales promotion in relation to new products and their successful launch will have as its objective a general widening of distribution and an establishment and subsequent increase in the stock or use of the product.

In industrial selling, promotion may take the form of exhibitions, displays, demonstrations or even the practical use of the product for a specific job or period of time. It is intended that users gain experience of the product and find a continual use for it. Promotion can also offer opportunities for wider demonstrations. For example, a manufacturer of earth-moving equipment may agree to lend a machine to do a job, providing that they are allowed to invite other potential customers along to watch. When we launched one of our display systems we lent one to a major national carpet warehouse for a special event, but arranged to have photographs taken of it in use; copies of these were then used by our own salespeople to demonstrate its use by a prestigious firm.

In whatever way a company decides to promote the new product, the objective will be two-fold:

(a) to bring it to the attention of, and stimulate, market interest;
(b) to induce users or stockists/distributors of the product to buy the product.

In these ways, sales promotion is a powerful tool of sales management, helping to stimulate interest, encouraging enquiries from potential customers who provide sales leads and publicising the benefits of the product.

41. Trade promotions

Manufacturers offer incentives to the trade to purchase their products:

(a) a *percentage discount* or a cash allowance for a specified quantity (a case, gallon or whatever) on purchase is given;

(b) an *extra product* is given with each order. This has the advantage for the manufacturer that it ensures the distributor passes on the allowances to the retailer;

(c) *gifts* may be given in return for a certain quantity of orders (it must be pointed out, however, that the line between inducement and bribery is a very fine one and so companies have to be careful not to infringe the law).

42. Consumer promotions

These are aimed directly at the consumer and have as their objective the stimulation to try, or to purchase more of, a product:

(a) *Coupons* are vouchers of a specific value that are passed direct to the consumer who obtains a price reduction on their presentation to the stockist and the manufacturer expects to gain certain benefits from coupons, including the fact that:

(i) they will act as an incentive to consumers to sample products;

(ii) the retailer will be encouraged to stock the product in expectation of demand; and

(iii) the sales force will have an opportunity to obtain additional display space for the product:

Clearly, these benefits can only be realised if the stockists, whether retail or trade, are aware of them. It is therefore imperative for sales management to ensure that the sales force tells the trade or keeps it informed by telephone or mail-shots.

(b) *Self-liquidating offers*: in this form of promotion the consumer is invited by the manufacturers to send a sum of money and a number of package tops or tokens for a particular product. The article is normally at a bargain price, which the manufacturer is able to do because of the favourable discounts received due to the bulk purchase of the offer item. Very often the manufacturer uses the offer to help the sales force obtain window or store display space. The method suffers from a difficulty in assessing results, as the number of applications received is not always a sound criterion of product acceptability.

(c) *Bargain packs*: the manufacturer offers a product for sale at a reduced price for a short period. Normally the reduction is clearly marked on the package, e.g. 20 per cent. It is really a temporary price cut and is frequently used as a counter to a competitive product. For example, in the 'margarine wars', numerous products offering a variety of benefits, such as taste, low fat, slimming, healthy etc., appear and then one or other of the established brands will reduce their price to try to persuade consumers to stay loyal to their brand rather than try a new one, which they might prefer. Invariably these reductions are in the form of 'money off' rather than actual price cuts, because no matter how temporary or publicised the temporary cut, consumers always react unfavourably to the return to a higher, even if it was the original, price because it still looks like a price rise.

(d) *Sampling*: consumers are given a small, free sample as an inducement to try the brand in the hope that they will like it and be persuaded to develop a brand loyalty. As the sample distribution must be large if it is to be effective, the method can incur considerable expense in:

(i) the production of special-size sample packs,

(ii) the cost of distribution of samples; and

(iii) the cost of 'lost sales', as some consumers who received the free samples would have bought the product anyway, but will now defer purchase until they have finished the sample.

43. New territory exploitation

Sales promotion has a particularly important role in developing the company's products in new territories. There are two general aspects of this:

(a)   home trade; and

(b)   export trade.

In home sales, development of a territory will usually have some continuity with adjacent territories as it is unusual for a product already selling successfully in one area of the home market to be completely unknown elsewhere in domestic trade. Sales promotion would serve here as an extension of the sales force in the role of a quick stimulus to develop trade to a profitable level as soon as possible.

44. Home trade

The methods adopted will vary according to the nature of the business. In retailing it may be store promotions, shop-within-shop arrangements or window displays linked with advertising or it may be linked to the methods suggested in 3:42 such as special offers, bargain packs and so on.

Industrial sales promotion differs essentially from retailing in that almost always it is a *derived demand*, that is, the products are only required for the benefits they can confer in meeting some other objective. For example, an automatic lathe, although expensive to buy, enables overall production costs to be cut; farm tractors increase the efficiency of food production; and word processors produce cheaper and more efficient printing. They all require industrial promotional techniques to be more positive in their appeals. The following are some of the benefits listed for Trailerbition exhibition systems:

(a) *instantly available and portable* display system that can be taken anywhere;
(b) no erection costs;
(c) low cost and *maxium efficiency* exhibitions and presentations;
(d) saves valuable executive time before and after an exhibition;
(e) because it is totally self-contained, the system *reduces transportation costs.*

These are just a few of the benefits claimed for the system but they all communicate *ideas*. All industrial promotional techniques must transmit ideas that spell benefits to the user, such as:

(a) saving time;
(b) reducing labour costs;
(c) lowering handling costs;
(d) quicker movements;
(e) harder wearing; or
(f) less downtime etc.

The ways of achieving results will necessarily vary according to industry, but the following are typical methods:

(a) *Demonstration*: cooperation of an operator is sought to apply or use the product practically. A demonstration is then staged to which other users, or potential users, are invited.
(b) *Trade show*: products are shown in a hotel or similar premises, such as a manufacturers' or stockists' showrooms, in fact, wherever practicable. The buyers are invited to view and discuss their problems with the company's representatives who may include the sales director, sales management or member of the sales force. It is usual to provide drinks and a buffet as an added attraction.
(c) *Individual demonstrations*: manufacturers will take a stand at prominent national exhibitions, such as the Motor Show, International Boat Show, NAIDEX (National Aids for the Disabled Exhibition).

45. Export promotions

Export markets offer companies a wider sales potential than the home market alone. That doesn't mean, however, that a company necessarily has to be over a certain size before tackling export markets. It may be to a small company's advantage to export, if, for example, secure financial arrangements can be made, perhaps by letter of credit (arrangements made with banks and making sure that payments will be made on time). A company can, with shrewd financial planning, generate a useful cash flow by exporting that can aid the firm's growth at home. Export orders can also be more formal, in the sense that they are often larger than in the home markets where similar-sized firms tend to buy in smaller amounts but more often. Another advantage is that orders are also frequently placed in plenty of time for production to be arranged. However, exporting can be complicated and may actually be less profitable than home business although, to repeat the point, it may be useful sales strategy to aid growth even for smaller firms.

Assuming the decision has been taken to export, a certain amount of market research would have to be undertaken to discover the best market in which to begin — it is better to take them one at a time. Market research would then be used to learn the best way of tackling that market.

46. Using promotions

A small firm entering a foreign market is at a disadvantage compared to larger firms that can afford to spend heavily on advertising to make their name as well-known in France, for instance, as it is in Britain. Of course, foreign firms do the same here, e.g. Peaudouce, Chambourcy, Elf etc. A comparatively cheap way of doing this for the smaller firm is to attend exhibitions in the chosen country. For example, a clothing manufacturer could exhibit at the International Men's and Boys' Wear Exhibition in Germany. Although it might seem expensive, it does offer an immediate way to meet the important buyers and to bring the company's products to the attention of as many customers as possible.

There is no fundamental difference between promoting products at home or in foreign markets, although there may be differences in social, legal or cultural details. For example, there are strict rules in Germany covering what can be said to promote children's toys. In some countries, different colours may have different significances. In the West, generally white is associated with happy events — weddings and christenings for instance — but in many Far Eastern countries white is associated with death and funerals. Slogans, too may have to be re-thought, not simply translated. There is the example of the American car that was promoted with a slogan to the effect that it 'went like a dream'. Unfortunately, it ran into trouble when translated into Arabic in which the nearest equivalent wording claimed that it went like a nightmare!

47. Stimulating sales at particular periods

With few exceptions, all products whether consumer or industrial, tend to be seasonal to some degree. Sales promotion can be used to stimulate trade in anticipation of a likely decline at a given time. Promotions may also be employed at periods of intensive buying when competition will be greatest. This may be at Christmas when manufacturers will want to positively direct consumer spending power towards their products or in industry when major maintenance work will be carried out.

In recent years, many firms in the home furnishing and carpets business have overdone 'sales' and special events to the extent that there is always a 'sale'. This has a negative effect and only stimulates a general price-cutting or special offers war, resulting in lower profits all round. It is important for all sales directors and managers to realise that additional sales achieved as a result of increased promotion are only obtained at increased cost. If the increased (or marginal) cost exceeds the increased (or marginal) revenue, then the operation will have failed.

48. Encouraging the sale of particular products

Suppose that Company A has been selling a range of popular products through its sales force. It is well known and accepted by customers and the sales force are making a good increment from the trade, whether through commission, bonuses or just a good basic salary. The company, however, wants them to concentrate on one particular product, perhaps because they have large stocks or because it is seasonal. It may be that the company is introducing a new product to the range or maybe a different kind of product to reach a market segment to whom they are not yet selling. What will the effect of these decisions be on the sales force?

Sales people generally will sell products that are easiest to sell and which generate income for them; that is human nature. The company, however, has perceived that the market is changing, perhaps because:

(a) demand for the existing products is declining;
(b) competitive products are cheaper or more modern;
(c) legislation is going to affect demand, price, design etc.;
(d) new production methods or company investment in equipment make it desirable to introduce new products.

All these factors may necessitate that the sales force sell the new product range in preference to the existing range or in addition to it. In such circumstances, the company may aim the sales promotion at the sales force to encourage them to sell the new range. This is particularly effective in industrial selling.

Example
A firm making a wide range of animal feeding stuffs has an extensive range of products, for cattle, sheep, pigs, horses and pets. The company has bought a bulk supply of grain at a very competitive price and feels that, with winter approaching and the demand for horse feed certain to increase, it can sell its production at the regular price, thereby increasing its profit margin by virtue of its cheap grain purchase. This decision, however, means that the sales force will have to concentrate on horse and cattle feed products in preference to other animal feeding stuffs. A competition is organised among the company's ten sales people. Each product is awarded a number of points per unit sold within a given period, say the following six weeks. At the end of the promotional period, the winning sales person receives a gift, such as a Christmas hamper. The products the company wishes to 'push' are given additional weighting in points and, as the sales force can improve their individual competitive positions with these, they are motivated to sell more of them.

Horse feed	per 25 kilo bag	10 points
Pony mix		10 points
Cattle feed		8 points
Calf mix		6 points
Sheep feed		4 points
Pig feed		3 points
Dog mixer		1 point
Rabbit mix		2 points

The concept has advantages in that it stimulates sales of the required products to users (farmers) to whom the company may not have sold before, some of whom may become regular customers. In this instance, it will also encourage the sales force to concentrate on the bulk users, farmers, horsebreeders and riding schools, rather than the easier sales option — the shops. There are generally disadvantages to every scheme and, on the debit side of such a promotion are the following:

(a) it may lead to large numbers of small orders, at least initially as new customers try the products;

(b) the competitive spirit may lead to less cooperation among members of the sales force who may not pass on information and tips to one another;

(c) it can be a short-term concept, ignoring the importance of selling forward and of spending time in negotiating long-term and larger-scale business (unless sales management takes steps to ensure otherwise);

(d) the 'opportunity costs' of (a), (b) and (c) may exceed the marginal revenue.

Nevertheless, properly managed and controlled, an internal sales promotion, such as this example, can be a powerful way to motivate a sales force towards particular products and markets.

Pricing

49. Introduction
Following the view expressed earlier, that sales tools are alternative investments, then pricing becomes an obvious factor in adjusting the company's sales strategy.

50. Pricing problems
Setting the level of one's prices, is a fundamental decision in any company. Essentially it results from consideration of several influences:

(a) how much profit you want, or need, to make;
(b) what the market will pay;
(c) the total supply costs; and
(d) what competitors are charging.

In reality, the pricing decision is an amalgamation of all these, as is shown in Figure 3.8 (a flow diagram showing these and other influences). However, if we take as a starting point a new company just setting out, clearly it is caught between two basic pressures:

(a) *How much do we need?* This figure will take into account the workers' pay, whether just one or several; how much will be needed to pay rent and meet fuel costs, such as electricity; and how much profit must be made to enable the purchase of further supplies.

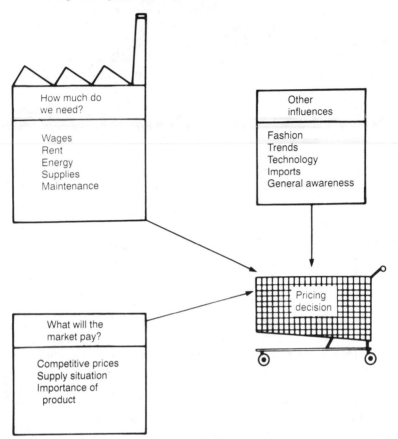

Figure 3.8 *Pricing decisions*

(b) *What will the market pay?* This figure will be deduced from looking at the prices of competitive products. However, nobody should be automatically put off if it appears to be impossible to make them so cheaply. For example, a company making clothes may find that its original idea, to make bulk clothing, is impossible because they will never be able to compete with cheap imports from the Far East. Perhaps the company should therefore aim to make fewer, but better quality clothes. All businesses are faced with these kinds of decisions concerned with market segmentation (as was discussed in Chapter 1).

The other factors — supply costs and competitors' prices — are equally manageable, provided the company decides on the basic point — which market it should be in.

51. Pricing as a policy decision

The levels at which prices are to be set will determine the broad strategy of the company, and vice versa. If the policy is to aim for the mass market, which is served by large volume production, then the general price level will be low.

Henry Ford did not achieve low prices by making his cars in quantity, but achieved quantity production at low cost by a deliberate policy of creating a mass demand for a low-priced car.

In this respect, the pricing decision will have to take several factors into consideration:

(a) the nature of the product;
(b) the importance of the product;
(c) the market for which it is intended;
(d) the form of production needed to manufacture;
(e) economies of scale; and
(f) ease of distribution.

The level of prices is determined by the policy of the company.

52. Fixing price levels

Manufacturers will wish to know at what levels their competitors have set their prices and will certainly be influenced by them, but the decision on fixing their own prices is the company's alone.

For most manufacturers, this decision of fixing price levels is an extremely difficult one. In many cases the manufacturer not only has to determine the company's selling price, but also, if the products are going to be distributed by a wholesaler or factor and sold to the customer by a retailer, the manufacturer may have to determine the suggested price at which *they* will offer the products for sale (e.g. manufacturer's suggested retail price, MSRP). In a very competitive market, the decision may have to be taken 'backwards', that is, the company looks at the particular market in which they would like to sell and works out if it is possible to make products at a determined price. For example, supposing there is a growing demand for a product, perhaps a convenience food, and there are already two on the market retailing at 65p and 68p respectively, can the manufacturer compete at that price? The kind of information that would need to be considered would be:

(a) what the total size of the market is for the food;
(b) what share of that total market the company can reasonably expect to obtain and at what promotional and selling cost;

(c) what investment will be needed to make the product to retail at between 64p and 70p (these are considered to be the outside parameters of that market);

(d) how long it will take to recover that investment — e.g. if the manufacturer estimates that it will take three years to sell enough to pay off the investment and make a worthwhile profit, will the market last that long? Many 'popular' products have very short lives.

When all these questions have been accurately answered, then a decision can be taken on whether to enter that particular market. In this situation, the pricing decision has been on the basis of competition. What is true of large competitive markets is also true of smaller market segments. Indeed, for many new or small companies, the correct decision will be to select a less competitive market segment where price may be relatively less important compared to service, design, quality and flexibility.

53. Competition pricing
Direct competition pricing, generally, is not a satisfactory way of differentiating a product and, as a concept, it is not usually favoured by manufacturers. There are several considerations to be taken into account:

(a) pricecutting is a simple operation and competitors may carry it out rapidly, but as one manufacturer's initiative in price-cutting will certainly be followed by others, competitive positions will be re-established at the lower price level;

(b) there is a psychological reluctance among manufacturers to increase prices and it is also true that once prices have been cut, customers even resist a return to former price levels — this has been noticeable in the petrol market where price cuts are generally kept to major adjustments following changes in crude oil prices, the competitive edge being maintained by sales promotions;

(c) there is a tendency for manufacturers and re-sellers to favour competing from a 'high price' as advantages will be sought by means of advertising, promotion, selling or distribution;

(d) among smaller manufacturers, there is often a realisation that pricecutting cannot succeed against much larger competitors, so they may decide to 'upgrade' their product and aim for a smaller but less competitive segment of the market.

54. Price revision
Manufacturers will have an objective for the company's product and, in assessing this objective, they will have been guided by mar-

keting research. In deciding on the tactics to achieve the objective, the 'tool' of pricing will have been considered:

(a) they will know the price structure of the market that is considered to be the most advantageous for the product;
(b) price will be closely related to brand image, such as the high-class cosmetic manufacturer, oozing sentiment and promiscuity for the company's creation, will not offer it at a 'bargain price';
(c) the planned objectives must be flexible enough to react to a constantly changing market;
(d) there will be fluctuations in commodity prices, as there will be in other raw materials and packaging;
(e) a periodical review does not, of course, necessarily mean that a change in price levels is called for.

55. Selling as a part of the promotional mix

Within the elements of marketing there is a common thread between those known collectively as the promotional mix:

- sales force;
- advertising;
- sales promotion; and where included,
- public relations.

These elements are all means of communicating with the market, but they are also alternatives to 'pricing' as a way of stimulating demand. Sales management should be aware of their relative advantages in deciding upon sales and promotional strategies.

56. Marginal analysis of selling costs

It is possible to use economic models of varying degrees of complexity to analyse the effects of advertising, sales promotion or sales force expenditures on the firm's profits and sales in alternative market situations. However, in a decision-making situation concerning marketing-mix allocations this can be difficult because the predicted results would depend on whether objectives could be clearly stated and whether the relevant variables could be identified in practice and were measurable. For example, look at Figure 3.9, which shows a simple, but typical sales graph. Sales have fallen in Area C, but what does that indicate? How can we identify cause and effect?

The basic purpose of selling costs is to shift the firm's demand curve to the right, so that more of the product is bought at any given price. Referring to Figure 3.9, at price p, quantity d will be demanded,

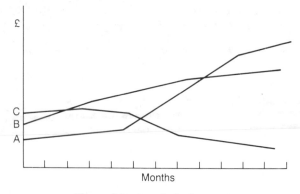

Figure 3.9 *A typical sales graph*

but if the price is reduced to p^1, then demand is extended to d^1, but at a reduced profit level. But if *selling/advertising* are used as an alternative to *pricing*, then it may be possible to increase the quantity demanded to d^1 while still retaining the price at p, only, however, by increasing the *selling/advertising* costs. However, while increasing demand by reducing price will have a short-term effect, and may initiate a price war (as in petrol prices), increasing sales through *selling/advertising* should have a long-term effect which will enable the firm to spread the increased costs over a much longer period and, once demand has been increased, maybe to reduce the *selling/advertising* costs while maintaining the higher level of demand; this is what happens through successful advertising when a new product is launched.

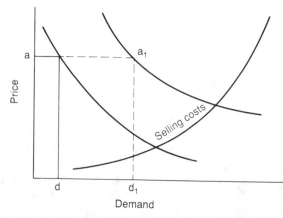

Figure 3.10 *Shifting the demand curve*

Selling costs may, therefore, be viewed as an alternative to price reduction as a means of expanding sales and is concerned with the relative elasticity of demand of different tools (*see* Figure 3.10). If promotional elasticity is high and price elasticity is low, selling costs will be preferred to price cuts as a means of expanding sales and vice versa. It should also be borne in mind that promotional elasticity will vary over the life cycle of a product, declining as the product reaches the stage of maturity. A proportionately, and possibly unacceptably, greater promotional activity will be needed to maintain sales volume as the product grows older, which is why in the decline stage of the cycle, pricing is generally a more effective tool to maintain sales. This, however, can only be done in the short term, because although it is not increasing selling costs, it is reducing profit and is therefore a viable strategy **only** while a replacement product is developed.

> "Marketing decisions which involve alternative strategies, such as the choice of advertising or the sales, apply the criterion; which solution is likely to yield maximum profits?"
> (*Marketing Techniques for Analysis & Control*, Allen).

Expenditure on the sales force is based on two premises:

(a) that it will increase the costs of the firm; and,
(b) successful application will increase the revenue of the firm.

The decision on how much to spend is one of equating the marginal cost of the sales force with the marginal revenue.

Marginal analysis expresses certain relationships, e.g. that an increase in selling cost is acceptable if there is an equal or greater resulting increase in sales revenue. In practice it is not so simple to determine what is happening, especially in the short term. An increased expenditure on the sales force through better training is not easy to equate in terms of improved selling in the short term, although in the long term a better trained and qualified sales force will *probably* result in higher sales revenues. Any expenditure and results are difficult to isolate and measure and the usual statistical problems of identification will be encountered.

Another important consideration to be borne in mind in this type of analysis is the influence of competitor activity, which will be in evidence in any oligopolistic market.

As we have seen, industrial buyers purchase goods to solve problems concerned with their own production or operations. Products are bought for their utility and efficiency. The sales of such products, therefore, are rarely influenced by promotional activities such as advertising and sales promotion, except as a means of drawing attention to them and inviting further information. Sales are expanded in such markets by negotiation processes which often involve discounts of some kind. Such negotiations cannot be effected by advertising or promotional means and must involve face-to-face communications.

Consumers, on the other hand, are influenced by factors other than efficiency and problem-solving characteristics; they are influenced by packaging, promotional messages and status, and these can best be communicated through advertising and promotion. The selling task is accomplished by creating consumer demand for a product and relying upon that demand to oblige retailers to stock the product.

Looking at this complex decision-making process it should be apparent that the elements of the mix are interrelated and interdependent. To reach the correct levels of investment in the alternatives is a matter of blending the proportions correctly, as was suggested in **Fig**ure 3.2.

Progress test 3

1. There are a number of alternative ways in which money might be invested that together, make up the 'tools' of the selling function. List them. (**3**)

2. What developments have influenced the role of the sales force in recent years? (**8**)

3. What is meant by the 'business purpose'? (**12**)

4. There are two terms used in discussing distribution to describe the ways in which goods and materials are collected together and then distributed; what are they? (**14**)

5. What information does marketing research endeavour to provide? (**21**)

6. Advertising is only one of many causes of customer purchases. How many others can you list? (**33**)

7. What factors of policy should be taken into consideration when taking a pricing decision? (**51**)

4

The role of the sales force

The importance of the sales force

1. Selling skills
It is a truism of selling that the process consists of two parts:

(a) sales management; and
(b) selling skills.

By selling skills we mean the whole bundle of techniques and knowledge that, together, ensure the ability of individual members of the sales force to efficiently and satisfactorily complete a sales transaction.

We have already seen, in Chapter 3, that the sale is not complete until the goods are in the hands of the user and are giving satisfactory service. This concept in itself is rather larger than the general perception of what constitutes a 'sale'. For example, if a salesperson calls on a new customer, perhaps a manufacturer, and persuades that company's buyer to place an order for a product, that would seem to be a sale. However, supposing that the order has been obtained by 'clever selling', maybe by exaggerating the product's attributes and making extravagant claims for it, will the buyer *remain* satisfied? What happens when an operative in the works complains that the product doesn't work as it was expected to? The most likely result is a complaint to the seller of the product, perhaps even its return and a demand for a refund of the money if it has been paid for or a refusal to pay if not. In any case, the sale is not definite and will probably result in dissatisfaction, plus, almost certainly, there will be no further business from that source.

2. Looking to the longer term prospects
How can the situation just described be avoided? Isn't it necessary to exaggerate product claims to clinch a sale? The answer is that it is often tempting to do just that, but skilful sales people will consider the longer term prospect, balancing the possibility of a quick order now and no further business or no business now but perhaps more business in the future if a sensible approach is adopted. Of course, in a well-planned sales campaign based on

sound product knowledge, it will be realised that few products satisfy everyone.

Take, e.g. a salesperson selling chemical cleaners. Asked if the product would do a particular job in a hospital, it would have been easy to say 'Yes' and hope for the best, but the sales representative admitted that the product wasn't really suited to that particular task and offered to discuss the hospital's problem with the company's technical people. In a few days, the salesperson returned, offering a modified product and was able to assure the buyer that it would do the job satisfactorily. The order was obtained and, in addition, the hospital's buyer was satisfied as to the expertise and integrity of both the salesperson and the company and had gained enough confidence in them to buy other products as needed.

3.   Discovering the customer's needs

There are several important aspects of the salesperson's job relating to satisfying the customer:

(a) to ultimately discover the customer's needs;
(b) to interpret them into clear needs for his or her company's products or services; and
(c) to ensure that the goods delivered provide continuing satisfaction.

In industrial selling, the sales force has an important role in identifying product/market opportunities. The aspect raised in (c), in particular, is all too frequently omitted. Even if the product is correctly sold and is specifically intended for the customer's problem, dissatisfaction can still arise if the salesperson neglects to make sure that the customer *uses* it correctly. Many modern products can be unexpectedly complicated and, even if the process has been explained to the buyer, and instructions are printed on tins, packages, wrappers or whatever else, people at shopfloor level can still use them wrongly, sometimes with disastrous results. So, ensuring satisfaction means seeing the product right through to completion in use or to providing continuing service.

4.   Buying–selling interface

Ultimately, the entire marketing process is about selling products, which is why the sales function plays such a major role in any company's organisation. This role has been heightened in recent years by:

(a) the increased competition from wider supply markets, that is, more exporting countries;
(b) the increased technology of many products; and
(c) cost pressures on all aspects of business, but especially production.

It must be remembered that *every* manufacturing company is 'double-ended' in the sense that raw materials and components are purchased at one end of the manufacturing process and sold at the other. So, the sales function of one company (the supplier) sells its products to the buying function (the customer) of another company.

During the 1980s, especially, there was enormous pressure on industry throughout Europe, beginning with high unemployment and a search for cost-effectiveness and modernisation that decimated many older labour-intensive, energy costly industries, added to which were vastly increased levels of competition. Manufacturing industry is now finding itself squeezed from both sides, as shown in Figure 4.1.

All these pressures have forced industry to seek efficiencies wherever possible and none more so than in purchasing and supply, for several reasons:

(a) to cut down on inventory costs;
(b) to reduce goods in work;
(c) to improve quality;
(d) all with the aim of maintaining a competitive edge over rivals to hold or, preferably, increase market share.

In all these situations the answer has been to better communications between purchasers and suppliers, both with and between companies, and that means better and more highly trained sales forces.

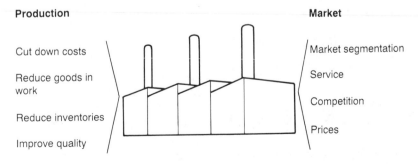

Figure 4.1 *The efficiency squeeze on industry*

In order to obtain the cost-efficiencies in purchasing, the buyer companies have frequently turned to supplier companies for cooperation in developing raw materials, components and supplies of all kinds. This need for cooperation at all levels has meant a higher degree of communication in the buying–selling interface.

In the entire field of industrial purchasing, choosing the right source of supply is a key decision and the sales task is to influence that decision so as to secure markets for the sales company's products (*see* 6:**1**).

5.   Influencing customers

The salesperson exerts one of three important forces to influence customers:

(a) advertising;
(b) experience of customers; or
(c) the sales force.

Advertising (and, in its widest sense, 'publicity' generally) will inform the customers of the existence of the company and its products or services and then motivate them to want them.

Experience of the customers will stem from satisfactory service, enabling satisfied customers to influence other would-be purchasers.

The sales force, by its skill in display and presentation, will effectively introduce the product to would-be customers and will so create new customers by making new sales.

6.   Need for selling skills

The term 'selling', implying the making-over of à product or service in exchange for money, has many unfortunate connotations. Past experiences of some consumers have caused fear and resentment to surround the concept and implications of 'salesmanship'. Unfortunately, there has been adverse publicity in recent times about the way in which specialist salespeople for fitted kitchens, double glazing and others use undue pressure to persuade people to buy. Therefore, in very general terms, some consumer resentment of selling methods may be justified. What isn't justified is that *all* sales and selling be tarred with the same brush. Clearly most firms and salespeople do *not* exert undue pressure, simply because it is counter-productive and against the professionalism of the sales force. Nevertheless firms are often uncomfortable with the term 'salesman or saleswoman' because of the negative connotations and so use euphemisms such as consultants, advisers, counsellors etc. The common term 'representative' is also frequently being used to disguise their real occupation, although this word, too, is starting to fall from favour.

This is just a matter of attitude. Selling is a skilled, professional job and the job itself should never be hidden behind other titles, although it may be the practice of the trade to use other titles. It is also true that titles such as 'consultant' may be effective in conferring more status or may emphasise a higher degree of technical ability in certain industries, which is fine as long as the accompanying training doesn't allow salespeople to forget that their primary objective is to *sell*.

The people who make up the sales force are a vital element in any company's total business activity and, as we shall see in Chapter 18, the organisation of a company must take their role and status into consideration in relation to planning and business policy as a whole. Any company must have customers and those customers can, ultimately, only be obtained and retained by an active, skilled and professional sales force that is fully integrated with the other operations of the company.

Selling is a matter of dealing with people and the salespeople will be effective if they:

(a) act using their common sense; and
(b) have a basic understanding of psychology.

7. The psychological basis of selling

Many successful sales people have an innate ability to respond to people and understand them; they are sensitive to attitudes and responsive to the moods of others. Such an ability is of great help to salespeople and it can be developed by an understanding of the basics of psychology.

Psychology is the study of human behaviour and what motivates people to behave as they do in different situations. Obviously a salesperson who understands something of why people behave as they do, will be more responsive to the attitudes and maybe the intolerances of others and be more able to handle them. In other words, an understanding of psychology helps the salesperson to know *why* people behave as they do. It is essential, in particular, to possess an understanding of:

(a) the mental processes;
(b) the elements of motivation and people's needs;
(c) the way in which people are likely to react to propositions; and
(d) the psychological basis of leadership.

8.   Understanding the buyers' decision processes

By itself however, this is not sufficient. We shall see later, in Chapter 7, that people responsible for buying have to take decisions but are, themselves, confined by the boundaries, or parameters, of their particular job. The buyer working for a large department store, for example can exercise discretion in buying but only within the policy laid down by the company. That policy may, for instance, limit buying to not more than £10 000 or may lay down certain clear guidelines about quality or even suppliers. Appreciating this can help any salesperson to avoid wasting time trying to convert people to a point of view that the very limitations of their job prevent them from accepting. The buyer may agree with you on a personal level, but is prevented from acting by the company's constraints or policies.

Here is an example to illustrate the point. My company negotiated the sales of nine presentation systems to a medical company for use by their sales force. We designed and priced the systems as competitively as we could to secure the order. The company liked them and agreed to place an order, but the buyer asked whether we could offer them a discount for quantity. We knew it wasn't really justified, but, as the buyer put it, 'I have to do the best for my company'. What he really meant was that he had to justify his buying decision to his boss and needed to show that he had negotiated a good deal. Suspecting such a situation might arise, we had, however, built into the price a figure that we could 'give away' in the form of a discount. The buyer was happy and so were we.

To fulfil the needs of salesmanship then, salespeople must also completely understand the business in which they are occupied. They must:

(a) be familiar with the business;
(b) comprehend the policies of their firm;
(c) understand the practices of the particular industry or profession;
(d) know something of the practices of the organisation to which they aim to sell;
(e) be aware of the policies of their competitors; and
(f) endeavour to create a harmonious relationship between their company and their customers.

Although these suggestions have been introduced in the context of understanding behaviour, there is the question of *acquiring* the information that is implied in the above list. It can be obtained without too much difficulty; for example, if you are going to sell to a government department, there are usually official publications that will give information on the buying structure of the organisation. If there aren't, it is worth spending some time on research or telephone calls to discover the right approach. It may be that the official you should see can take a buying decision only to a certain level of expenditure, after which he or she must seek permission or sanction from a superior. Understanding this can help you sell because you can ease the buyer's path when you discretely make it known that you are aware of the procedure. You may seek his or her advice in taking the matter higher or, indeed, provide the information that will enable the buyer to go to his or her superior. This also adds to your appearance of professionalism in the eyes of the buyer.

From the discussion of selling ability above, it becomes apparent that, while some people will have greater *natural* abilities in selling than others, good salespeople are, nevertheless, created by good *training*.

9.   Satisfactory service

Satisfactory service is the most important element in the completed transaction.

Many so-called 'super-salespeople' who boast about being able to sell anything, fail to realise that their high-pressure selling arises from dissatisfaction. That is, they *have* to be able to sell to anyone because they frequently cannot return to a previous customer. If you work hard and sell an article to a customer *knowing* that it is not what he or she really wants, then the result will be an unsatisfied customer. The customer will not become a repeat buyer. A reaction begins:

(a)   the customer will not buy again; and
(b)   the salesperson has to create further dissatisfied customers.

In the distributive industries:

(d)   the retailer will not buy more of that product from the wholesaler;
(e)   the wholesaler will not re-order from the manufacturer; and
(f)   the manufacturer may eventually cease production.

The product has failed, but worse, no goodwill has been created for further transactions. The situation can be avoided if, as we saw in 4:**1**, the salesperson seeks information from the potential customer that will help the company to improve or adapt products where necessary. This is particularly true if you are selling abroad. My own company, as I mentioned in an example earlier, manufacture an exhibition system mounted on a trailer. When selling it in the Netherlands, some initial research revealed that there were some legal requirements applying to trailer construction that weren't required in Britain. This

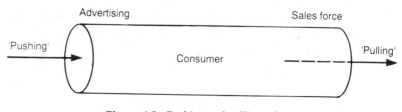

Figure 4.2 *Pushing and pulling sales*

would have put off Dutch customers, without them necessarily telling us why, but as we had found this out in advance we were able to overcome it.

10. Dependency on the sales force

Advertising's job, in general terms, is to promote knowledge and acceptance of the product by potential customers. The sales force, ultimately, have the task of introducing the product to customers and ensuring completion of the cycle from knowledge to satisfaction.

We can, in the selling process, talk in terms of 'pushing' and 'pulling', as in Figure 4.2. A salesperson–customer relationship is vital to the accomplishment of a sale. The necessity of this relationship is clear when it is realised that the impression the customer receives from the salesperson will usually form the opinion held of the company.

Example

A manufacturer of tools may make a considerable investment in time and finance, perfecting a new electric drill. The company will spend further effort and money in marketing activities (market research, advertising, publicity, distribution and transport costs) to put the drill into widespread outlets, such as the plethora of DIY superstores. If the machine is not 'sold' in the correct manner, this entire process collapses.

For example, if a customer goes to a DIY store for a drill, he or she generally asks an assistant's opinion of the range of electric drills and requests information. The assistant mentions a brand by name, but makes no move either to take the customer to the drill or to tell the customer where to find it. The customer gives the assistant every opportunity to introduce the drill but the 'salesperson' remains apathetic and negative. The customer leaves.

It is important to separate the two aspects of getting goods into user's hands and getting them sold. Until they are the responsibility of salespeople, everything that has happened to the goods is distribution. The selling does not begin until the salesperson takes over and meets the customer.

In the past the salesperson was either:

(a) an order-taker; or

(b) a persuader.

Todays's salesperson has to become more knowledgeable in his or her dealings with customers who are, themselves, becoming more knowledgeable and less credulous. Present-day salespeople have to more than equal their customer's knowledge if they are to be successful.

Maximising sales efficiency

11. Selling by proxy

Manufacturers who recognise their dependency on their sales force will have a more competitive position, and a healthier prospect of growth. There are, essentially, three types of selling.

(a) *speciality selling* — selling direct to customers;
(b) *industrial or technical selling* — selling to industrial or specialist users;
(c) *sales representation* (what used to be known as 'commercial travelling') — selling to a distributor before the product reaches the final consumers and users.

It may happen that salespeople have to perform more than one type of selling. For example, someone selling power tools may sell to large, DIY stores, which conform generally to type (c), and also to industrial users, such as manufacturers or contractors, which are type (b). What is important, though, is that the salesperson understands the *difference in purchasing reasons* between the two types. Using the wrong selling approach will lessen the effectiveness of the presentation.

12. Different approaches to suit different customer types

Consider selling directly to the three different types. What information will they be seeking and what information will influence their decision? Look at the matrix in Figure 4.3.

13. Bases of difference

Consumers are looking for personal benefits in terms of price etc. as well as what they consider to be a reasonable price. Users are also seeking benefits, although they are related to the impersonal advantages to their companies, that is, they are seeking cost-reducing advantages in terms of faster production time, less labour employed, more reliable work and so on. Distributors, retailers, and other re-sellers are seeking profit and so want to know how much money they will make by selling the product. They will be considering your

Customer type	(a)	(b)	(c)
	Personal benefits:	Economic benefits:	Commercial benefits:
Information sought	status colour ease of use guarantee simplicity reasonable price	reduces work load reliability durability cost-efficiency servicing	profit margin rapid stock turnover reliability attractive packaging and display

Figure 4.3 *A matrix of selling benefits*

product and its margins against those of other manufacturers or suppliers. If your product offers only limited profit margins and a slow turnover, it won't be acceptable, no matter how good it claims to be.

14. Selling through intermediaries

In selling through others — whether the company's own sales staff or those of distributors etc. — the manufacturer must ensure that their salespeople are also familiar with the product's selling points and benefits and can represent them to their customers. If the product is technical, it may be of advantage to run a training course for the distributors' staff as well as the firm's own people.

This is what is meant by 'selling by proxy'. Most small businesses know this problem because, as firms grow, they reach the point where the owners can no longer do all the jobs themselves; they then have to entrust their sales to others and have to be very sure that they are well trained. They must:

(a) be able to give good service to the customer;
(b) possess an accurate and full knowledge of their products; and
(c) know and understand their customers.

15. The salesperson

There exist, in every sales situation, two variable factors, which are:

(a) the seller or the seller's representative; and
(b) the buyer.

Any study of the effectiveness of salespeople as part of the workings of business, and distribution in particular, must include a consideration of these two factors.

As mentioned, there are three basic types of selling — speciality selling, industrial or technical selling and sales representation. Whatever type of selling is embarked on, the personality of the salesperson will be a major influence on the outcome.

Although a person may move from one type of selling to another, nevertheless, particular personalities may be more suited to one kind of selling than another. For example, a person may perform well as a technical representative, being able to converse well on technicalities, to understand the customers' technical problems and to inspire confidence; the same person, however, may not be as good at specialist selling because it requires a different approach.

Having obtained business, the salesperson's task is to retain it. He or she will therefore adopt a different attitude towards the customer.

16. Retaining business

The main task of the salesperson in retaining business will be to make it easy for the customer to keep buying from a known and trusted supplier, rather than risk changing. Salespeople can ensure that customers are retained and service maintained by:

(a) a good relationship;
(b) checking on order details, such as their quantity and quality; and
(c) familiarising themselves with delivery details.

By attention to details, salespeople may succeed in changing a buyer's source of supply or having a specification altered. A salesperson's success, however, can also be a weakness, because, if he or she has succeeded in changing the buyer's mind once, who is to say the buyer won't change it again?

Example
A few years ago there was a lot of business to be had in the development of motorways. For those in the metal protection business, there were large orders pending from treatment to the miles of balustrading on motorway bridges. It was quite usual for the specification to be laid down by surveyors and engineers when the original designs were approved. Later, when construction was progressing, a salesperson could introduce new, cost-effective types of protection and, providing the effectiveness of these treatments could be proven, he or she could get the specifications changed. Very often, however, other technical salespeople would then go along with an 'even better' treatment and succeed in changing them again. Once engineers had agreed to

change the original specification in favour of something demonstrably better, it wasn't too difficult to get them to change it again.

The example reinforces the idea that salespeople must be alert to competitors' activity and defeat it by diligent attention to detail.

17. Intensive and extensive selling

Intensive selling is employed where a product is highly priced and of limited appeal. Such selling requires a great degree of preparation and a high degree of selling skill.

Extensive selling is necessary where the product appeals to a wide range of people; the product is usually low priced and the salespeople cannot profitably occupy too much time trying to sell it.

18. Two-way representation

Within the structure of the selling process, salespeople occupy an important and unique position, interposed between customer and company. Communication of information, knowledge and opinion between customer and company is of vital importance to the selling task. Figure 4.2 shows the two-way task salespeople have and the intricacies of their responsibilities.

Example

A manufacturer made a wide range of animal feedstuffs, including a rabbit mix sold to pet shops in 20-kilo bags. Because of the popularity of rabbits as pets, the market for the product was very competitive and so literally came down to differences in pennies per bag. The Sales Manager thought about this and, after some analysis of the market, made a bold proposal to the directors: 'Reduce the price by ten pence a bag', he said, 'and bulk sales will increase to the point where the increase in demand will more than offset the reduction in profit per bag'. Using graphs and figures, he won the day and a mail shot went out to all the stockists and the salespeople, too, were told to concentrate a special effort on selling rabbit mix. The result was excellent and the larger stockists ordered in one tonne loads, thereby reducing delivery charges and enabling the ingredients to be bought in more economical quantities, and manufactured into feed in larger and cheaper production runs. So far so good. However, within a few days, complaints began to arise when stockists insisted that the mix was of poor quality with too much cheap grain and not enough of the better quality ingredients. Much alarmed, the Sales Manager went to the directors and found that they had 'cheated', because, although they had lowered the cost, the firm had *also* reduced the quality. After a furious row they agreed to restore the quality to that expected by the customer and the day was saved, but only just!

In this example, the Sales Manager was acting for both his company, by proposing a clever selling ploy, and also for the customers who, rightly, demanded the same quality.

At other times, salespeople may find it necessary to advocate changes proposed by the company even though they believe they will cause dissatisfaction among their customers and ultimately, lose the company business. Common examples are unavoidable price increases or product changes.

19. Management's responsibility

Salespeople, by the nature of their job, must work away from their company, home and family. An export sales executive may find it especially onerous to be away for weeks or even months at a time. It can be a mental strain to salespeople to be working alone, unable to express opinions or confide problems to family or firm.

Good sales management will be aware of this problem of isolation and insecurity and make provision for the sales force to meet at regular intervals. On these occasions, salespeople will make contact with colleagues, management and production and will be able to discuss problems and receive information and the experiences of others. Management will endeavour to assist the salesperson to enjoy successful personal selling skills by developing:

(a) proper attitudes;
(b) knowledge; and
(c) practical applications of skills and knowledge.

It is sales management's responsibility to provide alert leadership and adequate supervision to ensure that the sales force as a whole operates in the same direction and in accordance with agreed policies.

Progress test 4

1. What two parts make up the selling process? (**1**)

2. The salesperson exerts one of three important forces that influence customers; what are the other two? (**5**)

3. In what ways does understanding the psychological basis of selling help salespeople? (**7**)

4. Why should you adopt different approaches to suit different customer types? (**12**)

5

Behavioural aspects of selling

What behaviour is and its role in the selling process

1. Introduction

Selling goods and services is more than a purely economic activity. Whether individuals or companies are concerned with selling to consumers or to organisational buyers, it is very much an activity involved with human behaviour.

2. What is meant by 'behaviour'?

Morgan and King in *Introduction to Psychology* describe behaviour in the following way:

> 'Behaviour, rather than mind or thoughts or feelings, is the subject of psychology as we define it, because it alone can be observed, recorded and studied. No one ever saw, heard or touched a mind, but one can see and hear behaviour.'

This is an important consideration for all those involved in selling because selling is rather a combative activity. For example, one person selling a product to another person has to try and predict the other's attitude: will this person like this product? How will he or she react to what I'm going to say? As the description makes clear, we cannot see or 'plug into' another mind, so the best we can do is interpret a person's behaviour as a guide to what they are thinking. Clearly this is a very imprecise activity; we may wrongly interpret behaviour or we may not understand all the behaviour we observe.

3. Behaviour as a guide to understanding attitudes

Understanding behaviour can never be more than a guide to the attitudes of others and it is often 'attitude' that salespeople are most concerned with. We can see and measure what a person does or hear and record what a person says; anything else must be inferred. Applying behavioural knowledge to selling, though, is not an attempt to psychoanalyse someone or even to have pretentions of being a psychologist, but a useful aid to predicting the way others involved in selling may react or behave and can be useful in gaining an insight into why people react the way they do. For example, if a buyer rejects your sales presentation, it is possible that he or she is reacting to pressures or stimuli other than those being generated by you alone. We do infer that, in reaction to our actions in selling or promoting, a mental process has taken place and the buyer has thought and felt, but we can only gauge this by the person's *behaviour*.

A knowledge of behaviour can help salespeople control a sales presentation as well as providing a valuable guide to a whole range of promotional activities.

4. People's behaviour in relation to selling is not isolated from other events

People's behaviour as users and consumers of a wide range of products and services has to be seen and studied in relation to their other roles in life. For example:

(a) as parents;
(b) as workers; and
(c) as students or schoolchildren.

In this way, behaviour also has to be seen against an environmental background, e.g.:

(a) *social environment* — where people live or work;
(b) *cultural environment* — what a person's religious background, place of origin etc. are;
(c) *educational environment* — whether or not people are educationally equipped to understand or use this product and whether or not this will affect their attitudes towards it;
(d) *economic environment* — the level of income, standards of living and available disposable income will affect buying decisions of the individual or the firm.

Consumption and use of products, therefore, must be related to the structure of society and the interactions of individuals within the various groups that make it up.

5. Whose behaviour are we concerned with?

Everyone exhibits behaviour and that includes everyone involved in the selling process, including:;

(a) salespeople;
(b) sales management;
(c) consumers;

(d) industrial/commercial buyers;
(e) designers; and
(f) advertisers.

It is important to see all these people as interchangeable and interactive. For example, consumers of toothpaste may also be buyers of industrial oil, graphic designers may buy art materials for their firm as well as selling their services and salespeople and sales managers all have homes and are private consumers.

Therefore, when salespeople go into the offices of industrial buyers, they are meeting people who, at that time, are playing the role of 'buyer'. Buyers have private lives and private problems as well as those relating to their job role and, if you find it difficult to sell your new word processor or display system, it may be because the buyer can't pay the mortgage or because there is the possibility of redundancies in the firm or industry. Of course, salespeople, no matter how efficient and effective, cannot be expected to deal with every problem buyers have or even know what they are. It is sufficient to have an insight into their existence.

6.   The uses of behavioural knowledge
An understanding of human behaviour as applied to selling and marketing has many uses. It can be applied to:

(a) preparing a sales presentation;
(b) making the sales presentation;
(c) dealing with customer objections;
(d) overcoming customers' resistance to buying;
(e) planning sales promotions and advertising campaigns;
(f) developing and launching new products; and
(g) creating brand images.

In the wider context of selling, it also helps management and the sales force in their relations with one another, in the following ways:

(a) sales training;
(b) motivation and leadership;
(c) generally handling others in human relations.

7.   The bases of behaviour
Behaviour is a very complex subject, but it is sufficient here to outline the main factors that play a central part in determining customer behaviour. These are:

(a) cognition;
(b) perception; and
(c) the learning process.

8. Cognition
This term refers to those mental processes that enable us to experience and interpret the world in which we live. It embraces:

(a) perceiving;
(b) knowing; and
(c) judging.

The ways in which individuals react to a situation or a product will be influenced by the ways in which they perceive certain kinds of objects. They will have a personal view of the world in which they exist, which is derived from their environment and their frames of reference. A simple example is the way different people view smoking. This will be influenced by social and cultural conditions — where they live; how they were brought up; how the threat of smoking is perceived (as explained by medical, scientific and social information); and the effects of advertising and promotional information.

One can speak of a *cognitive map* of a person, which is an individual's own subjective view of the world. Consumption habits will be influenced by this agglomeration of cognitions and may influence people in many ways. For example in:

(a) Their choice of foods — should you buy only wholemeal bread?
(b) The choice of products — is it right to import foreign products?
(c) The choice of point of purchase — should you support the small corner shop in preference to supermarkets?

The environment in which we all live is extremely complicated and often very confusing — especially today when we are all bombarded with so much more information. Television, for example, has made us all much more aware of the greater world in which we live. It has also subjected us all to many more consumption pressures and a bewildering array of possible choices.

In selling, the job of the salesperson is often to clarify a complex choice for the customer by explaining the advantages and disadvantages and overcoming their perceptions of risk.

9. Perception
Perception is closely linked to cognition and is even regarded by

some psychologists as an element of cognition because it is by means of perception that a person 'knows'.

Perception occurs as a result of sensing. For example, an advertisement often makes use of a stimulus to attract attention, such as a startling image or a bright colour. Our senses are stimulated by unexpected or unusual events or objects. To perceive is:

(a) to hear;
(b) to see;
(c) to touch;
(d) to taste;
(e) to smell; and
(f) to sense something.

Generally we use these senses in combinations. For example, we see and hear an event on television and may additionally use insight to recognise or perceive what is meant or what is happening.

In selling, therefore, it is important to recognise the powerful stimuli created by such perceptions and use samples creatively. People can recognise and grasp ideas and propositions more readily if they can experience them. Food samples in supermarkets can, by the aroma, attract people from afar. Giving a customer a sample to handle, feel, experience and relate to, is worth a great deal of pure talk.

10. Learning process

If customers buy a product, use it and find it favourable, then it is likely that they will buy it again. This is because the experience (learning) of using it was favourable. Conversely, if the product did not, in their opinion, perform favourably, then they will not buy it again. It is from these experiences — learning through use — that brand loyalties are developed.

Learning may be defined as a 'more or less permanent change in behaviour that occurs as a result of practice'. It is through the learning process that buyers of goods develop attitudes, either favourable or unfavourable.

11. Different kinds of learning

What people learn can be classified in many ways, but they can be separated into two fundamental groups:

(a) perceptual learning; and
(b) response learning.

Perceptual learning is learning from stimuli picked up by the senses, while response learning is when one learns to make a particular response or group of responses.

12. Arousal and motivation

For learning to take place, the most fundamental condition is that the person be in a reasonably high state of arousal and, further, in a state of motivation. This means, for instance, that if a teacher is boring it is unlikely that the pupils will be either aroused or motivated. If we substitute 'salespeople' for 'teacher' and 'customers' for 'pupil', then the relevance of this to selling is apparent.

Good teaching usually involves the use of a variety of stimuli: examples, changes of sights and sounds, use of models and films etc. In the same way, salespeople should prepare to arouse their clients by a skilful use of these same stimuli, (see 5:8).

Good presentations are often successful because they arouse customers and motivate them to want information, that is they want to learn about the product being presented to them. The following examples contribute to successful presentations:

(a) if a salesperson has a boring or toneless voice, the presentation will not arouse interest in the customer, so varying the voice and showing your own interest and excitement at the product's use is helpful;

(b) using interesting stimuli, for example samples, and letting the customer see how it works, handle it and use it is very valuable;

(c) bringing creativity to the presentation is very effective, e.g. you can use a tape recorder or video to show a product in use or use display systems to create a small 'exhibition' in your client's office.

All these are intended to stimulate and, thus, arouse and motivate customers so that they will *learn* about your products. If they react favourably and use your product successfully, they will have reinforced that learning and be more disposed to use the product again.

Behavioural aspects of communication

13. Consumer expectation

Expectation is the biggest motivational factor in selling. Consumers are more likely to experience disappointment in their purchases, however, when they have a high expectation. The big purchases, which are given a greater degree of pre-purchase evaluation will produce the greatest post-purchase disappointment if they prove to be mistakes. Faced with a range of cars, domestic appliances etc., each claiming special features and each producing areas of doubt about them in our minds, how can we be entirely confident of our eventual selection? In psychological terms, the consumer will experience *cognitive dissonance*.

14. Cognitive dissonance

People's experiences of their environment can only be obtained through their senses in the process of perception. The ability to make sense of the information perceived is cognition. If the information received about a product is contrary to the consumer's beliefs, either the beliefs will have to be changed or the information rejected. For example, at election time people will be presented with several different sets of beliefs. People committed to party 'A' may be presented with a contrary view by candidates of party 'B'. The candidates may produce facts and figures to 'prove' a point, but they may in fact be providing information that would oblige the supporters of party 'A' to change their viewpoint if the information was to be accepted. What do the 'A' supporters do? If the information cannot be reconciled with their views, the supporters have to denigrate that information, perhaps claim it is biased. Very often a similar situation arises in selling.

Suppose you have always bought a particular product, say Shell petrol. If you are then faced with an advertising campaign urging you to buy an alternative brand of petrol and the arguments and benefits seem realistic and valid but you are a committed buyer of Shell, you either have to change your views and accept the new information or reject it as false.

Advertising campaigns sometimes make use of this phenomenon of cognitive dissonance by challenging the consumer to make a change. For example, women may buy particular brands of shampoo and marketing research indicates that they are reluctant to accept a new brand. The manufacturer has to choose from two alternatives:

(a) to make the new product similar to the competition in the hope that consumers will not see sufficient distinction between them to justify not buying it;

(b) to make the new product very distinctive, stress its difference and challenge consumers to try it and change brands.

The second choice makes use of cognitive dissonance, challenging people's beliefs and relying on their ability to choose.

15. Changing beliefs

It is recognisably difficult to change beliefs that are strongly held or felt to be important. Sales management will try to avoid attempting to change attitudes in those segments where the probability of change is low as this would be a waste of resources. They will, instead, allocate resources to segments where the probability of change is high. The question is then, 'Under which circumstances are attitude changes most likely to occur?'

16. Strengths of attitudes.

Broadly speaking, the probability of change varies inversely to the strength of the attitude. The stronger the consumer's predisposition, the less likelihood there is of changing that attitude by persuasion. There are four reasons for attitude strength:

(a) if the existing state of knowledge is limited, attitudes will be more susceptible to change and there will be less commitment to a particular belief;

(b) attitudes that are closely related to the person's self-concept, say, their morals, are more resistant to change and are strong motivational values;

(c) attitudes that are intimately connected with other attitudes are difficult to change, such as political or social attitudes;

(d) personality will also affect resistance to change to a high degree, people with strong beliefs being less likely to change attitudes in response to new information than those who have no strong beliefs.

17. Turning cognitive dissonance to advantage

Because a buyer has a strong belief it doesn't follow that a salesperson cannot use this to advantage. For example, there was an architect in South Wales who held the old-fashioned belief that it was far better to apply many thin coats of paint to a surface than just one or two of the newfangled modern thick paints. He could not be persuaded to change his ideas solely by being told about the benefits the new product offered. However, when a salesman agreed with him on his views of the need for many coats, but commiserated with him over the rising labour costs involved in painting the same surface many times, he reluctantly admitted that, despite his views, he had to reduce his labour costs and so agreed to buy the new products. Of course, once he had seen them applied and saw that they worked, he quietly continued to buy the new thicker paints!

18. Selling and commitment

The strength of commitment is the most important element in a particular attitude and has, therefore, a strong connection with resistance to change. Salespeople are constantly encountering such resistance and need a means for overcoming it.

Consumers and users who are strongly committed to a preference in products become dissonant when they feel that their preference is being challenged. This has important effects on the introduction of new or replacement products. Consumers who have developed a loyalty to a long-established brand are likely to become dissonant and tend to avoid or denigrate the new information. Thus, a large selling effort is needed at the outset of a new product launch. Manufacturers will often retain successful product and brand names, even when the product changes, such as Daz and New Daz, and Cortina I, II, III, IV and V.

An example of dissonance in response to a new product was Ford's introduction of a replacement for its Granada model. The Mark II Granada was a popular car but its replacement, first called Scorpio, was a very different configuration and not immediately successful. For a while, the car's name was changed back to Granada until the car had become more accepted in the market when it reverted back, first to Granada Scorpio and then to just Scorpio.

Figure 5.1 shows how attitudes may range along a spectrum, from a position that is most acceptable to a position that is most unacceptable. Between them is an area of non-commitment in which the possibility for changing attitudes is strongest. Sales management can

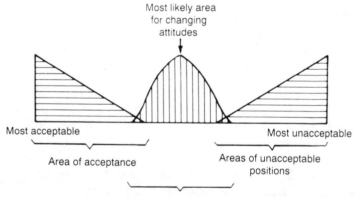

Figure 5.1 *Possibilities for changing attitudes*

use marketing research to discover which segments of a market would be most likely to accept a new or replacement product and target that segment for its sales and promotion campaigns, because that is the likely source of the greatest returns, at least initially. As the product becomes accepted and better known, it will then be possible to move outwards from this position to challenge less acceptable segments.

19. Motivating the purchaser

The concept of motivating a purchase raises the question, 'How far can a potential purchaser be motivated?' This begs the question 'What is motivation?'

Motivation is not something that we can do to others, but is, rather, the result of a situation in which people can become self-motivated. Motivation is a 'self-starter' rather than a 'tow-start'. For sales management it means that a favourable situation has to be created in which consumers or users will wish to buy the product and this means removing the factors that inhibit buying, the frictions to buying.

In behavioural terms, motivation is a state of tension created by a drive and the will to be satisfied by fulfilment of the drive, that is by buying something for which the drive — a need or want — has been created. Advertising and, indeed, other sales and marketing communication endeavours to provide information related to consumers' perceived needs, which will act as a cue and provide the drive. For instance, financial advertisements offering loans usually do this by suggesting uses for the money. Double glazing advertisements generally stress such factors as heat loss and the money spent on wasted energy that occur with conventional windows.

20. What are human needs?

Our needs broadly fall into two categories, which are:

(a) biogenic; and
(b) psychogenic.

In present-day society most of the biogenic needs — for food, shelter etc. — are satisfied, either by earning money to pay for them by working, or should be provided by social services. This leaves all our other needs to be categorised generally as psychogenic.

Eating out in restaurants has less to do with hunger (a biogenic need) than with its social importance (a psychogenic need). This can be seen in the many advertising campaigns that stress a social value rather than a physical need for their product, e.g. washing powder advertisements that imply that using such and such a powder enables a woman to be a good housewife or mother rather than simply producing cleaner clothes. Bedtime drinks, likewise, succeed in the market if the mother watching it perceives herself as satisfying her child's need for nourishment, goodness, sound sleep and other desirable characteristics by using the product. In reality, milk alone will do this just as well. Similarly, the choice of family toothpaste is now perceived as being important, because if a child has tooth decay it is implied that this is because the parent did not buy the 'right' toothpaste. This is a powerful, if negative, force in motivating purchases of products. Many claims that used to be made for 'healthy' qualities of products, such as 'Sleep sweeter Bournvita' or 'Guinness is good for you' are no longer permitted in Britain, but are still used in underdeveloped countries where a claim for health-giving qualities is a powerful motivator when children, especially, are suffering from severe malnutrition.

The need to conform is also found among organisational buyers, who prefer to stick to well-tried products rather than purchase newer products to which an element of risk may attach. This is not necessarily a *product* risk, but more a risk that the buyer may be wrong in changing an accepted practice. In selling, there is a need to find ways of providing sufficient evidence, recommendations and examples, to be able to give assurance to buyers that they will not be taking a risk when they buy your product.

21. Hygiene and motivation factors in buying

To what degree a sales proposition will prompt the customer to buy will depend on how that person, or people, perceive what the salesperson is offering. For example, if a salesperson presented you, the customer, with a hitherto unknown product for a purpose already fulfilled by alternative products, how would *you* react? Would you perceive there to be a need for their product?

There are two sets of factors in any buying situation, which are:

(a) those that do *not* encourage a person to buy, such as price, delivery etc.; and
(b) those that *do* encourage a person to buy, e.g. status, labour saving, prestige and other such factors.

The first are *hygiene factors*, so-called by analogy because hygiene does not make a person healthy but prevents a person becoming unhealthy. The second are *motivation factors* because they encourage people to take the buying decision.

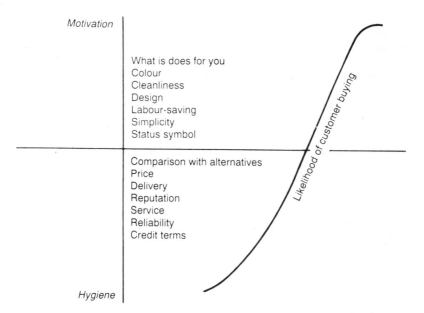

Figure 5.2 *Hygiene and motivation factors*

Figure 5.2 illustrates these two sets of factors. The hygiene factors should be recognised as characteristics that do not encourage people to buy and, indeed, are *reasons for not buying*. A salesperson must recognise such factors as those illustrated as being areas where customers will have doubts and deal with them in the sales presentation. For example, if the delivery date is recognised as being a factor that might dissuade the customer from buying, then dealing with it may remove an obstacle. You could say, 'Although the popularity of the product has created great demand, at the moment delivery is only two weeks'. Hopefully that will reassure the customer that delivery is not going to be a problem. In a similar way, all the other hygiene factors can be dealt with before they disquiet the customer.

Once the reasons for *not* buying have been removed and, with them, the customer's doubts, what is left are all the reasons *for* buying — those factors that the customer perceives as being desirable. For example, a new car gives prestige and status and a new machine offers the benefits of reduced labour costs and greater precision.

Progress test 5

1. What is meant by behaviour? **(2)**

2. What are the three bases of behaviour? **(7)**

3. What is the most fundamental condition for learning to take place, and how does understanding this point help selling? **(12)**

4. What is the difference between a hygiene factor and a motivation factor? **(21)**

6

Understanding the buyer

The buying–selling interface

1. The relationships between buying, selling and sales

The purpose of the sales function is to sell effectively and, therefore, the entire process is inseparably entwined with the activity of buying. To fully comprehend the total selling task, therefore, buying, or purchasing, must also be understood. Figure 6.1 illustrates this relationship.

A sale is never completed until the buyer decides to buy, therefore, effective selling must create favourable buying decisions. For example, someone selling office stationery does not succeed unless

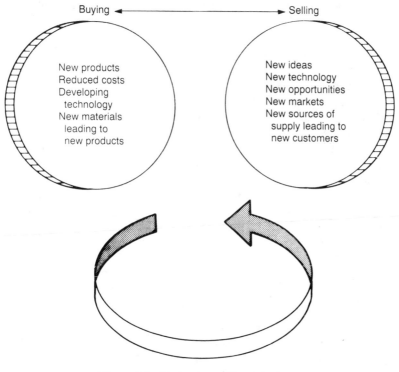

Figure 6.1 *The buying–selling interface*

buyers place orders for his or her products. Unfortunately, all too often, otherwise sound sales training omits a study of the buyer and buyer behaviour.

2. The importance of the buying–selling interface

A further point to be remembered is that the buying–selling interface is a self-generating process in which the needs of one (the buyer) become the purpose of the other (the seller). Of course, it also works the other way round, because buyers can be very dependent on the skills of those selling for the products and, often, the product development they need. For example, the technical needs of the car industry mean that it is very dependent on the innovative skills and product development of those industries that service it with electronics. In the spring of 1988, the electronics group, AB Electronics of South Wales, received much publicity for an entirely new electronic control system they developed for Jaguar cars. At a lesser level of business, many small companies develop special products for large firms. It is all a part of the process by which products and companies expand.

3. The different levels of the buying process

As seen in Chapter 3, distribution channels consist of a number of transactions — the whole process being termed a transvection. At each stage of this transvection, a buying–selling interaction takes place. If the entire production–marketing process is very long, e.g. in the production of a motor car from hundreds of beginnings, involving steel, rubber, electronics, paint, glass etc., and with each of them backed by a process of manufacture from raw materials to components, there will be thousands of buying decisions. The buying–selling interactions do not end until the car is sold to the final consumer.

Buying decisions for goods and services are made at four levels:

(a) the final consumer — usually termed *shopping*;
(b) retailing of goods — *wholesale buying*;
(c) buying of industrial goods — usually termed *purchasing*; and
(d) the securing of government supplies — usually known as *procurement*.

These terms, like so many in business, are not definitive, but are generally used. For example, if you want to sell to one of the many government departments, it is usually the 'procurement officer' who has to be seen.

4. How the final consumer buys

All marketing is ultimately fired by consumer demand. The influence of consumer demand or lack of demand has been seen all too clearly in the 1970s, 1980s and 1990s when rising unemployment has been the death-knell of many firms.

The process of shopping involves the consumer in hundreds of decisions a year. Buying for the house alone necessitates choosing between many different brands or versions of the same kinds of products. Choices are often made in an arbitrary manner in which the greatest influence for many branded goods is probably the perception of the product's advertising image. Indeed, many manufacturers spend millions of pounds a year to ensure that both consumers and stockists are favourably disposed towards the product.

Because consumers in their day-to-day shopping are faced with so many decisions, it is hardly surprising that they do not devote considerable time and effort judging each one. Of course, many people will compare prices and probably relate them to pack size, but even that will be tempered by such value judgements as taste and reputation. Because of the considerable choice and the number of choices, this type of decision making is termed *value attitudes*.

5. Value attitudes

It is fundamental to all selling that salespeople, and people in marketing generally, should try to put themselves in their customers's shoes, by asking such questions as, 'What do people consider valuable and important?' and 'How are their attitudes towards products formed?'

Values are not measurable in a mathematical sense. This is best seen in people's attitudes towards political propositions. One person may regard a state-run National Health Service a vital ingredient of a caring nation while another person holds an equally firm belief that those who can afford to pay should do so. How these attitudes are formed is probably the result of a lifetime's experience, as well as education and social and cultural influences. This is also true of people's attitudes towards products; what seems important to one may be trivial to another.

In present society, status and wealth are often measured by material possessions and this can be a major buying influence for some people. For others an appeal on the basis that neighbours, colleagues etc. have one, may antagonise. Selling necessitates its own value judgements in many situations and a little prior research, added to the experience of different people and their reactions to particular propositions, may alert a salesperson to likely responses.

6.   The bases for consumer buying

Consumers' buying influences are often complex and may even be irrational. If purchase influences are also important then the decision process will be even more complicated and not always apparent to the market researcher or salespeople. There are, nevertheless, a number of bases that influence consumer buying and sales management should ensure that their sales forces are familiar with them. They are:

(a)   personal product experience;
(b)   intended use of the product;
(c)   the needs of the purchaser influence;
(d)   consumers' knowledge of the product, either factual or believed;
(e)   comparison with other products;
(f)   fashion, novelty and a search for something 'new';
(g)   packaging and design;
(h)   group pressures and a need to conform, e.g. 'keeping up with the Jones's' or some valued opinion, 'as used by ...';
(i)   price image;
(j)   environmental pressures, such as aerosols damaging the atmosphere;
(k)   family or personal security needs.

7.   Buying for distribution — retail and wholesale buying

This level of buying is of special importance as the great bulk of consumer products are sold through the retail distribution network. Wholesaling has tended to change in recent years, largely due to the 'blurring' of the distinctions between retail and wholesale selling of many products, notably electrical goods, DIY goods, furniture and groceries with the development of out-of-town stores, supermarkets and discount stores.

A major change brought about by the growth in the size of retail outlets has been the development of buying committees. These are groups of buyers representing specialist areas of goods that meet once a week or so to analyse and discuss the items to be bought for the store. In many cases, though, the buying committee will discuss only products that have already been through a preliminary screening process, when many more will have been rejected.

The importance of the buying committee lies in the professionalism it has brought to retail buying. Manufacturers offering their products to such organisations can no longer rely on pure selling skill but will have to back up their offers with facts and technical information and, often, elaborate support programmes of advertising and promotion.

8. Purchasing — the buying of industrial goods

It has already been stressed that industrial buying is a complex process, often involving many different people with different jobs, including engineers, designers, works managers and buyers. This is sometimes referred to as *selling down the line*, implying the need to 'sell' to many people in different positions in the organisation.

Industrial purchasing is a very professional business and relies on a great deal of technical backup, often calling for tests, trials and development in conjunction with the manufacturer. This may involve:

(a) problem-solving assistance;
(b) cost and value analysis.

Problem-solving assistance is a two-way interaction between buyer and seller in which the technologies of two different companies are brought together to solve the buying company's problems.

Cost and value analysis techniques aid the buyer in expensive purchasing considerations, especially, for example, in the installation of new plant and machinery. If a company is contemplating spending thousands of pounds or more on new equipment, it must be certain that it understands the full costs and benefits. In these cases, the sales force, sales management, designers and development engineers may work closely with the client over many weeks or months to ensure that the most accurate assessment of the equipment is made. This is increasingly the case in electronics, where the installation and integration of computerised systems is both expensive and potentially risky if an entire process or information system is involved (8: **10, 11**).

9. Procurement — the securing of government supplies

Governments are major buyers of all kinds of products, from school and hospital supplies to military hardware. This type of buying, therefore, involves not only central government but local authorities and many other government departments.

Very often, government procurement is based on tight specifications and decided by competitive tender. This requires the sales organisation to keep a close eye on those areas of business interest, to note when tenders are issued and to ensure that their products meet government specifications. Of course, not all products are bought this way and much procurement resembles industrial buying, with the accent on selling benefits. In the present economic climate, with its emphasis on cost savings and cutting government spending, any product should, ideally, enable government departments to realise savings.

10. Sources of supply

Selecting a reliable and efficient source of supply is a key decision area in an industrial buyers' acquisition process. It involves:

(a) ensuring a supply of materials of the right quality, right price and on a reliable delivery basis; this may be for:
   (i) production purposes;
   (ii) maintenance purposes; or
   (iii) general administrative purposes, such as stationery;
(b) increasingly, sourcing involves close cooperation with suppliers in developing materials and components from early on in the product development stage.

From the sales management and selling viewpoint, it must be appreciated that the deliberate purpose of industrial marketing is to influence the buyer's decision in favour of their company's products over those of their competitors' and this necessitates:

(a) clear understanding of the customer's requirements and processes;
(b) detailed knowledge of both their own products, their characteristics and cost-effectiveness, and, also;
(c) detailed knowledge of competitors' products.

The last point is important as it will be the basis of successfully getting one's own products specified and of effective negotiation. Competent selection of supplies is purchasing's most important responsibility and overrides other purchasing contributions to the organisation. This relationship between seller and buyer is exemplified by the simple model:

Product marketing   ⟵———⟶   Supply sourcing

11. The buyer's decision making and information needs

From the buyer's viewpoint, the kind of decision making process involved regarding supply purchases reflects one of three possible situations:

(a) *straight re-purchase* — the repetitive purchasing of similar items from the same supplier, for such items as stationery, toilet rolls, small components;

(b) *modified re-purchase* — the purchase is modified in some way, for example a revised specification is applicable where, say, a producer of yogurt may have decided, for marketing purposes, to vary the size or shape of the plastic pot;

(c) *new task* — in this situation the buyer will have no experience of purchasing a particular item and therefore requires to search the supplier market for both suppliers and products, for example, a company may produce its own new product, requiring different raw materials or components, or decide to buy a computerised accounting system.

These three purchasing tasks can, and do, exist in every firm and, from the seller's viewpoint, represent situations requiring different kinds of negotiation and having different information needs. In situation (a), for example, it would be difficult to get buyers to change their source of supply purely on a quality basis because the items themselves are probably relatively unimportant. However, it might be possible to win the order by means of a price differential. In the last situation, though, (c), the buyer will need a great deal of product information and probably an assurance of continuing service and assistance with the new items.

The changing information needs and relative importance of selling points is shown in Table 6.2, which has been extracted from a table compiled by G. W. Dickson that appeared in the *Journal of Purchasing*, February, 1966.

Table 6.2 *Most important factors by situation*

Importance ranking	A — Paint	B — Desks	C — Computers
1	Quality	Price	Quality
2	Warranties	Quality	Technical capability
3	Delivery	Delivery	Delivery
4	Performance history	Warranties	Production capacity
5	Price	Performance history	Performance history

This clearly shows that the ranking of importance varies with the needs of the purchase. In industrial painting contracts, the nature of the problem and the potential cost of a wrong purchase decision far outweigh the relative costs of various alternatives. For desks, though, price becomes of major importance as the product differentiation will be of minor importance. In computers, the quality and technical capability rank high.

Managing the buyer–seller interface

12. The need to differentiate products

One of the problems in selling in very competitive situations is the ability to make your products different from those of the competition. Product differentiation can take many forms, including:

(a) brand packs and packaging;
(b) emphasis on specific benefits;
(c) cost differences;
(d) different image; and
(e) aimed at different market segments.

All these factors make your product different and in selling that is of the utmost importance. If buyers cannot readily distinguish your products from those of your competitors, the products are not going to compete. In presenting your products to buyers, samples, literature and other sales aids such as testimonials and reports should all be used to make the buyer believe that you are offering a unique product.

13. Customer expectation

As we have seen, expectation is the biggest motivational factor in selling. Consumers, therefore, are more likely to experience disappointment in their purchases when they have high expectations of them. Big purchases are given a greater degree of pre-purchase evaluation and so will lead to the greatest post-purchase disappointment when a bad choice has been made. For example, a government department wanted to buy a range of exhibition systems. They approached several companies and evaluated three different manufacturers' products, eventually deciding on one make that was created specially for them. When the first products were delivered, they were very disappointed. They met with the manufacturer's sales management, which was able to take along the original samples for comparison, after which the buyer admitted that they were as specified. After that they were quite satisfied with all subsequent systems and later ordered more. This type of complaint often occurs in post-purchase evaluation and reflects the buyer's own *cognitive dissonance* and his or her need for reinforcement of the original decision.

When we want to buy cars, washing machines, hi-fi systems or whatever, the range is substantial and each have special features. Even when consumers have chosen one, they may not be entirely confident about their selection. In these circumstances, it has been shown that more people read advertisements for such products, *after purchase* than before; again this is a search for reinforcement.

Salespeople can counter this dissonance by keeping in touch with buyers *after* the orders have been placed and delivered and, if need be, producing further evidence of the product's quality and benefits.

14. Buyer attitudes and beliefs

Attitudes influence everyone's lives — in the ways individuals react towards others, how they make judgements and how they behave towards objects and events. In terms of the buyer–seller interface, the attitudes of the buyer will be all important. (*See* 5:**16** and **18**.)

Because they are relatively enduring in nature, attitudes have particular interest for marketing strategists. They do not *guarantee* that certain types of buying behaviour will occur, but they are useful as *guides* to what buyers are likely to do in certain circumstances.

Interrelationships between attitudes are important as a means of enabling salespeople to assess the likely response of buyers to certain propositions. There are three significant aspects of attitudes to consider:

(a) Are the buyer's attitudes towards a product *specific* or *general*? For example, Buyer 'A' may be specifically interested in the performance of a computerised record system, wanting to know how it is programed and how the system works. However, Buyer 'B' may not be interested in the 'mechanics' of the system but only in how it can be used to improve the firm's information system. A presentation to 'A' will need to be technically based and require a sound knowledge of the *technology* of the system, whereas 'B' would probably be bored by the technology and require *benefit* information.

(b) What is the relationship between the buyer's attitudes and his or her *value system*? Value systems relate to the way a person sees a specific value as part of a wider role. For instance, if the buyer of a company sees his or her role as being one of conserving and protecting the company's reputation for high quality, he or she is not likely to be influenced to change to a new product by price inducements. Therefore, a salesperson trying to get that buyer to change to his or her products, needs to back up the presentation with sound product knowledge that will induce change because it conforms to the buyer's attitudes towards quality.

(c) Is the buyer's attitude towards your product likely to contradict his *self-concept*? How far does the buyer's attitude reflect his strongly held beliefs on a particular subject? For example, supposing you are selling an imported product, say a Japanese-made machine tool, would that create conflict for a buyer with a strong belief in buying British?

15. Strength of attitudes

Generally, the probability of change varies inversely with the strength of the attitude. The stronger the customer's predisposition, the less likelihood there is of changing that attitude by persuasive communications. There are four reasons for attitude strength:

(a) if the existing state of knowledge is limited, attitudes will be more susceptible to change and there will be less commitment to a belief;
(b) attitudes that are closely related to the person's self-concept, such as morals, are more resistant to change and are strong motivation values;
(c) attitudes that are intimately connected with other beliefs are difficult to change, such as political or social attitudes;
(d) personality will affect resistance to change to a strong degree: people with strong beliefs are less likely to change attitudes in response to new information than those who have no strong beliefs.

As we saw earlier attitudes range along a spectrum, from a position that is most acceptable to one that is most unacceptable. Between them is an area of non-commitment, which is where the probability of changing attitudes increases.

Progress test 6

1. What is the importance of the buying–selling interface? (**2**)

2. List as many of the bases for consumer buying as you can. (**6**)

3. How many of the many forms of product differentiation can you remember? (**12**)

4. What are the four reasons given for attitude strength? (**15**)

7

The need for product knowledge

Understanding the sales proposition

1. The need for knowledge

The entire selling spectrum has to be clearly perceived as fulfilling two kinds of needs. On the one hand there is *consumer selling*, where personal selling has given way in the last two decades to merchandising methods at one level and self-service and mail order at another. None of this move to impersonal selling, largely at the end of a motivation process that begins with advertising, relates to *industrial selling*, where the need for personal contact and a very high degree of product knowledge has never been greater. We have already seen how the roles of seller and buyer have become much more closely integrated and hinge on product knowledge.

Salespeople's knowledge of the products they sell is of paramount importance. Nothing betrays novices more or loses the confidence and interest of buyers more quickly than an incomplete knowledge of their products and, further, the industry in which they operate. At the industrial level, selling ability has to be matched with other knowledge, such as the workings of the industry and its technology, hence the greater demand for graduates of all disciplines in selling. This product knowledge must also extend beyond the limited range of the salesperson's own company and its products to encompass all those that compete with them.

2. The salesperson's job

To be able to face a prospective customer with confidence, salespeople must have a high degree of product knowledge. This depends on their ability to equate the need for product knowledge with:

(a) the need for *sources of information*; and
(b) his or her selection of *selling points*.

3. Industrial selling

The need to sell benefits to industrial buyers is of paramount importance. Salespeople must understand that industrial goods are a *derived demand* and that buyers are interested in what the products will do. Their knowledge must be related to this and they must recognise that dissimilar products may well serve the same ends. To improve a bad floor surface a contractor could:

(a) lay a new cement screed;
(b) lay granolithic concrete;
(c) lay an epoxy-resin screed;
(d) lay quarry tiles;
(e) lay thermo-plastic tiles;
(f) lay linoleum;
(g) paint with floor paint; or
(h) lay a woodblock floor.

Salespeople trying to sell any one of these floor surfaces would need to know the costs, durability and the advantages and disadvantages of all of them. If the customer countered their proposals by saying that they were interested in one of the alternatives, they could then re-spond, if they knew of its disadvantages.

This need to know about alternatives exists in all selling, whether to industrial customers, to wholesalers or to distributors and it is equally important for salespeople in a retail store too.

4.   Extent of product knowledge

If salespeople have a wide knowledge of their products, it can only help to broaden their ability to sell them, enabling them to:

(a) satisfy customer needs;
(b) innovate on product uses; and
(c) assist customers to innovate.

When salespeople's knowledge extends to a critical analysis of their competitors' products, it becomes their best defence against competition, enabling them to present rational counter-arguments. This knowledge, however, must extend beyond the narrow limits of their products alone and a model of this process is shown in Figure 7.1.

Salespeople will need to know about:

(a) competitive products that are *closely similar;*
(b) all products that, although not closely similar, could compete as *substitutes;* and
(c) all products that may compete for *customers' scarce resources.*

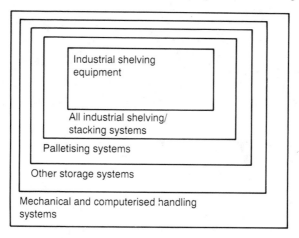

Figure 7.1 *Product knowledge model*

Sensible use of knowledge

5. Fact as opposed to opinion

One of the worst mistakes a salesperson can make in the course of an interview is to express an opinion: 'I think this will solve your problem' or 'I imagine you can sell a lot of this'. The buyer will not really be interested in, nor impressed by, the salesperson's opinion. Salespeople must be *positive*.

Buyers need advice and product knowledge to help them to form a judgement on which to base a purchasing decision.

To present a sound case, therefore, salespeople should be as familiar with competitors' products as with their own. If on occasion they must accept defeat, their technical expertise will have won them favour in the eyes of a buyer and so prepare the way for the next time.

6. Product knowledge requires fluency

Knowing your product is insufficient if you can't express it in fluent terms, coping with the technicalities and expressing them in a way that your client understands. There are many technically sound salespeople who suffer from faults, such as an inability to get a flow going or being unable to express the technicalities in simple terms. Salespeople must be capable of understanding technical terms and be able to express an idea in a simple but accurate manner to non-technical customers. Both faults can be remedied with practise and using a tape recorder helps in appreciating the effect of what is being said when you're on the receiving end.

7.   Industrial product knowledge

Industrial salespeople's interest and knowledge should be stimulated and broadened by sound technical training, which should include:

(a) the background to the product;
(b) related industrial problems;
(c) product research and development;
(d) manufacturing methods;
(e) methods of use; and
(f) service and servicing.

Salespeople will make greater progress and obtain increased job satisfaction if they have an interest in their products and a knowledge of their customers. Whenever possible, the objective should be to build on the salesperson's own experience, performance appraisal, cost analysis and experiments so long as he or she keeps within the broad parameters of corporate policy.

8.   Kinds of knowledge

Salespeople need to appreciate that buyers will have different degrees of knowledge about the products they are selling to them, often corresponding to whether it is, from the buyer's viewpoint, a routine re-purchase or a new task.

As we saw in (3:5), the product is made up of three components:

(a) the core product;
(b) the tangible product; and
(c) the augmented product,

and these attributes must form the basis of any sales presentation. However, we can define them a little further in terms of preparing sales information.

Essentially, three kinds of product knowledge are necessary to salespeople, which must be identified for each product. We can relate them to the product model:

(a) *The core product = behaviour in use.* The most important group of facts to the industrial salesperson. Industrial products are sold not on what they are made of, but, rather, on what they will do, i.e. the benefits. Thus, the key or core fact about an industrial paint will be its ability to confer benefits in terms of corrosion or abrasion resistance.

(b) *The tangible product = tangible qualities.* The facts that can quite definitely be proved or, equally, disproved, such as 'polyurethane', 'stainless steel', 'acid resistant'. They are statements of fact and can be supported by evidence. Documentary reports by relevant established testing authorities, such as universities, or the Ministry of Defence, will substantiate such claims and are helpful to the buyer.

(c) *The augmented product = intangible qualities.* Facts claimed for a product have to be substantiated by warranty or certificate, such as 'made in England', or that may be in support of guarantees, or delivery and service responsibilities.

As to which pieces of information are most important, you have to use your common sense. For example, buyers of electric sanding machines are concerned with the appliance's ability to sand or buff and its qualities in terms of capacity and power to remove wood and metal; they are *not* likely to be concerned with the quality of the metal used in its construction.

The speciality salesperson who relies to a great extent on demonstration is concerned with the first consideration almost exclusively.

9. Material costs

Material costs are not the same as the price of the raw material. For example, a company making steel panels 1 × 0.75 m for the building trade may buy the raw material, that is sheet steel, at £X000's a ton delivered to its works. It then has to process this material, including internal transportation, storage, delivery to work site, cutting and fabricating and storage of the finished goods.

On the other hand it may be able to purchase steel panels already cut to size and, perhaps, already colour-coated. However, these panels will cost much more than the sheet steel, say £X000 plus 20 per cent, but the internal handling and storage will be reduced. Pre-cut steel panels of the same size can be handled much more easily and require less mechanical handling equipment than sheet steel in bulk. Therefore, the advantages are reduced materials handling because of easier internal transportation, and that fewer manufacturing operations are involved.

The buyer, in cooperation with the works management, time and motion engineers and transportation management will need to cost the differences in handling and calculate whether the savings from buying pre-cut steel panels will exceed the lower price of bulk steel plus the extra handling and manufacturing operations.

The role of sellers in such complex purchases is often central and they often become very involved in the whole process. The sellers' take the view that the more involved they become, the more likely it is that a successful negotiation will be concluded.

Other considerations of cost during negotiations may involve delivery schedules. For example, just-in-time (JIT) deliveries lower storage costs for the buyer, but increase them for the seller.

These kinds of 'make or buy' decisions apply to most industries today and have given rise to component manufacturers for all kinds of items. For example, in the car industry, apart from buying in hi-tech components such as headlights and electronics, many firms also buy in seats. At another level, many canteen and school meals are bought in rather than prepared on site.

10. Sources of information
In most selling situations there will be many varied sources of information and the determination with which salespeople pursue this knowledge to its sources will, largely, decide the degree of their success. Salespeople should always be hungry for knowledge. Product knowledge may be obtained:

(a) by examining the products themselves;
(b) by trying out the products;
(c) by considering how the product is made;
(d) by asking others, including those who made or distributed the product;
(e) from catalogues, brochures, reports and other company-originated literature;
(f) from the consumers' or users' experiences;
(g) from trade journals and press reports;
(h) from advertisements;
(i) from books; and
(j) through information on labels and tags.

The sources and amount of information required will vary according to the nature of the product and the kind of people it is sold to. A simple criterion is that salespeople should always be able to give *concise* information about the product.

11. Comparisons of products
To be able to make a comparison with competitors' products is an important selling point.

Example ────────────────────────────────

A salesperson is selling a portable exhibition system.

Salesperson: '… and the *Felix* portable system unfolds to give you a display area of 5.6 square metres on both sides …'

Buyer: 'Yes, but the system I've used before can also be adapted to make various shapes, such as towers.'

Salesperson: 'I see you use *Slide*, well, that's an excellent system, but, to obtain those extras cost you twice as much as the basic system. With our system, *Felix*, which comes in its own carrying bag these "extras" can be constructed from the basic system, by adding only one extra panel. That saves you approximately 60 per cent of the cost of *Slide*.'

Buyer: 'I see. Can I have the same choice of colours?'

Salesperson: 'Actually, we can offer you a larger range, with more than one colour per set if that is what you want. What colours would you want?'

Buyer: 'We use blue and white. Yes, all right, your *Felix* seems a better proposition.'

────────────────────────────────

Salespeople must know how to expose points of superiority, which might include:

(a) economy;
(b) durability;
(c) safety;
(d) colour;
(e) scent;
(f) cost;
(g) service; or
(h) convenience.

The above example shows the sort of information good salespeople make themselves aware of and a situation in which it paid dividends. It is not overstating the point to repeat that good salespeople will know as much about rival products as their own.

Salespeople must also be familiar with problems arising from the use of the product. Salespeople selling metallisation treatments to shot-blasters will do better if they become familiar with the process and complexities of shot-blasting.

12. Selection of selling points

The purpose of investigating the product and its competitors is to select *selling points*. The salesperson must be aware of the limitations in applying knowledge. Inexperienced salespeople must beware of overstating a case or trying to teach 'experts' how to do their jobs by offering information to people who should, and probably do, know all about their jobs.

Main selling points for a typical product might be:

(a) materials used;
(b) construction;
(c) visual appeals;
(d) performance;
(e) maintenance; and
(f) reputation.

13. Tactful use of knowledge

Salespeople's product knowledge (of their own and other manufacturers' products) is acquired to put them on equal terms at least with the prospective purchaser. If this knowledge is superior to the customer's, it may be tactful to conceal the fact. A typical opening might be: 'As you will be aware, the use of this product produces a heating effect'. Customers may or may not be aware of the effect but the words will either flatter, because they don't know them or they will because their capability has been acknowledged.

It is wrong to offer too much information. If the buyer is told everything, it may exhaust the discussion before the prospective purchaser is convinced. You might then have to repeat yourself, at the risk of becoming boring. However, whether the information is offered or not, it must be known in case a question is asked about it.

14. Selling and the product life cycle

The concept of a product life cycle was introduced in Chapter 1. In terms of product knowledge, the position of the product within its life cycle can be important.

For example, when personal micro-calculators were introduced in the early 1970s, they were at the beginning of their life cycle. They were considered hi-tech and were very expensive, with colleges buying them at around £60 each. Today a calculator is frequently a give-away promotional gimmick for salespeople and may be bought for as little as £2. Furthermore, they are hardly regarded as hi-tech anymore.

This example illustrates the point that products *do* have life cycles and it is important that salespeople are aware that the knowledge they have of their products must be placed in a time context. Very often a company will continue selling a product long after it is no longer new and innovative, but is still very useful. In these circumstances, however, the product is often sold at a lower price to overcome competition from later, more modern, equivalents. For the salesperson to try and sell a product nearing the end of its life cycle as new and innovative or offering some unsuspected benefit, is wrong. It is far better to acknowledge that the product has been selling a long time, using such phrases as 'well tried and proven', 'reliable and trusted', and if need be, 'low cost because of its long production runs'.

Progress test 7

1. To be able to face a prospective buyer with confidence, salespeople must be able to equate their needs for product knowledge with what two factors? **(2)**

2. With what aspects of technical training should industrial salespeople be equipped? **(7)**

3. What are the different kinds of product knowledge that are important to salespeople? **(8)**

4. List some of the sources of information from which salespeople may get product knowledge. **(10)**

5. Outline the relationship between selling and the product life cycle. **(14)**

8

Techniques of selling

The selling process

1. The correct technique

Successful selling must depend on the use of correct technique, but what that technique is must, inevitably, depend on what is being sold and to whom. There is no one correct way, although there are certainly basic principles that should be applied in each situation. How the techniques are applied depends very much on two factors:

(a) the type of product or service; and
(b) the type of customer.

2. Salespeople and customers

A first step in all selling processes is to get into a face-to-face relationship with the customer. This isn't as easy as might at first be thought.

Example
A representative calls at a small factory at 10.30 a.m. to see the proprietor with the objective of selling electrical fittings. The proprietor is busy and cannot see the salesperson. At 1.30 p.m., however, the proprietor leaves the factory to visit a DIY superstore and spends an hour selecting electrical fittings for an extension to some equipment at his factory, eventually choosing the same type that he refused to see earlier.

The point being made above is that in selling, product, time and place are important considerations for both buyer *and* seller. Figure 8.1 shows this graphically.

3. The need for appointments

The need to make appointments to see people is vital because of their *preoccupation*, their mental and physical absorption in other areas of their job. The effects of this preoccupation are shown in the graphs in Figure 8.1:

(a) customers are most likely to buy when the *needs for the product are highest* and the *preoccupation is lowest*; the converse is also true;

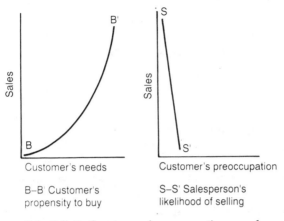

Figure 8.1 *Effect of customers' preoccupation on sales*

(b) Salespeople's likelihoods of selling are greatest when customers' preoccupation is lowest, but it will *rapidly diminish* as preoccupation grows;

(c) this tendency will hold true in most circumstances as it can be assumed that the greater the level of preoccupation, the lower the level of immediate need for the product in question;

(d) elasticity of demand does not influence these general assumptions because the degree of elasticity is implicit in the level of preoccupation, that is, when need is great, demand is great and elasticity is, therefore, affected.

The greatest influence on customers to lower the level of preoccupation at a given time will be the ability of salespeople to stimulate the level of immediate need. For instance, in the example given above, had the salesperson telephoned for an appointment and explained what he or she was selling, the buyer would have been interested in a meeting. So, if salespeople are to succeed in lowering preoccupation and raising need, several important points must be considered:

(a) When will be the best *time* to see the customer?
(b) Where will be the best *place* to see the customer?
(c) What will be the best *product* to show to the customer?

If adequate attention is *not* given to these fundamental points, all the subsequent steps in the selling process will be negated.

4. The buyer's needs
Industrial or organisational buyers are generally characterised as

buying for totally logical reasons, usually technical or economic, based on perceived benefits. Unfortunately, this belief ignores the fact that buyers are human too and, in making their institutional buying decisions, encounter the same kinds of personal doubts that they face in their private buying decisions.

If buyers are young or new to the firm, they will feel less confident than would well-established buyers with proven company records of successful buying. If buyers have recently moved to the firm's locality, are the sole earner with young families and are totally dependent on the firm, their responses to sales pressures will be different from those of older people, with no mortgages and grown-up families.

Salespeople have to recognise these behavioural factors in industrial buying decisions. They should appreciate the buyers' needs for reassurance, especially if the product is new to the company. Buyers may, in turn, have to 'sell' new products to works managers or a senior buyer and must, therefore, be adequately supplied with facts and evidence of success. These will include:

(a) specialist reports by well-known users;
(b) test reports by appropriate scientific institutions;
(c) samples and test pieces; and
(d) accurate, up-to-date cost analysis data.

All these items constitute sales aids that, correctly prepared, will greatly increase the likelihood of a sale.

5. The need for sales aids

What sales aids a person can carry obviously depends on what they are selling. For example, in the clothing trade, representatives will often carry the actual products with them or at least a sample of each type of garment, supported by cloth samples to show different colours. At the other end of the scale, people selling industrial processes have to support their presentations with all kinds of aids to introduce the customer to the product or service. It is, therefore normal practice for salespeople to carry various samples, which may include any or all of the following:

(a) actual products, such as clothing;
(b) samples of products, such as colour swatches, paint cards, small bottles of oils or other liquids;
(c) examples of work, e.g. examples of machined parts or sections of a product to show the quality that can be produced;
(d) copies or illustrations of previous jobs, such as photographs; and

(e) illustrations or designs of the type of work that can be done, e.g. drawings and plans.

Samples serve two purposes. First they illustrate what the company can do; second they get the customer's attention. As explained above, it is important to reduce the customers' preoccupations and one way of so doing is to give them something to hold, to examine, screw together or whatever else will bring about some physical involvement. As a basic principle, whenever possible, *get your customer involved*.

6. The selling process
The objective of the selling process is to persuade customers to buy products that will give them satisfaction. There are four major elements in the process that are fundamental to all the other factors involved:

(a) the company and its policies, especially sales policies;
(b) the customer;
(c) the products or services; and
(d) the salesperson.

It is an essential responsibility of sales management to make sure that the sales force appreciates and clearly understands these four major elements in the selling process before they embark on the subsequent steps in the process.

7. The steps in the selling process
These stages in a successful sale are:

(a) approach and greeting;
(b) determining the customer's needs;
(c) effective presentation of the products;
(d) countering objections;
(e) closing the sale; and
(f) developing goodwill after the sale.

Often it is possible to add another step between (e) and (f), which is the selling of related products. For example, the selling of brushes to someone who has bought paint or car polish to someone who has bought body repair materials. When the objective of the selling process is the satisfaction of a specific need or the winning of a substantial order, as is the case with much industrial selling, this additional step could have unfortunate results and would be omitted. Obviously the response in individual situations is a matter of using common sense.

8.   Are all selling processes the same?

The answer must be no. Not only are there differences between selling consumer and industrial products, but also between all kinds of products, whether to consumers or to organisational buyers. The actual process will inevitably vary according to the frequency of the calls. For example, someone representing an electrical wholesaler will probably call on the same group of contractors every week or so and, in those circumstances, relationships tend to become very informal and friendly, with both parties knowing what to expect. On the other hand, someone selling to the engineer of a local authority will no doubt be very formal and approach the event with careful planning and preparation. In describing the selling process, therefore, it must be pointed out that:

(a) a classification of steps must, by the dynamic nature of the selling process, be arbitrary;
(b) some steps may be unnecessary in accomplishing some sales;
(c) the actual sequence of the steps will vary depending on the customers and salespeople in individual circumstances.

9.   The mental processes in a sale

People do not make up their minds in a flash. Rarely do any of us instantly grasp the meaning of what we are told, let alone instantly decide how to act on it. A simple example of this process is to think about advertisements on television. A new product is advertised for the first time and, afterwards, most people would have only a vague recollection of what it was about. If it was interesting, then we may look out for it next time and then learn a bit more about it. After a few times, we may understand it, decide if the product is what we want or not and act accordingly. The point is, however, that all this understanding and decision making is part of the mental process of absorption of information and learning what it means.

Buyers, then, may progress through a series of stages before deciding to buy the product. We can identify seven stages in this mental process:

(a) arousal of interest;
(b) increase of knowledge;
(c) adjustment to needs;
(d) appreciation of suitability;
(e) desire to possess;
(f) consideration of cost;
(g) decision to buy.

Regarding arousal of interest, Figure 8.1 shows that customers have a higher propensity to buy when their preoccupation is at a low level. It follows that the first task is to arouse the customer's interest in the product. Until this has been achieved, the customer is unlikely to give sufficient or serious attention to the sales presentation. To do this salespeople might open their presentation (or, indeed, increase their chances of getting an appointment) with statements such as, 'I can show you ways to reduce your costs' or 'This new product will eradicate waste'. Alternatively, salespeople may produce an interesting sample or sales aid to arouse interest. Attention is *not* focused by telling jokes or talking about a football match.

The second stage, the increase of knowledge, occurs if salespeople have accomplished stage (a) as customers will be receptive to further information and will wish for further knowledge of the product. At this stage, salespeople may produce examples, photographs and figures to demonstrate cost savings and other benefits.

Then there is the third stage, adjustment to needs. Customers may find salespeople's product information interesting, but, unless it can be shown that the product fulfils their needs, the sale will not be accomplished. By this time, however, salespeople should have assessed customers' needs, preferably by some pre-call research, and be able to relate the product to their specific needs. For example, they might have recognised that customers have corrosion problems or packaging problems or need more regular flows of raw materials. By explaining the advantages of the product, salespeople should be able to make customers recognise that their product and their company's services could be of benefit to them.

The fourth stage is the appreciation of suitability. Following the adjustment to needs, customers will be considering whether it will be suitable for their use. Once again salespeople should not wait expectantly for customers to make this connection, but should be able to make the point, for example, by asking prompting questions. 'You are already using this type of cleanser, I believe. Of course ours is more advanced because it contains ...' and so on. If customers can see that the product is suited to their needs they will be receptive to the next stage.

This is the desire to possess. This should lead on naturally from the last stage. There are ways to stimulate the result, by emphasising the benefits to be obtained, for example. Do not assume that they are obvious — make sure customers can see them.

The sixth stage is the consideration of cost. By this stage, customers will be approaching the decision of whether or not to buy. The cost will then be important and, providing the benefits have been explained fully, customers will usually be able to relate costs to benefits.

The final stage is the decision to buy. This should not be a sudden confrontation, but should have been approached gradually, bearing in mind at all points that this stage is the ultimate objective. It can sometimes help if salespeople produce an order book early on and leaves it in sight while going through the whole process, but this depends on the type of customer and product. After all, not every successful sales presentation leads to an immediate order. The sale of large products or specialist business may take several meetings and involve producing more figures or designs. At the outset, salespeople should have recognised what their objectives are and be aiming for them. Whatever the close is to be, however, their knowledge and skill is aimed at making the movement to this stage as natural as possible.

These mental stages in the selling process (summarised in Figure 8.2) are important to the successful conclusion of a sale, but it must be

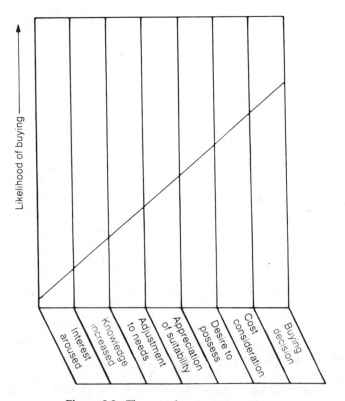

Figure 8.2   *The mental processes in a sale*

remembered that they exist only within the wider context of the selling interview.

10. Is there a difference between selling at home and selling abroad?

Essentially the techniques will be the same but, as happens with most aspects of selling goods abroad (exporting), the process is more complicated. This is because of:

(a) distance;
(b) foreign languages;
(c) different currencies;
(d) different weights and measures systems;
(e) different business practices; and
(f) different cultural patterns.

This is not to say that in every country all these problems will be present. For example, in the USA the language is virtually the same but weights and measures are different to those used in the UK. In the EC the weights and measures are the same but the languages are different (with the exception of Ireland), although English is spoken widely. In the Far East, the cultural patterns may be very different. All these conditions demand that selling techniques be varied and, as most businesses now operate in an international environment, it is important that salespeople understand the problems that might arise.

Progress test 8

1. How do customer's preoccupations relate to the need for appointments? **(3)**

2. 'Buyers may in turn have to "sell" new products to works managers or a senior buyer ...' How can salespeople help in that process? **(4)**

3. List some typical sales aids. **(5)**

4. What are the steps in the selling process? **(7)**

5. List the seven stages in the mental processes in a sale. **(9)**

9

The sales interview

How to ensure that things go smoothly

1. Introduction
The culmination of the preparation and research, and the crux of the selling process, is the selling interview at which buyer and seller meet.

2. Creating the right environment
Some kind of relationship always exists between company and customer, even if it is just a neutral relationship because neither has experience of the other. A buyer looking up possible suppliers in the *Yellow Pages* will probably know little or nothing of the firms listed. Their first contact establishes a more positive relationship, for better or worse according to the nature of the contact. If, for example, the supplier has a switchboard operator with an unhelpful manner, the initial relationship will not be as good as if the operator were helpful and interested.

In the same way, the initial contact between salesperson and buyer (or whomever the customer is, say, works manager or designer) will reflect the cordiality of the event. A cheerful greeting or a businesslike manner will set the tone of the subsequent interview. Of course, on most occasions both customer and supplier have some knowledge of each other, if not personally then at least by reputation, perhaps through advertising or a mail shot.

3. The opening moves
At the first meeting between salesperson and the customer's representative, we'll assume a buyer, a confrontation results. These two people will exchange information, views, opinions, possibly arguments and finally both will make a decision:

(a) the salesperson's decision will be on the prospect of a sale and whether it is worth continuing, and for how long, with the sales presentation;
(b) the buyer's decision will be on the suitability of the product.

Reaching their respective decisions will alter the relationship between seller and buyer. The manner in which this is brought about is

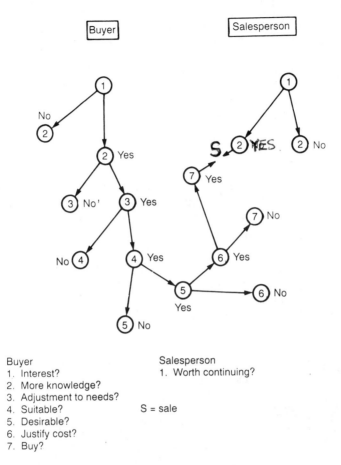

Figure 9.1 *Decision-making complex*

illustrated in Figure 9.1 and, using this diagram, the complex chain of decision making can be examined and understood. For the seller it is a simple consideration of continuing with the sale or not; but for the buyer it involves the seven mental stages discussed in 8.9, expressed here as decisions. At each stage, the decision will be influenced by the buyer's knowledge. For example, if he or she fails to appreciate the product's suitability, it may be because of faulty knowledge, some point having been inadequately, or even incorrectly, explained.

4. The sales interview

The mental stages are only a part of the sales interview which, itself, is a more complex process. It is possible to identify 15 steps in the typical sales interview.

Opening
- (a) Exchange of courtesies.
- (b) Salesperson's opening.
- (c) Interest aroused.
- (d) Interest developed.

Body
- (e) Commencement of selling proper.
- (f) Demonstration:
    - (i) presentation of product;
    - (ii) explanation of selling points;
    - (iii) operation of product by salesperson; and
    - (iv) operation of product by customer.
- (g) Discussion of price.
- (h) Countering of objections.

Close
- (i) Commencement of close.
- (j) Persuasion and trial close.
- (k) Decision making.
- (l) Order taken — purchase completed.
- (m) Completion of details.

Departure
- (n) Closing courtesies.
- (o) Departure.

5.   Opening remarks

The opening remarks in the exchange of courtesies are the beginning of the selling process. Customers may well draw conclusions about salespeople from their first words.

Example

A sales manager called on a customer in South Wales during a period of prolonged bad weather. The bluff sales manager in an attempt to be jolly began with what he thought was a humorous remark about the Welsh weather and how the customer must be enjoying the rain. The remark went over like the proverbial 'lead balloon' and tainted what remained of a tense interview.

A little prior knowledge can help. Does your customer play golf, garden, suffer from gout, watch birds? Salespeople help themselves by being observant. On entering customers' offices, successful salespeople can take in the room at a glance and learn about customers from it. The opening remark should succeed in getting the customer's agreement at the outset, such as 'It's rather wet', 'It's a nice morning',

'The flowers on your desk are delightful'. If customers can agree with you at the outset, they may be more inclined to go on agreeing.

Seek to guide and control the interview at all times but be prepared to be guided by circumstances. There will be a certain amount of manoeuvring for advantage in the beginning and younger salespeople often make the error of plunging into the sale too quickly. Be natural and nudge the conversation in the direction you wish it to go.

6. Developing interest first

Frequently sales are lost because salespeople are over-eager and fail to ensure that their customers' interest has been aroused before beginning the real selling.

7. Enthusiasm

It is important to make customers enthusiastic as early as possible — interest must be developed into enthusiasm. To achieve this, salespeople must be motivated by the products they are selling, as enthusiasm is infectious. Salespeople who can involve customers from the outset will succeed.

8. Commencement of selling

Once interest has been aroused, the stage has been reached when the selling proper may commence. Whether or not a sale is achieved depends on what salespeople then say and do.

Some time will have been spent in developing product knowledge and, by combining experience and sound pre-sales preparation, salespeople will have assessed selling points and arranged them in the best sequence.

If the product is one that can be demonstrated, a sequence will have been selected that will lead buyers to the point at which they will be prepared and keen for a demonstration, curious to see if the product will satisfy the company's needs.

Sales talk should be standardised but standardisation should concern facts and should never degenerate into a parrot-fashion recitation. Sound knowledge is always fluent and doesn't need to be learned by rote. At the beginning of the selling process salespeople should endeavour to inspire confidence by:

(a) sincerity and fluency of manner, as conveyed by voice and bearing;
(b) capitalising on the good name of the firm and its prestige and achievements;

(c) product knowledge;

(d) basing selling techniques on sound customer investigation.

9.   The demonstration

In the sale of most products, the demonstration (of the product itself or of some sales aid in its place) is the highlight, the point at which the selling process comes alive. Give the product or aid to customers, let them hold it, work it, investigate it and, if the demonstration is correctly carried out and backed with a good presentation, a sale or the probability of a future sale should result. Correctly presented, the demonstration will have two effects. It will show customers:

(a) the performance or quality of the product; and

(b) that the product is as good as the salesperson says it is.

To ensure maximum effectiveness, the demonstration should be practised frequently and new techniques incorporated wherever possible. The demonstration itself is a learning process for salespeople and, each time it is performed, it will be improved and modified as a result of the experience.

10.   The demonstration is a learning process

The demonstration must be informative and it is important that customers should be told what is happening at every stage. Too many salespeople are unsure themselves when it comes to the demonstration and so they tend to work too fast. It must be remembered that any learning process must be paced to suit the learner. If customers have no previous experience of this product or type of product, they may not be able to absorb the new information if it is displayed too quickly. To avoid this, salespeople should be alert to confusion and gently and patiently go over any part of the demonstration they feel have been missed or not thoroughly understood by customers. Of course, tact must be exercised in this situation to avoid patronising a customer. Learn to develop the demonstration so that natural pauses will allow customers to digest what has been seen and feel able to ask questions if they wish to. Remember that customers may not have seen the product before.

11.   Discovering customers' needs

The demonstration, on occasion, may be less specific than is indicated in the previous paragraph. Determining customers' needs and presenting the merchandise may sometimes be two aspects of the same operation. Among some salespeople, for example, those formerly termed 'commercial travellers', the presentation may be the means by which customers find the products they need. This is particularly true in the grocery and general wholesale trades and is also typical of retailing. To be effective in this situation, a demonstration involves:

(a) the knowledge of the location of products in the salesperson's bag or showcase;
(b) a sensible selection of what is to be demonstrated;
(c) a careful selection of selling points;
(d) the correct display of products; and
(e) an effective presentation.

An effective presentation is *not* one in which a confused salesperson inadvertently empties a briefcase of leaflets, which then shower around a showroom.

12. Handling price

In any sales interview there is a correct time to mention the price. More sales are lost by the incorrect handling of price than by any other aspect of selling. The following points should help price to be dealt with successfully:

(a) price is only *one* factor in the consideration of a purchase;
(b) the right price will not sell the wrong product; however, the wrong price will not prevent the sale of the right products;
(c) do not fear price — so long as it is approached in the same way as any other selling feature, the salesperson should be equipped to deal with price and counter any criticism;
(d) if price is mentioned by the customer at the outset, it should be dodged; the counter is to stress the *value*, that nothing is cheap, but you get what you pay for;
(e) all prices can, and should, be *related to the article* and to what the article can do.

It must be remembered that, on its own, price means nothing. It should always be considered in relation to other factors.

Example ────────────────────────────────
Selling a portable exhibition trailer.
 Buyer: '£2100! That's a lot more than the display panels I had in mind. No, I think I'll have to leave it for the moment.'
 Salesperson: 'Perhaps I should explain the benefits of our products again…'

Buyer: 'There's little point in that. You see, I don't have that much money available. I have to mount at least three exhibitions this year. We'll have to use the conventional displays.'

Salesperson: 'Let me reassure you on the point of cost. It's true, of course, that you can buy display systems at less cost, but don't forget that at most exhibitions you have to employ union labour to erect your stand, and then you have to be prepared to spend several hours before the exhibition opens preparing the display panels. All that is extra cost, whereas the mobile exhibition trailer requires no erection and is immediately ready for use, thus *reducing* labour costs.'

Matters arising from the sales interview

13. Disposing of objections

Even if a sale is correctly presented, there will almost certainly be objections. Indeed, you could say that a successful presentation *creates* objections because it arouses interest. Whatever the reasons for them, objections should be treated as *opportunities*.

Meeting objections correctly constitutes the most difficult part of the selling process. Many objections can be anticipated and countered in the presentation and, again, it is part of salespeople's experience and related to the learning process: 'Last time a customer queried such and such a point, so this time I'll present it more carefully'. Nevertheless, unexpected objections can also occur and can be divided into three types:

(a) general objections;
(b) specific objections; and
(c) excuses.

Experienced salespeople will have the knowledge and ability to deal with the first two and ignore or brush aside the last. Here are some helpful points to remember when dealing with objections:

(a) do not argue with the customer;
(b) anticipate objections and try to be prepared for them;
(c) counter objections firmly and completely;
(d) inspire confidence, by manner and general demeanour;
(e) do not denigrate competitors.

In the last case, objections prefaced with, 'Well, I always buy so and so's ...' are often made. The correct counter to this is along the lines of, 'That's a good product and you are obviously looking for real benefits, but do you know that we can actually do the job at lower cost?', or whatever other advantage is being sold.

14. Concentrating on the decision

The sales objective is to make a sale. Salespeople must not become too interested in the conversation and lose sight of their objective. Too many times a salesperson has allowed a customer to prattle on about personal interests, views or methods, only to be suddenly reminded that another appointment looms and there isn't any more time to spare! On the other hand, no attempt should be made to rush customers because the sale will then almost certainly fail. Again, it is a matter of common sense; a calculated decision of *time* versus *result*. The order of business salespeople should aim for must be to:

(a) state their case;
(b) demonstrate; and
(c) dispose of objections.

Following the completion of this sequence, salespeople should direct their efforts to closing the sale.

15. Closing the sale

Closing the sale is the most delicate point in the selling process. To achieve success, salespeople need to be aware of buyers' likely behaviour and be able to make decisions at the correct moment. One of the most useful ways of closing a sale is to suggest a finish, perhaps along these lines:

'Now, how much material will you require?'
'Will you want it sent here or to your Smith Street depot?'
'Will you send the order or can you place it now?'
'Blue and white are your company colours, so I imagine you'll want those ...'

Remember that the entire selling process is working towards the objective of closing the sale and it should be a smooth and natural progression.

16. Arranging further interviews

Industrial selling can be a protracted business and a sale is not always possible on every occasion. Frequently it necessitates repeat calls to secure the order or to develop further business. It is, therefore, always important to leave on terms that will permit a return visit. How this return appointment is obtained will depend on the particular circumstances.

17. Departure

Having completed the selling process, finalise any arrangements, ensure that there are no outstanding matters and make your withdrawal. Both customers and salespeople are busy and protracted departures can cause irritation.

Progress test 9

1. Why is it important to create the right environment before commencing a sales interview? (**2**)

2. 'Frequently sales are lost because salespeople are over eager.' How is it possible to overcome this problem? (**6**)

3. Why is the demonstration important? (**9**)

4. What points should influence the way a salesperson handles price? (**12**)

10

Negotiating with buyers

Knowing buyers

1. Buyers' knowledge

Buyers keep their jobs on the basis of their ability to buy only those products that can be resold at a profit or used to profitable or economic effect by their users. Buyers must have the widest possible knowledge of the types of products and materials being handled. Good buyers will be:

(a) aware of what their companies are interested in, or need;
(b) aware of what new developments will benefit their companies; and
(c) people who recognise that it is essential for the buying department to welcome new ideas.

We have already seen (at **6:1**) that, increasingly, buyers are involved with suppliers in materials and product developments, especially in hi-tech areas.

2. Meeting buyers on equal terms

The traditional view of the buyer–seller relationship has been one of protagonists, where both buyers and sellers attempt to gain advantages over each other. While an element of this conflict will always be present, nevertheless, a modern approach is more likely to be one of cooperation. This is particularly true in complicated industrial buying where salespeople are called upon for advice and, indeed, may actually participate in costing exercises to see the effects on buyers' businesses from changes in supply or the introduction of new materials and products.

If sellers, especially, are to be effective in this approach of competitive cooperation, then they must be fully equipped both in product knowledge and in the applications of their products and be able to communicate the cost–benefits of the products they are selling.

It is equally true that in a highly competitive business environment, buyers must also have an open mind to new product ideas or to new supplier ideas and not be so blinkered as to focus solely on known and existing suppliers. There has been an argument for

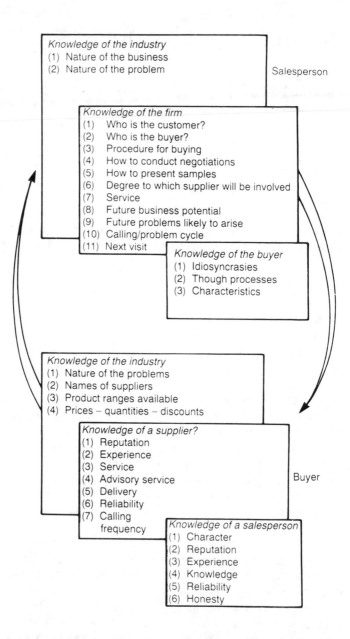

Figure 10.1 *Buyers' and sellers' reciprocal information needs*

single-sourcing of supplies, but, while this does have cost and supply advantages in industries with long and standard production runs, nevertheless, it can mean missing out on economies and perhaps better supply in the long term. After all, no matter how reliable a supplier, any firm can fall to unexpected catastrophes such as fires, and a single-source supplier can also fail to keep its products in the forefront of development if it has no reason to fear competition.

Therefore salespeople and, to a lesser extent, buyers should prepare themselves by finding out about the product and the conditions under which the selling takes place.

3. Reciprocal information needs

Buyers and sellers need to know about each other. They both have to know about the industry with which they are involved and they have a reciprocal need to know about each other, both as individuals and as companies. For example, salespeople need to know buyers' idiosyncrasies; buyers need to know salespeople's characters. When these reciprocal information needs have been satisfied, a sound working relationship can be built up between buyers and sellers. Figure 10.1 shows the type of information needs that must be satisfied.

4. Knowledge develops confidence

All knowledge develops confidence, conferring the ability to converse and express an opinion. There is *no substitute* for salespeople. Glib-talking salespeople might bluff their way along for a while, but, in time, buyers will see through it.

That persuasion still has its place is true, but it must be directed towards needs that may be satisfied by the purchase of particular goods and services.

If salespeople lack product knowledge, the responsibility lies in two directions:

(a) salespeople are to blame for failing to equip themselves adequately to meet their customers;
(b) sales management are to blame if they fail to provide sufficient training and motivation to salespeople or, when working through a personnel department, if they neglect to impress on the firm the need for such training — they have then failed:
   (i) to provide instruction; or
   (ii) to follow up initial training to determine that products are being presented to customers in a satisfactory way.

5. The organisational buying decision

Organisational buying is subject to many factors and takes place within the confines of these influences. They may be grouped under three broad headings:

(a) environmental;
(b) organisational;
(c) personal.

6. Environmental influences

These are the same factors that constitute the business environment in general (see Figure 1.1), but they can be further refined to distinguish more specific influences. These include:

(a) *Market sizes and market trends.* For example, a large company with high-volume production of a product for a mass market will seek larger supplies at better costs than a smaller firm making a more exclusive product for a small market. Also, if the trend is towards the expansion of that market, perhaps because of many new producers (as occurred in pocket calculators and in word processors), the buying department will be seeking longer term supplies than if the market is contracting or stable.

(b) *Demand levels.* This is really an expression of the last factor in individual terms. Stimulation of demand may be accomplished by extensive advertising, promotion and selling. It is another example of the close relationship that should exist between buying and selling. As an example of the disastrous results of lack of such cooperation, take the case of a clothing manufacturer that pursued a policy of export expansion, seeking customers abroad, especially in tropical countries. However, due to a breakdown in liaison between sales and buying, the specialist lightweight fabrics needed for these overseas customers was dropped from the range by the buyer who didn't think that they were selling well in Britain.

(c) *Cost of capital.* If the purchasing decision relates to large items where capital costs need to be balanced against other demands on the company's finance, the purchasing decision may be subject to careful cost–benefit analysis and a comparison with alternative expenditures.

(d) *Changes in technology.* Technology changes very rapidly these days. Buying decisions in such situations may have to take into account the 'life' of components. There is no point in having large stocks of a component that may be superseded before stocks have been used up.

7. Organisational influences

In any company there are specific rules, regulations and organisational policies that influence the way decisions are made and, in this context, purchasing decisions especially. These are illustrated in Figure 10.2.

8. Individual influences

These are manifested at two levels:

(a) personal attributes; and
(b) behavioural characteristics.

At the personal level, buyers are influenced by such attributes as:

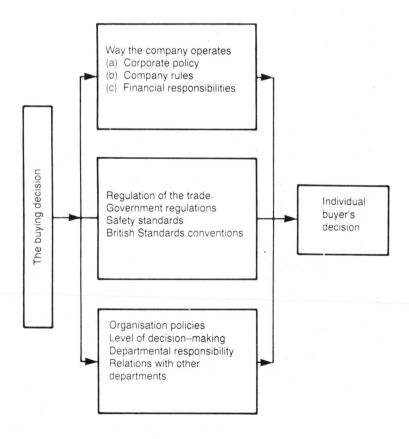

Figure 10.2 *Organisational influences on buying*

(a) age;
(b) job position;
(c) education;
(d) intelligence;
(e) income level;
(f) working experience;
(g) membership of other organisations;
(h) span of control and departmental responsibilities;
(i) decision-making style;
(j) purchasing criteria.

At the behavioural level the influences may include:

(a) personality;
(b) self-confidence;
(c) attitudes — towards challenge and risk, subordinates, peers and superiors in the organisation and towards life in general;
(d) motivations;
(e) perceptions of the job and responsibility towards the organisation.

All these factors will exert an influence on the individual's behaviour, both personally and in his or her perception of the job role. Salespeople represent an outside influence that modifies the role of buyers', for better or worse. For better, salespeople may be seen as an opportunity to enhance buyers' reputations, as useful connections and, maybe, as answers to organisational and personal problems. For worse, salespeople may be seen as intrusions, an addition to buyers' existing problems, a waste of time and cause personal friction.

How these two personalities and job roles interact will depend on the exchange of information, represented in Figure 10.1.

9. Buyers' levels of influence

Buyers have varying levels of personal responsibility and authority depending on:

(a) personal experience;
(b) organisational responsibility; and
(c) the level of complexity of the purchase.

Buyers new to the company or lacking in experience must have limited authority or it may be company policy to limit the role of buyer. Both these will be important factors in selling and salespeople should be able to make a judgement decision on this point fairly quickly if they are not to waste time. For example, if salespeople are attempting to sell expensive equipment or a process or treatment requiring a high level of decision making, it is essential that buyers' possible limitations are recognised early on. This does not mean that the sales interview should be curtailed, but, rather, that the purpose might change.

*Example*_____

A packaging company, we'll call them 'Presspack', invented a new process for applying foam materials for the packaging of delicate instruments. Initially 'Presspack' targeted a major manufacturer of scientific instruments and sent its sales representative to make initial contact. 'Presspack's' sales director knew that getting the target company to change to the new packaging system would be difficult because of the high initial cost and, also, as it would represent a major change in the customer's own marketing presentation it would be a major decision.

'Presspack's' sales representative met with a younger buyer, who, he discovered quite quickly from carefully prepared discussion, though helpful and pleasant, had very limited buying capability. He therefore pursued the line of research, finding out who took the buying decision; this turned out to be a divided responsibility between the senior purchasing manager (a notably difficult person), the works manager and the technical manager.

'Presspack's' sales representative went back to his company and reported the situation. 'Presspack' then planned a three-pronged sales drive; the representative to concentrate on the younger buyer and, through him, get an appointment to see their technical manager, taking along 'Presspack's' own technical director. Once they had the customer's technical manager interested, they then got him to introduce their product to the customer's works manager and arranged a demonstration followed by a trial installation of the new process. Three months later, when the trials had been thoroughly conducted and both sides had a great deal of technical experience and facts to go on, they then took the proposition to the senior purchasing manager.

This example illustrates the complexity of selling major processes and also how to handle complicated buying decisions, in this case an informal DMU (decision making unit). Figure 10.3 illustrates buyers' degrees of influence in various involved situations.

10. Negotiation

As we have seen, in a situation where purchases are routine, supply limited and products are low cost, the selling–buying process is often dominated by salespeople using persuasive communications.

However, in the past 30 years, buying has become more technical, with much greater emphasis on cost-effectiveness by means of judicious purchasing due to:

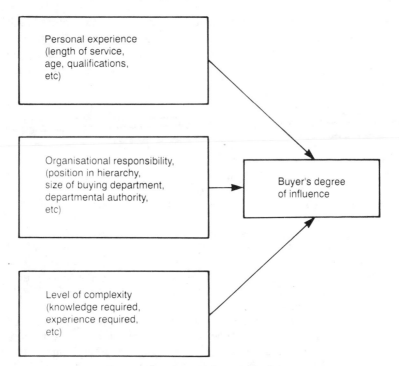

Figure 10.3 *Buyers' degrees of influence*

(a) more complex products;

(b) the higher cost of technology;

(c) the need for a higher degree of cooperation between seller and customer in product development;

(d) a greater need for awareness of economic pressures, such as
    (i) high interest rates,
    (ii) greater international movement of products,
    (iii) fluctuating exchange rates,
    (iv) advantages of spot and future buying of commodities;

(e) the greater involvement of non-buying executives (technical and works executives);

(f) greater investment in technology and, therefore, longer term recovery of investment.

In negotiations with buyers, as we saw earlier, increasingly buyers are involved with suppliers in materials and products developments (especially in hi-tech areas), but it must not be forgotten that buyers are essentially concerned with buying, and this means handling price but also non-price factors such as product knowledge on both sides.

Even before a meeting takes place between sellers and buyers, a degree of information exchange will have taken place. There is an on-going search for customers by sellers and for suppliers by customers. These joint efforts to establish trading contacts are referred to as 'pre-negotiatory double-search'.

Minor purchase searches by buyers might start and finish with the rapid selection of an item that appears quite suitable. In such a routine re-purchase situation, searching time and effort is often minimal. Sellers' searches in this situation may consist of ensuring that their products are known through literature, advertisements in appropriate business journals and by period calls from their salespeople.

At the other extreme, where a new purchase situation arises, the task may involve a carefully deliberated purchase after a prolonged and fully negotiated transaction. A components buyer, for example, may diligently search for market information, trade catalogues and directories, literature, information articles in trade and industry journals, advertisements in trade journals and so on. The buyer may be influenced by this information, but may also consult with others in the trade who have negotiated purchases for similar products. For example, buyers for Local Authorities will consult on the use of materials and treatments and some authorities have pooled their purchasing knowledge to achieve efficiencies in this area.

Because of these added complexities, and an undoubted increase in the professionalism of buyers and purchasing officers, negotiations have also tended to become more protracted. On both sides, the participants have a high degree of technical knowledge within their particular fields as well as a corresponding degree of commercial experience.

11. The negotiation process

Negotiation is the process of bargaining to reach a mutually acceptable agreement and is the basis of much industrial selling. It is a more formal process than a sales interview and often takes place over several occasions. Both parties usually come to the negotiations with prepared positions, thus:

(a) sellers have a sales objective — a product to sell at a predetermined price.
(b) buyers have a purchasing objective — a need or problem to satisfy, at a predetermined cost.

The negotiation phase of a transaction entails further communication about terms of exchange. To reach agreement, buyers and sellers have to agree on the amount of money to be exchanged for a product. Broadly defined, this includes:

(a) time and place of delivery,
(b) time and place of payment, and,
(c) the services that the buyers and sellers agree to exchange after negotiations are over.

In a fully negotiated transaction for an item, such as machinery requiring repair and maintenance after purchase, it is usual for buyers to agree terms under which this maintenance will be carried out.

Other conditions of buying may include sellers' firms supervising plant installation or operator training. The largest single order this country has ever won involved the supply of Tornado fighter bombers to Saudi Arabia, supported by Hawk trainers and a full support-training programme of personnel to train the Saudis in every aspect of installation and operations. In highly competitive markets, such as defence, these ancillary services often have to be provided at cost or even below cost to secure the order.

For complex machinery without which the plant may not operate, as in refineries, sugar mills, paper mills etc., this may involve sellers agreeing to a 24-hour standby maintenance agreement, whereby sellers' firms will have engineers always available.

For other items, such as electronics, this may involve sellers agreeing to take away the item for repair, and, perhaps, lending another piece while it is being repaired.

Experienced sellers will prepare their presentations carefully, perhaps producing graphs, charts and detailed cost–benefit analyses, and also having an agreed 'flexibility' in the presentation so as to be able to give a certain amount of ground. In the same way, buyers will also have cost–benefit analyses, details of their production requirements and buying schedules. The negotiation process will aim to bring the two sides together at a mutually agreeable level.

12. The need for high-quality sales training

The higher standard of negotiation underlines what has already been said about the need for product knowledge and a high standard of selling skills. It also means that, in complicated product areas, salespeople must have an appropriate level of technical and commercial experience if they are going to be able to cope with highly experienced buyers or DMUs.

Progress test 10

1. What are the three broad headings under which one can group organisational buying decisions? (**5**)

2. What are the determinants of buyers' levels of influence? (**9**)

3. What is involved in the negotiation process? (**11**)

4. Why do higher standards of negotiation call for better sales training? (**12**)

11

Telephone selling

What telephone selling involves

1. The fundamentals of telephone selling

The basic techniques of selling to customers by telephone do not differ fundamentally from personal, face-to-face selling, although the medium obviously has certain limitations:

(a) it is a non-personal medium;
(b) the conversation is completely dependent on a single line of communication — other important sensory channels of communication (touch, sight, smell) are missing; and
(c) it is not possible to observe people's physical reactions, observations that are very important to effective responsive selling.

In today's business world, however, the telephone has become one of the principal lines of communication between companies and customers and the correct use of the telephone is essential to good customer relations. It must be remembered, too, that anyone in a company answering the telephone to customers is communicating, if not positively selling, regardless of what their job title is. If customer relations are good and customers find it a pleasant experience to deal with the firm, they will call again, so, in a sense, a 'sale' has been made.

The techniques of telephone selling can be divided into two parts:

(a) the basic techniques of handling telephone calls; and
(b) actual telephone selling skills.

Sales skills can be coupled with good customer relations techniques to make a very effective combination that will boost telephone sales. Selling skills on the telephone can be applied in four ways:

(a) to incoming calls with a query, an enquiry or a prepared order;
(b) to outgoing calls to regular customers, say two days before the regular van delivery in their area, to induce new orders, or to remind customers to place their regular order;
(c) to make appointments for salespeople to call on them;

(d) to outgoing calls to potential customers to introduce and sell the company and its products in a 'cold call' sense or to obtain orders from established or semi-regular customers.

2. The incoming caller

People don't usually make a telephone call to an unfamiliar company unless that company has a unique product or it is experienced at establishing good customer relations. However, a number of potential customers may call when 'shopping around', perhaps testing the market and comparing prices or delivery dates. Therefore we can identify two types of incoming callers:

(a) previous customers;
(b) potential customers.

Many callers do not properly introduce themselves so, if the customer launches straight into his or her requirements without introduction, at the first opportunity politely ask for a name, company and telephone number before progressing with the call. It makes good sense to avoid taking orders or giving data without obtaining the caller's name and company, just in case you forget to ask later. It also sounds much more businesslike if you get this information at the beginning, providing you don't sound officious. It is important, though, because, for instance, not realising you are speaking to a regular customer who is entitled to a discount (due to volume ordering), you may quote prices that do not allow for that discount and so you could lose the order.

3. Handling the telephone enquiry correctly

There are a number of basic steps to handling telephone customers. The person handling the in-coming call should:

(a) use open-ended questions to elicit information;
(b) use polite persuasion to achieve the selling goal;
(c) effectively close the sale;
(d) offer alternative products if necessary.

Open-ended questions are those that require an informative answer. 'I'm interested in some switchplugs …' is a very broad statement of the requirement and does not give the telephone salesperson anything specific to work on. In this case it is necessary to draw out the facts from the customer. Use open-ended questions to do this — ones beginning with 'what', 'when', 'where', 'how' and 'who'. An example would be to ask, 'What size switchplugs do you want?', which obliges the caller to give some information. Even if the customer answered that he or she didn't know, it would lead constructively on to other open-ended questions such as, 'What are they to be used for?' etc. Remember to avoid asking, 'why', however, as it implies criticism. Here are some further examples of open-ended questions:

(a) 'What colour switchplugs do you want?'
(b) 'How many have you been using per month?'
(c) 'When do you require them by?'
(d) 'Who else in your company would be interested in electrical fittings?'

Customers may not always be as technically competent as might be expected or may be unaware of recent product developments or new lines. Therefore, it is always worth asking customers, even ones who state their requirements clearly at the beginning of the call, 'What are you going to use this for?' or 'How are you going to use this material?' This ensures that the right product or service for the job is being discussed. It can be useful to keep a list handy detailing additional items to sell with key products; it will act as an aide-mémoire.

Having established customers' needs, the selling and persuasion can start. If customers ring up with specific requirements, is it possible to increase the quantity, augment the breadth of the range bought or to sell an additional item or an associated article? For example, having taken an order for paint, why not ask if the customer needs thinners or brushes? This technique of enlarging the order can be practised by using the information gained from the client. Again, staying with the paint example, if the customer has ordered stone paint, can they be persuaded to buy special applicators or solutions for sealing absorbent surfaces? However, although the examples given are not technical, the basic principle can be applied to all trades and professions.

It should be remembered that, if at the end of calls customers have ordered no more than they originally rang up for, they have not been sold; they have placed orders. (Of course, the orders may be a result of previous sales efforts.)

When customers only ring up for information, the seller's job is to convince them to buy *now*. The key to persuasion is to use benefits, that is explain how you can help them and why they should be buying from your organisation. Relate these benefits to their requirements. For example, if a regular supply is needed, demonstrate how you can meet this need, by daily deliveries for instance; or perhaps your product offers cost-saving benefits.

When selling an additional item to callers or when trying to persuade new customers to buy, it is essential to close the sale. The technique was explained in Chapter 9 on sales interviews and, although the principles are the same for telephone selling, there is the obvious difference that neither the customer nor the product can be seen. Therefore, conversation and the ability to impart knowledge and apply persuasion with confidence are very important.

It is wrong for salespeople in any situation to feel embarrassed in asking for the order. After all if you never asked, you couldn't be sure you'd have got it. It is the *manner* of asking that has to be refined. Nevertheless, it can be approached persuasively to lead the customer to a natural close.

It is useful to *lead* customers towards a natural acceptance that they will order. For example, try using 'trial closes' such as, 'When will you want this delivered?', 'Will you want it sent to your Green Street depot or to head office?', 'Do you think the green will be better for you?' etc. All these lead the customer gently towards a positive decision, such as, 'We need it by the 15th', 'It will have to go to Green Street', 'The blue will be best'. After that, it's relatively simple to get the final decision.

The question of dealing with price is also examined in detail in Chapter 9, however, bear in mind that, before closing the sale, you must mention the price but surround it with benefits to help justify it. This way the price seems reasonable. For example, 'The price, to include a, b and c which will give you the flexibility that you require, is £x, which includes delivery on the required date'.

It is important to note that, if you are unable to supply the product that the customer initially mentioned, there may be plenty of opportunities to supply alternative products that may do the job just as well, if not better. Having asked open-ended questions in the initial stages of the telephone conversation, the information obtained will give you more opportunity to introduce other products. By using benefits, you may well be able to persuade the caller to buy an alternative product. Assuming you handle this skilfully they will be delighted that their requirements have been satisfied.

To summarise, remember to:

(a) explore the customer's needs with open-ended questions;
(b) make notes;
(c) if you haven't got what customers ask for, offer the nearest alternative that you have available;
(d) have the information to hand;

(e) give the price with extra information;
(f) stress the benefits;
(g) meet price objections with value answers;
(h) check back over important details;
(i) explore other sales possibilities.

4.   Cold calling

This expression describes a situation when you pick up the telephone to ring up an organisation with whom you have not previously dealt. Your aim is to find out who takes buying decisions in that organisation, to speak to him or her and discover the company's buying requirements, to introduce your organisation and to sell your products or services. A tall order, some may say — but it works. This can be quite a difficult technique to master and is often dependent on the attitude not only of the customer, but also of the intermediaries, such as switchboard operators and secretaries, who frequently have instructions to *prevent* sales calls being put through to the decision maker.

There are a number of stages to go through if you want to be really successful in this type of selling.

5.   Before making the call

Obviously the initial consideration must be *who* to ring up. So where can leads be obtained? There are numerous sources of sales leads available, it is just a question of looking for them. For instance:

(a) national press;
(b) regional and local press;

> look at editorial columns, contracts and tenders; and advertisements (i) for product, (ii) for jobs; these may give clues to changes, developments or products used.

(c) trade and technical press;
(d) *Yellow pages* and other directories;
(e) names given by existing customers;
(f) ex-customers — old records may provide useful names that are now 'cold calls' because of lack of recent contact (for 12 months or more).

And so the list goes on. Any sales manager should ensure that someone in the sales office is continually updating such sources of leads for the organisation.

6.   The correct approach

Having found sales leads, the next stage is to think through the correct approach. One of the first things to consider is to whom you want to speak — who is the decision maker? It has been shown in Chapter 6 that the term 'buyer' covers a very broad spectrum of activity — from ordering paper-clips to multi-million pound nuclear generators. So who is the most likely person to make the decision about your product or service? Find out, for this is the person to speak to.

It is vital that the telephone salesperson aims to contact the most senior relevant person. It is much better to *attempt* to speak to the works director and be passed down by him or her to the works manager, than to speak to the works manager who then tells you that decisions are made by their works director. It is then much harder to get to the works director. It is often a good idea to ring up in advance of a selling call just to get the name of the right person, asking something along the lines of, 'We are doing a mailing list of …' etc. In most cases the information is forthcoming. One of the following may be the right type of person for you, depending on the style, size and structure of the organisation you are calling:

(a) works director;
(b) works manager;
(c) production manager;
(d) chief buyer;
(e) specialist buyer, such as for plastic or timber or machine tools;
(f) general manager;
(g) personnel director/manager;
(h) sales director;
(i) publicity director or manager.

7. Who makes the buying decision

Having found a lead, and thought through who is most likely to make a buying decision, it is worth considering additional information. For instance, do you know anything about the organisation you can use as a talking point, such as:

(a) Are they opening a new factory?
(b) Have they recently been awarded a major contract?
(c) Have they just published their annual report?
(d) Have they invented a new process?
(e) Have they launched a new product or service?

If one or other of these points is relevant, then a bit more research or careful consideration of the implications may prove beneficial, especially on points (a), (b) or (d).

8. Getting through to the decision maker

When a salesperson makes a call, it is often a far from simple process to get through to the decision maker. As mentioned, many switchboard operators and secretaries have been told not to put calls through from sales people. So it is up to the salesperson to exercise professionalism to bypass any opposition.

If the information hasn't been previously obtained or isn't on record already, it is always advisable to ask the switchboard operator for the name of the person *responsible* for buying say, medical equipment, rather than just asking to be put through to the buyer of medical equipment. Asking for the name first will make sure that you know if the person who answers the telephone is the person you want. By asking straight away for a connection to the buyer, without a name, puts the caller at a disadvantage, if, when the extension is answered, a voice simply says, 'Yes, Thompson here ...' The caller then has to question Mr Thompson to see if he is the decision maker.

It may be that the switchboard operator gives the name and then promptly connects the caller, perhaps too quickly. On the other hand, other operators will cross-question the caller along these lines:

Caller: 'Can you tell me the name of the person responsible for buying medical equipment?'
Operator: 'Who is calling?'

The answer to this question is to try countering with just your name and, in this case, a title — Mr, Mrs, Ms or Miss — can be useful as it sounds formal and important, such as 'This is Mr Brown.'

In answer to the 'From where?' question which often follows this, it is a good idea to give the company name and location, especially if the salesperson really is calling long distance, saying for example, 'from London' or 'from Birmingham'. Although it is probably not the expected answer, the operator will often put the caller through. On the other hand, the switchboard operator may persist by asking what the call is about.

If the salesperson admits that the call is concerned with selling, the response may well be a suggestion to write in for an appointment or to send details. Neither option is satisfactory from the viewpoint of selling so it can be a good idea to try to avoid a direct answer by offering just an outline of what he or she wishes to discuss, such as, 'I want to talk to him/her about new developments in medical equipment'.

This explanation may sound too complicated to the operator, and often the caller will be put through. Of course, the switchboard may also be congested with other in-coming calls, which puts pressure on him or her to connect the caller with the extension. Salespeople should always avoid discussing their products or giving even a brief sales talk to the operator or the secretary however helpful they appear or how many promises they make to pass on messages.

9. Make an appointment

Sales discussions should only ever be made with the decision maker; anything else is time-wasting. However, you can use a secretary's offer of help to get a telephone appointment with the decision maker. For example:

> *Caller*: 'I'd like to speak to Mr Taylor, please.'
> *Secretary*: 'What is it about?'
> *Caller*: 'Is he not there? What time are you expecting him back?'
> *Secretary*: 'Well, he's at a meeting. Can I help?'
> *Caller*: 'It's a bit complicated because I need some information from him; perhaps it would be better if I called back this afternoon or tomorrow morning?'
> *Secretary*: 'Well, later this afternoon should be all right.'
> *Caller*: 'I'll ring back about three-thirty then.'

10. Selling by telephone

Once you are through to the decision maker, then the selling process begins. In essence it should not be any different from the process described in Chapter 8 and the priority is still to establish facts about potential customers' businesses, but this is especially vital in telephone selling. A few discreet conversational remarks will often enable salespeople to find out about customers' buying requirements and patterns before they reveal all the details of their company. If you give all the facts away about your organisation to begin with, it is very simple for customers to decline and dismiss you or say that they are quite satisfied with existing suppliers.

Beginning to sell too quickly may also mean that the seller chooses the wrong product or service to talk about or, at least, not the most relevant. So establish some facts first.

11. The opening remarks

When the caller gets through, it is good practice to make an introduction, giving his or her name and a brief description of the company, for example:

> *Caller*: 'Good morning Mrs Archer, my name is John Brown from

"Presspack". We're specialist manufacturers of form-packaging. I read in the *Financial Times* that you have just won a major contract to supply medical equipment to Saudi Arabia. I think we might be able to help you.'

Topical pieces of information as may be found in press cuttings, for example, can be useful talking points to open a telephone sales conversation.

12. Plan your call

If selling calls are planned in advance, the element of surprise works to the advantage of salespeople. The person being called, though, may be occupied with other tasks, such as dictating letters or involved in a meeting. If the caller is to attract and hold the buyer's attention, then the presentation needs to be stimulating and interesting enough to achieve this or at least to the degree that the caller may be asked to call back.

13. Establishing the facts

Once salespeople have made their introductions and some formal opening remarks, such as, for example, about the company's new process, the next stage is to try to establish some facts and information about the potential customers' business. In a similar way to the method of handling the incoming caller, who perhaps does not explain his or her requirements very well (11:3), use open-ended questions to establish facts about customers, that is questions beginning with:

(a) what?
(b) when?
(c) where?
(d) how?
(e) who?

These open-ended questions are useful as a means of gaining information. If such questions are asked in the past tense, you will find that there is less opposition to giving you factual replies and it is still possible to refer to things that have only recently happened, such as:

(a) 'What has been your buying requirement?'
(b) 'How have you been obtaining supplies?'
(c) 'Where have your goods been delivered to?'

Assuming that a conversational tone of voice and open-ended questions are used, on the whole, people will respond and give answers to questions. Generally speaking, people will discuss facts about their organisation because they are interested in their company and like to talk about it.

14. Making the sale

Once callers have established conversation with the decision maker, the selling process should be much the same as any other kind of selling, albeit with the difference of not being able to see one another. This obviously limits the salespeoples' abilities to sell a new product or one customers haven't seen. In these circumstances, the purpose of the call is generally to arouse sufficient interest to enable an appointment to be made to see the person. Inevitably there will be requests and suggestions to send literature and so on and it is sometimes hard to avoid doing so. When this happens, though, it is essential to follow up the literature with another call and aim for a personal appointment as soon as possible.

Progress test 11

1. What are the three fundamentals of telephone selling? **(1)**

2. What are the two types of incoming caller? **(2)**

3. What is meant by cold calling? **(4)**

4. Why is it important to use open-ended questions to establish facts? **(13)**

12

Sales records

Information needs

1. The purpose of sales records

Sales records are written statements of a salesperson's activities during a specific time period in a particular area and are used by sales management as a means of controlling the activity and expenses of the sales force. They are also used as a means of collecting information about the market, present sales activity and anticipated activity. They fall into two categories:

(a) control of the sales force; and

(b) an aid to market research and planning.

2. Records help effective selling

A person with natural abilities, some experience and the correct degree of training should prove to be a good salesperson, but will not, by these virtues alone, become an *effective* salesperson. Effective selling is made possible by a sensible routine, an understanding of the territory, a predetermined presentation and, most important, clear objectives and a personal goal. Salespeople who leave home in the morning, wet a finger to see which way the wind is blowing and then follow it, will not be effective. Factors that will determine effectiveness are:

(a) efficient coverage of the territory;

(b) sensible use of selling time;

(c) effective journey planning;

(d) an ability to combine regular calls on established customers with the creation of new customers;

(e) the ability to recognise customers' needs;

(f) the correct use of territory customer records; and

(g) an ability to vary selling techniques according to the situation.

Of course salespeople alone cannot be responsible for combining all these elements efficiently. Sales management must ensure, by continuous supervision and training, that they understand their goals, their products and are acquainted with the methods known to be most effective in reaching objectives. Management of the sales force will not be effective without regulation, the element of control, that will be used:

(a) to determine where the faults lie that inhibit salespeople from reaching their goals; and
(b) to show how techniques may be used more efficiently.

3. Controlling the selling effort

Sales management is ultimately responsible for any weaknesses in the sales force or in individuals within it. The sales force cannot display periodic or sudden bouts of efficiency but must be trained, equipped and motivated to run continuously at optimum efficiency. If the sales force and the organisation is large enough, then specially trained group leaders, supervisors and managers will be responsible to higher management for assessing the performance of those they control. This assessment will be carried out by:

(a) determining suitable goals;
(b) establishing sensible control systems; and
(c) appraising subsequent performance.

Here we are concerned with the second factor, establishing and maintaining sensible controls. These will be guidelines to goal achievement and, following the assignation of the salespeople's goals, the next step will be to devise a quantitative method of comparing achievement against the set standard.

Monitoring salespeople's ability to achieve their sales targets is a control measure that sales management can use. This will enable the managers to determine the overall efficiency of the sales force as well as that of individual salespeople. While this is effective as a means of keeping a check on the force and discovering the less efficient, its more important purpose is the positive one of providing *motivation* through a spirit of healthy competition and challenge, with a bonus to those who attain the largest increase over their targets.

Control begins with the allocation of sales territories to salespeople. This establishes an individual sales area that allows for adjustment of personnel, if needed, without the loss of existing sales records or customer records; in other words, the control is kept on the *territory*, not the individual salesperson.

4. Territory organisation

The organisation of the sales force is usually on a basis of allocating specific territories to individual representatives. This enables salespeople to specialise in one territory, with its customers and conditions, and leads to a development of the customer–salesperson relationship. The territory is also a basis for planning and budgeting of the sales force and for allocating quotas.

For example, if a company had a number of people selling in different areas, say, North London, Birmingham and Southampton, it would have to realise that the sales potential of each is different. North London and Birmingham are both large, urban areas with a great deal of industry, but Southampton is a relatively small and largely rural area. How the salaries of salespeople in each area are calculated is a problem, unless one links the quotas to the possible sales. If, for the sake of argument, the sales potential of North London is estimated to be £100 000 per annum, Birmingham £80 000 and Southampton £35 000, then the targets set will be reasonably equable at the same salaries, because the larger territories will have a much higher potential without requiring any more effort than the smaller areas.

5.   Using records to exercise control

The sales records, and statistics derived from them, enable sales management to exercise control over the sales force by making use of the figures that will be recorded and available whenever they are required. These figures will also be kept in terms of areas or groups into which the sales force is organised and will also be a check on the efficiency of the managers responsible for them.

It is important that a continuity of records is maintained and it becomes necessary to distinguish between the results of the salesperson on the territory and the territory itself as a facet of the organisation structure. This need necessitates separate information being compiled that can be analysed independently. This differentiation is important to avoid discontinuity, which may arise from:

(a) changes in territorial organisation;
(b) increasing the size of the sales force; and
(c) changes in salespeople, due to them leaving, dismissal, promotion, retirement, illness or other reasons.

Each of these factors will require decisions to be taken on the continuity of the sales records.

6.   Territory planning

For sales management to plan for the development of the sales force and the entire selling function, it is essential that comprehensive sales statistics are available. These will enable an in-depth study of the facts and discernable trends to be made.

Very often, sales managers will take decisions based on the size and parameters of territories on the basis of personal experience or that of their superiors or predecessors. This does not always make certain that industrial, urban and social changes are recognised and accounted for in the system. It is important for these changes to be noted whether the company is selling products direct to consumers, via stores, industrial users or agricultural buyers. The relative size of towns, populations etc. will also be important.

7. Changing territorial conditions

The calculation of the size of a territory will normally be based on a prediction of the volume of business it should generate.

In the 1980s in Britain there were massive changes in the structure of industry. Areas that were formerly industrial, some specifically involved in heavy industry, changed almost beyond recognition. The North East, West Midlands and South Wales are examples of regions that were once known for particular kinds of industry but today much of their industrial structure has changed. In the 1960s, South Wales had around 30 collieries and perhaps 12 iron/steel works; today it has 3 collieries and just 2 steel plants.

In terms of territory planning, these changes in industrial structure must be examined and their effects on sales predictions and so on reviewed. Companies selling to specific heavy industries (such as the mining or steel industries) have almost certainly suffered a decline in sales; however, there has been an increase in lighter industrial work, especially in electronics and assembly work, offering sales opportunities in these fields. Several areas have also seen an increase in the number of foreign-owned firms, attracted by government incentive grants, but very often the companies establish manufacturing or assembly plants only and the buying function remains at a head office in another part of the country.

Anyone reviewing territorial structures should periodically consider:

(a) changes in the economic and industrial structure of areas;
(b) changes in the type of work being done;
(c) changes in the location of centralised buying offices and head offices; and
(d) changes in the ownership of companies resulting from concentration, takeovers and mergers.

8.   Bases of assessment

In assessing territories, sales managers must consider different factors that would influence sales. These will naturally differ according to the type of operation. For predicting results in both a consumer trade, such as the grocery trade, and industrial trade, the following would be guides:

(a) consumer suppliers will require information about the:

(i) general levels of income in an area;

(ii) distribution of customers and potential customers among large and small buyers; and

(iii) consumer trends for the type of product;

(b) industrial suppliers will need information about the:

(i) general level of business activity;

(ii) nature of the business — whether it is heavy industry, light industry, chemical processing or whatever and the relative percentages of each; and

(iii) number of firms with *local* authority to buy or with buying departments in *other areas* (many companies, especially in development areas, are solely manufacturing units, all administrative functions being performed at head offices in major cities).

From these assessments, estimates can be made of the general level of business activity and the likely turnover; predictions will be subject to periodical review, using current sales and sales-recorded information as a comparison check.

9.   Journey cycles

A journey cycle is the period taken by a salesperson to make a complete round of their territory following the most logical and efficient route. A recorded system of journey cycles will:

(a) ensure that any territory is worked completely and logically within a prescribed time;

(b) enable prior planning of the journey;

(c) facilitate the arrangement of appointments with important customers in advance;

(d) provide customers with a known frequency of calls, during particular weeks or even days; and

(e) aid a new salesperson to take over an existing territory with the minimum of disruption.

All these points help salespeople to work their territories efficiently. In consumer selling, the regular calling frequency is most important if the customer is going to develop a loyalty to products or brands. They must know when particular companies' salespeople will call. Planned schedules of calls will ensure that salespeople have a clear understanding of who to see, enable firm appointments to be made and ensure that they have the right samples and any additional information they may need.

10. Planning the journey cycle

Planning the journey cycle will depend, essentially, on customers' ordering frequency. If customers buy every week, for example, hotel provisions, then the salespeople need to call every week. In some cases, such as fresh meats, it may even be every day. It must be obvious, therefore, that the buying period, by determining the frequency of calls, also affects the sizes of territories. For example, salespeople selling fresh meats must call on customers every day, so their territories must be small enough to be covered in a day.

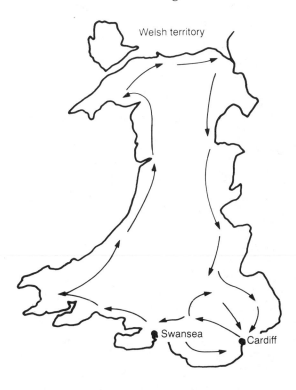

Figure 12.1 *Continuous journey cycle*

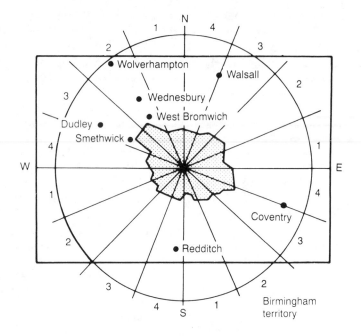

Figure 12.2 *Quadrant journey cycle*

Alternatively, people selling industrial products may only make a regular call on customers every three or four months or more. In that circumstance, the territories can be larger and the journey cycle much longer.

There are many ways of planning the cycle. Figure 12.1 shows an example continuous cycle for a manufacturer of quality clothing, men's or women's wear. The more expensive end of the clothing trade tends to buy twice a year; for the winter and pre-Christmas trade and for the spring/summer trade. The cycle, therefore, has to ensure that the salespeople see all their customers at least twice a year to book their major orders and the rest of the cycle will be for filling in, answering queries and non-regular calls. If a firm wants to order between calls, they can contact the sales office directly.

Figure 12.2 shows a system where there is no set ordering time and so the salespeople have to ensure coverage in an orderly way but there is in-built flexibility to allow them to reach customers with unexpected problems or urgent needs. This system divides the territory into four quadrants, corresponding to north, west, south and east.

Each quadrant is divided into four again and numbered one to four. These numbers correspond to the first four days of the working week. Salespeople using this system will begin a cycle by calling in the areas numbered 'one', that is north one, west one etc. To cover all four number 'one' divisions will take until Thursday. Friday is left free for any special calls or non-selling calls, e.g. dealing with problems, seeing non-buyers who will specify products for purchase by other departments etc. Thus, the entire territory can be covered in four weeks. This scheme also means that the salesperson is never very far from any part of the territory as each quadrant is visited every week. In the event of an urgent need to see a customer, the call can be made without upsetting the whole cycle.

Communication needs

11. Report writing

Throughout the sales organisation structure a certain amount of essential reporting will be required, from the individuals of the sales force upwards, through the intervening levels of responsibility and authority, to the sales manager and, from there, to the directors. The amount of report writing salespeople will have to do will tend to increase further up the organisation structure and will be necessary if each element is to work effectively. While this should form a relatively small part of the total work, particularly at the lower level, it is, nevertheless, important. The main responsibility of salespeople, however, is to sell and so they should not be overburdened with an excessive amount of report writing.

The sales organisation depends a great deal on sources of information, both on customers themselves and their reactions to the products. Salespeople serve an important role in providing such information to aid sales management in planning and controlling. They also fulfil an important part of market research, especially in industrial selling where the usual market research questionnaire techniques are less effective.

How all this information is used is shown diagrammatically in Figure 12.3. It shows how a plan is revised, implemented, measured, compared with its predicted effect and subjected to revision. Reports from the sales force, along with achieved sales figures, are a source of information for comparison of actual results with predicted effects and will result in subsequent revision if necessary.

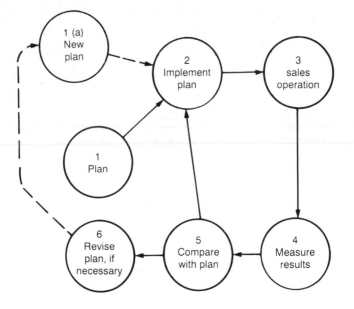

Figure 12.3 *Management information circuit*

12. Preparing a report

Reports should be clear, concise and conclusive and facts should be used whenever available. Opinions can also be valuable but, when they are given, it should be made clear that they are only opinions.

Reports need not be long and should generally not take the writer longer than a quarter of an hour to prepare. Ideally they should be written as soon as possible after a sales interview and, when this cannot be done, rough notes of the essential details should be made. Many firms issue report pads or memo pads and salespeople should always make use of them.

13. Who needs information?

All the elements in a sales organisation need information. It flows in two directions:

(a) *upwards* from sales force to management; and
(b) *downwards* from management to sales force.

Figure 12.4 shows the main flows in an organisation structure and the nature of the information being communicated.

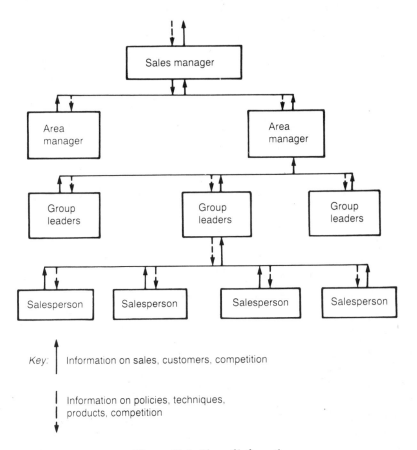

Figure 12.4 *Flow of information*

14. Levels of management

The different levels of management have particular needs for the information drawn from sales records. At the top level it will be for a broad analysis of results as an aid to strategic planning. Lower management will want much more specific information as a means of operational control. The different needs (summarised in Figure 12.5) are:

(a) *sales/marketing directors* require a summary of analysed results of performance against planned performance, which involve:
   (i) sales figures;
   (ii) selling and related costs;

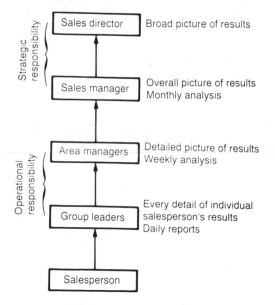

Figure 12.5 *Differing record needs*

  (iii) market trends;
  (iv) activity of competitors;
  (v) anticipated business for next period; and
  (vi) variations from plan;
(b) *sales managers* require details of overall sales organisation's performance, including:
  (i) areas;
  (ii) customer categories;
  (iii) new accounts;
  (iv) lost accounts; and
  (v) selling costs;
(c) *area managers* require detailed analyses of area results on a weekly basis:
  (i) by territory;
  (ii) by number of calls per day;
  (iii) by number of new contacts; and
  (iv) by breakdown of sales by product range;
(d) *group leaders* require comprehensive information on the performance of the salespeople under their direct control on a daily basis:

     (i) number of calls per day;
    (ii) percentage of new contacts;
   (iii) number of interviews;
   (iv) number of presentations;
    (v) number of sales;
   (vi) size of orders;
  (vii) future anticipated business;
 (viii) name and status of contact;
   (ix) if salespeople are working to plan; and
    (x) if salespeople are making effective use of training in presentation, technique and samples.

15. Summarising information

Salespeople are the source of the information needed by management to determine whether its sales policies are being applied successfully. It is necessary for salespeople completing records and reports to give explanations for any variations in their work from the prescribed plan. Similarly, any results that indicate that sales are down on the planned level should also be explained.

Reports must give sales management the necessary information and, where it is needed, an interpretation of the facts. Management will need this interpretation if the facts are to be correctly translated. Only if management has all the information can it take the correct decisions.

16. Reporting by exception

Management by exception can be summed up in the phrase: 'If everything is all right, don't tell me.'

If management is to be free from unnecessary clutter so that it can concentrate on the really essential details, it must increasingly delegate the routine matters. Reporting by exception is an adaptation of this concept for the sales force. Essentially, it leaves the day-to-day operations to the person on the spot so long as it can be sure that it will be informed of any problem that is either beyond the salesperson's authority or jurisdiction.

17. Records and motivation

The two-way system of communication is an aid to motivating the sales organisation. At the top level, sales managers will want assurances from the board that it is satisfied with the way its policies are being interpreted into action and positive results. Area managers will want assurances that their area's results are in line with quotas and other areas' performances. Salespeople will want to know how they stand in relation to other salespeople in the group, the area or nationally. This will affect the individual's sense of security, income and prospects and give assurance that their interests are being cared for in terms of assistance and will show the company's appreciation of what they are doing.

18. Types of records

Salespeople will complete a number of forms or records in the period of a month. Some will be daily, others weekly and usually an aggregated monthly summary of activity will be produced. Types of records include:

(a) *Daily report.* This is usually completed during the day's work and sent to the superior each evening. It will provide the information needed to enable management to keep abreast of daily progress.

(b) *Customer record card.* This is a filing system that each salesperson will be required to keep and which will be returned to the company in the event of termination of employment. It will record the names and addresses of customers, or potential customers, the person to see, the nature of the business, a record of orders placed or likely to be placed and details of previous calls. Salespeople should consult this before each journey to refresh their memory before visiting each customer. It must be kept up to date and should be regularly inspected by management.

(c) *Weekly activity summary.* Usually combined with a vehicle report (where a company vehicle is supplied) it will summarise the week's events, orders, new customers, special events, distance travelled etc.

(d) *Monthly report.* This will aggregate the weekly records and will also predict likely business for the coming month and possible business for the following month(s). It is a guide for sales management in determining production requirements and longer term trends.

(e) *Expenses forms.* Salespeople will be expected to keep records of any expenses incurred and submit them on a regular basis. Sometimes a firm will give a fixed amount in expenses that is calculated to be sufficient for the salesperson's needs.

Progress test 12

1. The purpose of sales records falls into two categories; what are they? **(1)**

2. How do sales records assist in controlling the sales force? **(3)**

3. How may records be used to exercise control? **(5)**

4. In assessing a sales territory what bases may be used? **(8)**

13

Increasing sales

Measuring profit

1. The business purpose

A company's success is ultimately judged by its ability to make profit. Profit, therefore, is the objective of any commercial organisation. It is also the means by which the company, in the long term, continues to exist. It follows that as a company expands, its profits should, logically, increase, although it is sometimes difficult to ascertain whether expansion increases profit or vice versa. A company may, by better sales, grow larger and that will increase its profits, but equally, a profitable firm has the means to expand. Perhaps the real test of the importance of profit is that if a firm does not make profit, it eventually dies.

2. The business objective

For a company to realise a profit it is necessary to make a sale. This creates a need for customers and, more important, satisfied customers. The objective of business is profit and its purpose is the creation of satisfied customers.

It is a management myth to define the business objective as being to maximise profit; in reality the prime business objective is often survival — to attain long-term resilience by means of customer service. Profit as a term, however, can mean different things, such as:

(a) an increase in the overall profit of a company over a period of a year; or
(b) an increase in the amount of profit earned on a particular product.

In (a) the company is endeavouring to sell more, possibly by creating a wider range of customers. In (b) the concern is with increasing profit, getting more out of each transaction.

3. Different concepts of profit

Different companies may put differing interpretations on what is meant by profit. A company may define profit as being:

(a) the *total expenditure* over a period of a year, deducted from the *total income* over the same period; or

(b) a *percentage* deducted from all expenditure, which would include depreciation, from the *total income* in the same period; or they may

(c) *aggregate all expenditure* on obtaining business over a period of a year, ignoring expenditure on advertising aimed at gaining business in the next yearly period and deduct this sum from the *total income* of the period, plus all *outstanding* money from sales effected during the year.

From the above definitions it is clear that profit is not an absolute concept, but is what individual management defines it as.

4.   Volume versus profit

It might be thought that as sales increase, profits will increase by the same factor. For example, if the profit from a product is £10, then the profit on 100 of those products should be £1000. In reality, though, the increase in profit rarely rises constantly. It may be that by making more of a product, the firm can buy raw materials or supplies on more advantageous terms, which will lower the total cost and so enable the firm to operate with a higher margin of profit. Alternatively, to obtain the higher volume of business, the firm may have to lower its prices or offer some other inducement, such as free delivery and, in these circumstances, the percentage of profit might actually fall.

The problem for sales management in calculating price and profit levels is to predict what the market response might be at different volumes of sales and also at different volumes of output. Is there an advantage in selling more products at a lower profit rather than fewer at a higher profit? How far is such a decision related to forecasts of future sales?

If the market is expanding and forecasts predict rising demand, it will probably be sensible to take a lower margin of profit to obtain a growing share in the expanding market. If, on the other hand, a firm is entering an existing market or already has a small share of the existing market, it may have to maintain its prices but perhaps spend more on advertising and promotion to improve, or hold on to, its market position. If a firm has a new, innovative product for which a growing market can certainly be created, it will probably decide to take a high margin of profit, perhaps even an 'excessive' profit, while competitors are trying to catch up, in the knowledge that as competition grows its own profits will inevitably decline.

5. Achieving the business objective

We have seen that the business objective is profit and the realisation of this objective is the criterion by which success is measured.

The formulation of commercial policy within the company is the basic concern of sales management in their declared strategy of increasing sales.

Management's prime functions of planning, organising, motivating and controlling (*see* Chapter 16) are all directly applicable to the work of sales management. To set realistic objectives and individual goals, sales management has to be aware of the divergent aims of the company in meeting its ultimate responsibility of achieving the required profitability. Unless sales management is aware of the overall commercial policy, its strategy will not be congruent with the overall corporate strategy. Conversely, top management, if it is out of step with a customer-orientated sales management objective, will aim for the greatest possible profit return from the business, which, if pursued to extremes, can bring about the demise of the business.

6. Profit maximisation as a false objective

Example ———————————————————————————————

In the 1960s, the export manager of a menswear manufacturing company pursued a policy of customer-orientation and established the company's products in about 40 different markets world-wide, although some were small and specialised. This was achieved by carrying out marketing research to find out what influenced customers' taste in clothing, e.g. what effects climate, economic conditions, legal restrictions and cultural factors had on each market. These findings were examined and, put together with internal company matters such as production ability, design, cloth availability etc., used to help the company produce what each market wanted (as far as possible). Like most exports, they were less profitable than comparable products sold at home — because of increased selling costs, high standards of manufacture and competition abroad — but overall exports contributed between 25 and 30 per cent of the company's sales. Not a bad result considering the small departmental staff involved.

After some years, there was a change in the top management of the company and the new directors were highly profit-oriented. In the home market, the company's long-established reputation was allowed to lapse as they sought bulk sales to mail-order catalogue companies — quality was sacrificed in favour of quantity. Long-established franchises were scrapped. The company then turned its attention to the overseas markets, using the same methods and concepts. When these 'strategies' failed to achieve the level of profits demanded, they opened 'factory shops' selling their own clothing directly to the public. This act offended the remaining stockists, who refused to carry the brand. The company then switched to importing women's and children's wear in the desperate search for profit and finally went out of business — with the loss of around 500 jobs.

The maximisation of profits by any company may lead to:

(a) employment of low-grade personnel at low pay;
(b) purchasing of cheap materials;
(c) retention of obsolescent equipment;
(d) cut-backs in research and development;
(e) cut-backs in product promotion;
(f) the minimum of product development and innovation; or
(g) the imposition of a policy of variety reduction, that is reducing the range of products leading to less choice, as in the case of the motor industry (although there can be some justification of this when an excessive number of models are available).

Due to a policy of low investment in labour, capital and resources, profits may be increased in the short term, but, in the longer term, the company will be overtaken by its competitors and lose its markets. This kind of activity was unfortunately practised by many British firms in the 1960s and led to the loss of much export business, as well as encouraging the purchase of better quality imported products.

The business should have as its objective not the maximisation of profit, but the least profit that it must earn to meet its costs.

7. Commercial considerations

The problem of defining and measuring profit is a difficult one. Accountants, business people and economists disagree on a suitable, definitive solution. Two commercial considerations are:

(a) increased-net-worth theory;
(b) cost and revenue theory.

In the increased-net-worth theory, the profit a business has accrued over a set period of time is the difference between the net worth of the business at the commencement of the period and at its termination.

It is necessary to make adjustments for the withdrawal of capital and the introduction of any additional capital. One of the many problems associated with this theory is deciding which assets and liabilities are to be included. It also has the particular drawback for sales managers that the theory confuses 'windfall' and 'planned' profits. Windfall profits arise purely from chance while planned profits are the result of management planning and decision making. Clearly, if profit is to be a criterion by which sales management is to be judged, it is necessary to have a means of distinguishing between windfall and planned profits.

The cost and revenue theory reasons that the profit accrued during a period is the difference between the revenue earned and the cost incurred. It is difficult, however, to measure revenue exactly and what precisely constitutes costs can also be a problem.

If an item purchased is totally consumed during the accounting period, for example, a measured length of aluminium, the amount of cost to include is straightforward. However, if some of the raw materials are left or the cost relates to a machine that will be used for several years, the matter becomes more complicated.

In spite of problems, the cost and revenue theory has merits. The difficulties of distinguishing between windfall and planned profits for instance are lessened.

8.   Profit

If a company's success is to be judged by the amount of profit earned, it follows that the higher the profit, the more successful it is judged to be. However, in the short term, the concept of profit is *not* a suitable criterion for measuring success.

Consider a company that recognises it can win a major share in a market if it reduces the prices of its products. This price reduction can be achieved by increasing the amount of capital equipment or machine tools used. The investment needed may reduce or even eradicate any profit in one period and, if success is judged solely on profit, one would say the company had been unsuccessful. However, over the longer term, it may recover its investment and turn the temporary loss into a major profit. Too many companies fail to set realistic profit objectives:

(a) it is as serious to set the sales targets and profit goals too low in the short term, as it is to set goals too high;

(b) top management, by imposing objectives and exerting pressure on subordinates to achieve goals, frequently leads middle management to underestimate its profit targets;

(c) managers must be motivated to determine realistic goals that will encourage their needs for self-fulfilment;

(d) a realistic use of management by objectives enables short-term planning by managers to be made more consistent with top management's long-term strategy, which is a necessary correlation for sustained success.

A company's resources have a value and the profits earned during a given period of time have to be related to this value.

9. The profit returned on capital employed method

If a company accepts this concept of profit, it may restate its objectives to be: 'The maximisation of the profit return on the resources invested in it.'

To sales managers the concept is important as it means that the resources of a company are limited and should be put to their most profitable use.

Achieving profit

10. Selling up, selling more

To sales managers, these terms may both be applied to the problem of getting a better return on the investment in stock or selling techniques. The choice of technique will depend on:

(a) the nature of the product; and
(b) the nature of the market.

If the price of the product is raised in order to obtain a higher margin over costs, it follows that a better return will result.

Example

Product 'X' cost £1.00: margin of 25 per cent	= profit of £0.25
Sales of 1000 of product 'X'	= profit £250.00
Product 'X' cost £1.00: margin of 30 per cent	= profit £0.30
Sales of 1000 of Product 'X'	= profit £300.00

If the problem was as simple as this example suggests, increasing profits would be a straightforward matter of increasing prices, but economic laws operate that fundamentally affect the outcome of such apparently simple attempts to increase profits.

Concepts of demand

11. Demand contracts as prices rise

This principle is shown in Figure 13.1. From this economic fact of life, it follows, therefore, that if we increase prices in order to maximise profit, we face the prospect of selling fewer products. The amount by

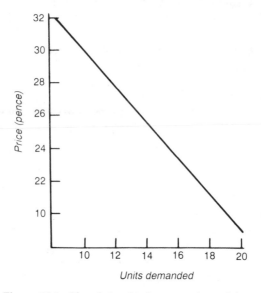

Figure 13.1 *The relationship between price and demand*

which demand falls will depend on the 'elasticity' of demand, which is the responsiveness of consumers' or users' demand to an increase in price.

12. Elasticity of demand

If things are elastic they stretch; the more they stretch the greater is their elasticity. If a small change in the price of a product leads to large changes in the quantity of the product demanded (bought) it is subject to elastic demand. Conversely, if a change in price leads to little change in demand it is held to be inelastic in demand.

If demand is elastic, an increase in price will produce a fall in demand. For example, if ice-cream suddenly increased in price by 20 per cent, people would buy less, although they may begin to buy again when they've grown accustomed to the increase. If demand is inelastic, a rise in price will not result in an immediate fall in demand — although, in the long term, consumers may seek alternative supplies or substitutes. This is what happened to demand for oil-based products in the 1970s. When the price rose dramatically, the demand for petrol, for example, did not fall very much simply because people with cars had to have petrol, but, in the longer term, it did result in a search for alternative forms of energy. The following examples illustrate differing consumer demand responses:

(a) in the event of salt increasing in price by 10 per cent, demand would remain constant; everyone needs salt, there is no substitute and, in any case, the level of demand is low and steady — *demand is inelastic;*
(b) should bread increase in price by 10 per cent, demand would probably fall in the short term — consumers might try baking their own — but it is an essential product and demand would soon rise again — *demand is inelastic in the medium to long term;*
(c) if the price of beef increases by 10 per cent, demand falls immediately as people can do without beef because there are many substitutes, so only a fall in price will induce people to buy beef again — *demand is elastic.*

13. Why sales managers should recognise elasticity

If management is to handle price increases, whether because of rising costs or as a means of increasing profit, it must consider the elasticity of demand for its products. In general, as price increases, demand falls (*see* Figure 13.2).

The concept of elasticity can also be applied to price cutting, but sales management must know what effect price cuts will have on demand. For example, a cut in the price of pepper or oil drilling equipment is unlikely to increase the demand by much, simply because these kinds of products are only ever needed in particular

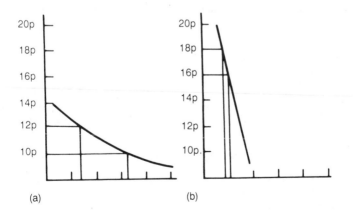

Figure 13.2   *An elastic demand curve (a) and an inelastic demand curve (b)*

quantities. A cut in their price would therefore lead to lower overall profits. On the other hand, falls in the prices of many consumer products and industrial and commercial consumables such as electricity, would probably lead to increased demand for them and greater profits.

14. Increasing profits
To increase profits, sales managers have two alternatives:

(a) *To lower costs.* This may be achieved in various ways, depending on the nature of the product or service:
    (i) increased utilisation of machinery or equipment;
    (ii) by reducing variety in the product range, for example deleting the less popular colour options for a range of goods;
    (iii) rationalisation of staff, for example employing fewer representatives, office workers etc.;
    (iv) by using capital equipment to replace higher labour costs.
(b) *To sell more effectively.* Sales management must constantly ensure that a higher proportion of sales is achieved per sales interview. More effective selling is a marketing problem and involves all the different tools of marketing being used in conjunction. For sales managers it is an especially important task and they must:
    (i) think out the strategy;
    (ii) evaluate alternative plans;
    (iii) make decisions on possible solutions;
    (iv) ensure policies are put into practice; and
    (v) monitor results.
An essential aspect of the sales manager's role is to constantly seek out new sales opportunities and this creative task must by dynamically performed.

15. Creativity
Marketing implies a serious study of market trends in an attempt to obviate as many problems as possible and to enable more positive sales predictions to be made. By using market, economic and consumer research, it should become possible to aim products at specific market segments, enabling better market targeting and promotions, resulting in lower sales costs. In this process, various sales aids may be employed:

(a) sales promotion;
(b) advertising; and
(c) public relations exercises.

16. Increasing sales

To sell more often simply requires more effort; more attention to the needs of the customers, more thought going into the selling process and, perhaps, longer hours and greater effort being put into improving customer relationships and service. Widening the customer product mix will ensure that more sales can be achieved. Clearly any such exercise must be closely monitored to ensure that the extra *costs* do not exceed the additional *sales* made, or the results will be negated.

Progress test 13

1. There are several different concepts of profit; what are they? (**3**)

2. Why may profit maximisation be a false objective? (**6**)

3. What is the difference between selling up and selling more? (**10**)

4. What two alternatives do sales managers have to increase profits? (**14**)

14

Customers and communications

Understanding customers

1. Consumer research

The modern business environment has created and refined many ways of obtaining the information necessary for the prediction, planning and more exact understanding of conditions, both present and future. These include market research, product research, motivational research and research into employees. Consumer research exists to investigate consumer trends generally and to find out what consumers are doing rather than to discover essential facts about customers as individuals.

Available consumer information consists, generally, of a series of precise but lifeless statistics, recording what has happened, rather than estimating what customers will do.

2. Results of research

Much of consumer research derives from the activities of advertising, which needs to know how people might react to advertising and sales messages and accentuating the essential diversity of human nature. The general concepts inferred from advertising research of consumers' behaviour are that:

(a) human beings are self-motivating and complicated;
(b) they are reasoning and intelligent, but equally capable of making irrational *and* rational decisions;
(c) their motivations are largely a result of emotion, custom or prejudice;
(d) they differ in nature and personality;
(e) as seen from the above, they form widely differing desires and buying behaviour; and
(f) their differences in buying behaviour will be great, even within one particular society.

3. General trends

It is reasonable to assume that distinguishable relationships will exist between buying behaviour and changes that arise in society and between the behavioural influences that affect individuals. It is possible to recognise general trends. For example:

(a) particular models of motor cars have varying degrees of success largely due to the visual impression they create or their styling, not necessarily the mechanical performance they give, which is a reflection of consumers' attitudes to the modern world;

(b) sales of package holidays rely on the general feelings of holidaymakers about certain countries and resorts, rarely on specific details, such as degrees of temperature, rainfall and the facilities they all provide.

4. Significance of consumer trends

It is essential for a company to try to appreciate the underlying significance of apparently trivial consumer trends, such as the choice of bright colours in men's shirts or trends in women's lipsticks, which often gain a momentum of their own and defy the fashion houses' attempts to dictate alternatives.

There has developed in recent years a need for self-expression that, if related to the hierarchy of needs (*see* 15.**13**), may have come about because our physiological and security needs are generally satisfied. This self-expression is manifested in new hobbies, homes, do-it-yourself holidays, sports and the wider range of leisure activities.

It becomes important not only to research basic reasons for patterns of consumer buying, but also to examine the wider implications of human behaviour patterns as a whole. Consumers are not simply persuaded by rational considerations of price, utility and presentation, but also by basic motivations arising from expectations, by behaviour determined by attitudes, experiences, social responsibilities and so on and by the way in which the person's particular peer group considers the object of his or her interest.

5. Individuality and communications

It is easy to regard consumers acting *en masse* as being something apart from the rest of humanity — a woman in a shop buying an article is often considered to be different from a woman at home or work. It must be remembered that both the buyer and the seller, after all, are individual human beings, prone to individual thoughts and opinions, even though research on consumer behaviour usually reduces them to rows of statistics. The needs of customers will alter with changing social conditions, while consumer trends may alter with changing life-styles.

Advertising does make attempts to relate its messages to its concepts of particular customers although, even then, it usually fails to present the customer as a believable human being. Thus it fails to make the most of its communicatory abilities. The success of an advertising message must depend on more than the obvious rational content, as much of the communication of meaning is conveyed in ways other than verbal.

6.   Personal characteristics

Research into the factors influencing customers' buying decisions invariably reveal that the critical element in buying or not buying is distinctive personal characteristics. This has been revealed especially in areas where the population is formed from distinct groups of widely differing origins, race, religion, education, income etc. and yet it has been shown that decisions about the purchase of cars, clothing, even foodstuffs, derive from variances in personality and not expressly from the other factors. If a man buys a bright red shirt, it is generally because he has an extrovert character and not because of any particular background; similarly a man who insists on a formal striped tie is also displaying a particular behaviour pattern related to his personality.

7.   Confidence of consumers

It has been evidenced from recent studies of consumer behaviour in buying that confidence is a strong determinant of whether a purchase is made or not. It does not rely heavily on how much money a person has, but, rather, on how he or she views the future. In this, consumers' behaviour reflects fundamental attitudes concerning their appreciation of the economic picture.

During the early 1980s there was a general rise in unemployment throughout the developed world and in Britain this was largely caused by a drastic restructuring of traditional industries. The uncertainty caused by economic depression and high unemployment was reflected in the low demand for many consumer goods.

8.   Systematic consumer knowledge

To correctly interpret consumer attitudes, especially in relation to the needs of business, it is necessary to provide systematic knowledge about:

(a) the ways in which consumers form attitudes;
(b) methods to determine the fundamental attitudes;

(c) how negative attitudes can be changed; and
(d) the way in which particular attitudes are self-selecting for communications about products or services.

There are overall behavioural attitudes, such as consumer feeling about the state of the economy, but, in addition, there are specific attitudes that apply to all consumers' reactions to product propositions. For each product and for each brand name, there will be positive and negative reactions from consumers, but frequently the manufacturer will not detect these. People presented with decisions as to whether or not they will buy a product will be significantly influenced by their fundamental attitudes. Attitudes to colour in clothing may derive from earlier experiences when 'flashy' might have been the current description of colourful, rather than 'trendy'.

A manufacturer desperately trying to promote a product with little success may not have fully understood the underlying attitudes of consumers to the product that although they appear trivial, are important to their ultimate buying decision.

Motivating customers

9. Communicating the message

A tremendous amount of money is spent annually by manufacturers on advertising or other means of communicating messages about their products. If the message is to succeed, it has to have an impact upon the customers or users that will motivate them to buy the product. Whether or not customers will be so motivated will depend on three factors:

(a) how people *react* to the message;
(b) how frequently they are *exposed* to the message;
(c) how effectively they *recall* the message.

The ability to recall the message effectively is dependent on memory.

10. Memory

Memory is connected with imagery insofar as it depends on the ability to recall images of something that has already occurred. An experience does not simply happen and get forgotten; a vestige of it will be retained in the mind. These vestiges may be no more than ephemera or they may have a lasting effect and be recalled with great intensity. Exposure to an advertisement or other sales message may pass almost without recognition and yet a person can see something in a shop that promotes recall and may lead to an impulse purchase.

11. Recognition and recall

Recognition is a much simpler process than recall. The sight of a product, or even a similar advertisement, may bring back memories of the original experience. Recall is a voluntary effort to remember an image. A consumer faced with a problem attempts to recall a relevant product or a brand that has been seen somewhere, but it has not consciously registered deeply enough. It is important for sales management when promoting products to recognise two important factors that will influence consumers' ability to recall messages. These are that:

(a) *repetition* of an experience enables it to be recalled more readily (important to note when demonstrating products); and
(b) *the intensity of the original stimulus* will make recall easier.

Any promotional campaign must therefore ensure that the message:

(a) conforms to customer attitudes;
(b) is repeated sufficiently to form strong images in customers' memories; and
(c) is intense enough to register positively, enabling certain recall.

12. Benefits to customers

All goods, whether industrial or consumer, are really bought for the benefits they confer. Even consumer products are bought to satisfy needs — thirst, hunger, fashion requirements — and for the effects they induce, such as television for relaxation and coffee for a stimulating hot drink. Before individuals become customers for particular products, they must have a perceived need that they want to satisfy. For example, a mother who buys healthy food for her child perceives the benefit this will confer in health terms. This will create a 'notion' for something.

When people have conceived a notion for something, they are thinking in terms of how the product or service will provide the desired benefits. The following process will occur:

(a) anticipation of benefits;
(b) desire for the product/service;
(c) desire grows into a positive need;

(d) the person is stimulated to seek information;
(e) the person becomes a potential customer for a particular product or service.

Customers are therefore motivated by their conception of what the product will do for them. The management of customers makes it essential for this aspect of derived demand to be thoroughly understood and implemented through an understanding of what customers believe they want, and then so directing communications that they fulfil these personality needs, no matter how trivial they may appear to the manufacturer.

The total communication need

13. Communication needs

The purpose of sales and marketing communications is to provide information about the product or service in a favourable way, to motivate customers to want the product and to inform them where it may be obtained. To be effective, however, communications must go further than simply explaining the company's products. They must also distribute favourable information about the company, its policies and activities. Sales and marketing communications should include all those activities that dispense information, such as:

(a) the sales force;
(b) advertising;
(c) promotions;
(d) public relations and publicity;
(e) exhibitions and conferences
(f) literature, brochures and newsletters;
(g) stationery, including business cards, letter headings, invoices etc.; and
(h) vehicle signs.

All of these methods of communication will be directed towards:

(a) creating an environment in which the *company's products will elicit favourable reactions* from consumers or users; and
(b) *encouraging sales of the company's products by stimulating demand* and so achieve a satisfactory return on investment.

14. Communication and sales objectives

Sales objectives result from corporate strategy and long-term planning being translated into departmental objectives and will have been determined by market, economic and social research. Once the objectives have been determined, the role of communications in the marketing mix will be decided.

There is a range of activities that sales management can employ to realise its objectives and, together, they will make up the marketing mix; they will be blended to give the most satisfactory combination to reach the actual or potential customer (*see* Figure 14.1.)

The actual composition of the marketing mix will depend, among other things, on the strategy of the company and how it regards its role of satisfying customers. Sales management will use these variables in different ways, reflecting the type of product, the market, the competition and the distribution costs:

(a) a company dominating the market for a particular range of goods may rely on its *reputation and public relations* for communication and competitive pricing to maintain its share of the market;
(b) a company selling products with little differentiation in a highly competitive market will be forced to *advertise heavily and promote extensively* to ensure that its position in the market is maintained;

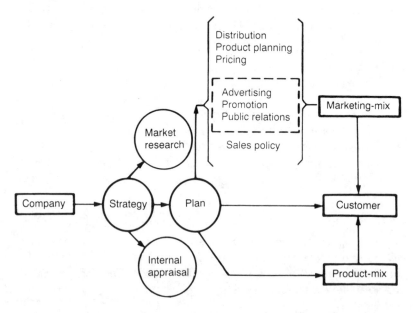

Figure 14.1 *Communications in the marketing mix*

(c) industrial suppliers may place *less emphasis on competitive pricing if their product is specialised*, and their communication may be limited to advertising in restricted-circulation magazines so their communications will be largely by means of the sales force and through public relations.

15. Changing needs for communication

Communication needs will change as market conditions change and according to the way a company perceives its market situation.

In this assessment, market share plays the major role. This is because the company with the largest share of a particular product line's market will be in a very strong position to take advantage of any promotional push by its competitors due to the fact that most product advertising raises the *general* level of awareness for a *type* of product, rather than for a specific brand. This situation exists in most branded grocery business. For example, Heinz has the largest share of the multimillion pound baked bean market. If any of their competitors advertise their own baked beans, Heinz will also benefit because it has this largest share.

This phenomenon presents a problem to companies striving to increase their own market share against a major competitor and calls for communication strategies other than direct advertising. One way in which a company with a small market share can grow without passing on a share of its effort to the major market shareholder, like Heinz, is to develop specific varieties aimed at specific market segments. Cross & Blackwell, for example, faced with strong competition in the tinned spaghetti market, introduced a brand aimed specifically at weight-watchers. Advertising for that brand in that particular market segment was, at that time, a segment in which its main rivals did not compete.

The firm's or the product's position in the market, therefore, will be a major decision-making influence on the choice of mix (*see* Figure 14.2)

A company's communication strategy will also change according to the position of its products in the product life cycle (*see* Figure 3.7):

(a) initially the company will communicate by advertisements and sales promotion to ensure that as many potential customers as possible learn about the product in a favourable way;

(b) later, when a strong market position has been established, the company will need to maintain a certain level of advertising to keep the product in consumers' minds;

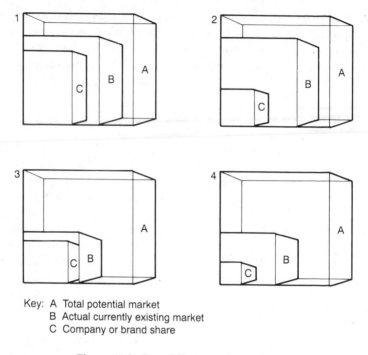

Key: A Total potential market
B Actual currently existing market
C Company or brand share

Figure 14.2 *Four different market positions*

(c) when competitors begin to affect the company's share of the market, it will have to adopt a different communication strategy — it will then see the need to develop sales promotions as a means of lowering the price to customers without changing the listed price and setting off a price-cutting 'war' (this effective use of sales promotion is a communication technique);

(d) at some time, competitors will possibly develop a rival product with undoubted improvements and, for a time, the company may not be able to offer its own improved version or new product, so at this point the kind of communication will again change, with an advertised decrease in listed price and a concerted promotional campaign.

Planned communications

16. Planning the communications campaign
Sales and marketing operations must always be controlled in a

way that allows flexibility because so many of the factors involved are beyond the company's control.

Sales management need to take an analytical approach to problem solving that will obviate inspired guesses as a basis for action. As all objectives are easier to understand and problems resolved more readily when set down, it is as necessary to establish a plan for a communications campaign as it is for a selling operation.

17. The communications plan

Any campaign must be planned in order to avoid misunderstanding among the personnel involved in its operations. It will also serve to coordinate the various activities that will be concerned in its successful implementation: sales management, advertising, sales promotion, public relations, finance, production and distribution. The communications plan must ensure that all are working towards the same goals. The essential requirements of the plan are that:

(a) it can be understood quickly and simply; and
(b) all the necessary information is available.

The plan will also be a record of the way in which the campaign was undertaken and its effectiveness can be measured against it. In this way it provides a basis for future campaigns and a relative measure of their overall effectiveness.

18. Selected strategies

Communications can include advertising, sales promotion, public relations, exhibitions or the use of the sales force. Each method will require a similar set of statements to make sure that efforts are coordinated.

19. Communications plan structure

All the separate plans involved in the overall campaign will have a similar basic structure of objective, method and explanation:

(a) *the objective* will have been determined by the overall sales strategy, of which communications will be a part;
(b) *the method* of achieving the objective will be set down in a concise, factual manner;
(c) *an explanation* of the purpose of the objective and reasons for the proposed methods of achieving it will be given.

Planning in this way delegates responsibilities for particular aspects to specialist groups or departments, within or outside the firm.

Of course, such delegation is based on an ideal organisation structure, which would only exist in the largest firm. Nevertheless, as will be seen in Chapter 17 about organisation, it is the *allocation* of responsibility that is important and, in smaller firms, these tasks may be done by one or two people, dividing their time between their different functions.

20. Communications copy proposal

The purpose of the copy proposal is to ensure that the advertising agency or department create ideas in line with the overall communications plan. Those responsible for the creative work, the text or graphics, must be familiar with the essential points of the product — its purpose, any special points of merit or originality etc. The sales presentation plan will detail the proposal in the same three ways:

(a) *objective* — which will outline the creative objectives in terms of method of appeal, underlying behavioural reasoning, type of customer and the way the product fits in with the company's policy;
(b) *methods* — how it is proposed to communicate the creative ideas to the market;
(c) *explanation* — the underlying company policy, essential product knowledge and points of superiority.

21. Media proposals

The media to be selected for communication of the plan will be the responsibility of a special planning section. They, like the creative section, will have to operate within the parameters of the company policy and objectives:

(a) *objective* — details of the customers, who they are, industrial or consumers, home or abroad, high or low income, and how they may be reached and the frequency needed;
(b) *method* — the proposals will include details of how the plan will be achieved within the limits of the budget, the media selected and their respective costs;
(c) *explanation* — details of why the plan has been so designed.

22. Ancillary information

Ideally the plan will require the collection of a wide variety of information on the market, with examination of products, customers, distribution, media and market and economic research. The amount of research done, however, must reflect the financial strength of the firm. What is collected should be compiled in the form of a report that will be circulated to all the departments, sections or people involved in the fulfilment of the plan. The report ensures that continuity will be established with future plans and that the data it contains can be modified as the market evolves or experience increases.

23. The total communications concept

The communication of information is central to any sales or marketing campaign, whether it is conducted on an international, national or purely local basis. It creates the need for information by the requirements of understanding the product's market position. It then disseminates information in answer to customer information needs and to create a favourable attitude in the market towards the company and its products.

An example of a total promotional concept is the way in which McDonald's, the American-based fast food giant, promotes itself. With an annual promotional budget of around $1bn, it can easily out-manoeuvre its rivals in straight advertising, but it also employs all the other elements of the promotional mix. It uses media advertising to 'swamp' any competitive campaign and to launch new products. It links these new launches to money-off promotions to stimulate brand loyalty and also uses a wide range of promotional games that encourage customers to eat more often at a McDonald's. Finally it has a large publicity strategy aimed at reinforcing a favourable and caring corporate image among its public, which includes sponsoring sporting events, such as the 1988 Olympic games, and providing free family rest accommodation at children's hospitals. The company's giant promotional budget for a mix of advertising, sales promotion and publicity ensures that it remains the largest promoter of a brand in the United States.

Progress test 14

1. List some of the results of advertising research into consumer behaviour. **(2)**

2. How can good communication affect customer motivation? **(9)**

3. When people conceive a notion for something, what are the steps in their process of determining its benefits? **(12)**

4. List the eight activities that dispense information. **(13)**

15

Managing the sales function

Some initial considerations

1. Introduction

Being concerned with the selling function and its management throughout this book, many of the duties of sales managers are examined in depth elsewhere in the book. This chapter, therefore, will look at the broader responsibilities of sales management, avoiding the specific areas discussed in other chapters.

2. Who should be sales manager?

In most companies, there will be a selection procedure for the post of sales manager. Choosing somebody for this position can be a very important decision and, all too frequently, the most successful salesperson is selected. Examining the sales figures of the members of the sales force over a period of time generally reveals who sold the most. However, as there is no direct correlation between sales figures and management abilities, it is not a satisfactory basis for choosing. There are several reasons for this:

(a) the salesperson who sells the most is probably the best member of the sales force;

(b) removing that person from effective selling may harm sales results, especially if he or she has a close working relationship with the customers in the territory;

(c) the qualities that characterise the best salesperson are not necessarily those that make the best sales manager; and

(d) a sales manager needs experience of, or capability to learn, those techniques that make a good manager.

3. The principles of effective management

Before concentrating on the specialist activities of sales management, as a function of the business organisation, it is important to understand the basic principles of management and how they relate to sales management in particular.

It is all too easy to think in vague terms of 'management' as a general term covering certain work in the administration of business as the title seems to be so widely and arbitrarily applied. Management is a profession, like that of a doctor or an engineer, and members of all professions must accept certain rules and follow specific principles. 'Management' within a company may not be encompassed by any formal rules but it is based on fundamental principles common to all types of management.

Management's responsibility can be determined as combining four essential elements. These are:

(a) planning;
(b) coordinating;
(c) controlling; and
(d) motivating.

These four elements of management are interrelated and each exerts an influence on a particular situation. When that situation alters, the manner in which the elements are used will also change. Management's skill is in the recognition of the situation and in responding with the correct action to rectify any difficulties.

Elements of management

4. Planning

Planning is an essential element of management and will be carried out in all management's differing functions. It is an answer to the question, 'what must be done', and will also determine 'who will do it'. The basic requirements of all plans are that:'

(a) they must be based on fact or on rational assumptions;
(b) they must be realistic;
(c) they must be comprehensive;
(d) they must incorporate sufficient flexibility to allow for reasonable variation; and
(e) they must be known to all involved in carrying out the task.

5. Coordination

Coordination is the essence of management. It is an accessory to planning and is largely what a manager makes of it. It derives from the manager's personal sense of cooperation and requires tact, understanding and guidance. Coordination helps the staff to see the total picture of the task rather than just their own part in it and to combine and integrate their activities accordingly, turning a group of individuals into a team.

The following points should be noted about it:

(a) it will encourage direct personal contact within the organisation, particularly in lateral relationships;

(b) the cooperation concept must be fundamental to the business operations and will be basic to, and arise from, the planning element;

(c) it will encourage the free flow of information that is relative to the objectives of the business;

(d) it will see that no personal problems arising from the business operation are ignored but will endeavour to help, through a free exchange of ideas.

6.   Controlling the sales force

The need for control arises from the activity of planning and checks that set targets, budgets or schedules are attained. It will also instigate procedures to bring to light a failure to attain targets. Sales management's role in controlling is especially onerous as many of the targets are the results of forecasts. Salespeople's targets are predictions based on estimates of their forthcoming sales. Not only does the control system have to determine whether targets were achieved but also whether the system of prediction is accurate enough. It must:

(a)   prepare sales and market forecasts;

(b)   determine the level of the sales budget;

(c)   determine the sales quotas for each salesperson;

(d)   continue the review and selection of distribution channels;

(e)   organise an efficient sales office;

(f)   establish a system of sales reporting;

(g)   establish a system of statistical sales control;

(h)   establish a stock control system;

(i)   establish a delivery control system;

(j)   continue the review of performance of the sales force; and

(k)   establish periodical training programmes.

Example ————————————————————————————

A company was set up to sell a range of bath lifts for the disabled, selling to social security and health departments, hospitals and specialist disabled aids shops. Using market research, the Sales Manager calculated the size of the market, both for new lifts and for replacement lifts, and from this decided on the size of the sales force necessary to cover the country. Each salesperson was allocated a territory reflecting both the market potential, the geographical size of the market and the density and distribution of outlets, for example London needed four people but the whole of Wales only one. Each territory was also calculated on the basis of generating sufficient revenue to cover the salesperson's costs. Each salesperson was then set a target for a specific period and the weekly sales results were used as a basis for a control scheme to monitor whether the system was working satisfactorily.

7. Motivation

Motivation is an important role of leadership and is, essentially, a human relations concept concerned with understanding human behaviour and providing the right environment and conditions to stimulate employees to become self-motivated. This requires a degree of understanding of psychology and its application to the working situation. The responsibility of sales managers for motivation may be summarised thus;

(a) if the members of a sales team are not motivated to achieve the goals of the company, then the goals will not be reached;

(b) motivation is accomplished only by the fulfilment of the needs of those whom it is intended to motivate.

8. The role of sales management

Management should conform to established practices, applying its expertise in ways relevant to the specific field in which it works. It exists both to fulfil the needs of the enterprise and to identify and stimulate those needs. A study of management in its many aspects reduces its work to three fundamental tasks:

(a) the economic use of scarce resources;

(b) making decisions requiring judgement;

(c) ensuring that the work gets done.

9. The economic use of scarce resources

Management's task is to ensure that resources are used at optimum efficiency so that the return on their use is at least equal to that which could have been realised in any other way. In all economic decisions, managers must consider the *opportunity cost*, that is the loss of whatever else the money would have provided. For example, the opportunity cost of mounting an exhibition costing £10 000 is, perhaps, a new machine tool also costing £10 000 and the benefits derived from it.

The selling function of a company should be the first to discern changes in the environment in which it operates. No commercial firm should be so committed to a single purpose that it cannot change it when all the evidence suggests that it should. The manufacturers of motor cycle sidecars no doubt kept a keen watch on *each other's* developments, but failed to watch the rise of the small motor car.

Sales managers with limited budgets, faced with many alternatives must consider the return from each possible alternative and make decisions between them. Many times they will be able to quantify the problem in terms of pounds and pence or units sold, but, at other times, a decision must be taken that is part intuitive, part derived from experience and part a personal value judgement.

10. Managers judgements

Management's responsibility is greatest in decision making. Managers may delegate work to subordinates, but they always retain the ultimate responsibility for the deputy's work — they cannot delegate their essential decision-making role.

Decisions cannot be made until clear objectives have been determined. These will have been derived from company policy, which sales managers will have translated into departmental, group or individual goals. The decision-making process may be summarised as:

(a) specifying the objective;
(b) analysing the objective;
(c) selecting the information;
(d) collecting the information;
(e) evaluating alternative solutions; and
(f) deciding on the solution.

The final decision may not be precise or exact, allowing no doubt, but it will be, on the available evidence and in the sales manager's experience, the best and most viable option in the circumstances.

11. Ensuring the work gets done

Responsibility for ensuring that the work gets done is an involvement with the total problem of motivating workers. Sales managers need to see that the personnel reporting to them accomplish their goals efficiently. Further than this, however, sales managers must aim to ensure that the personnel under their control do more than the compulsory minimum allowable. This is especially important in such unsupervised jobs as selling. The task should not be seen negatively, as a disciplinary measure, but, rather, positively, as a responsibility to encourage people to develop their own capabilities.

Every employee costs money. A salesperson will cost £x per year to employ and there will be a minimum acceptable return on that cost (at least £x to break even). If a salesperson's salary is £8000 plus a car and expenses, a total cost of £15 000 a year, the minimum value of sales generated that will justify the appointment to the company may be £40 000 a year. That figure does not, however, represent the sales potential of the territory, but only the recovery of the cost of employing the salesperson. That target is the minimum that can be expected and, although the company may not be unhappy with that return on their investment (in salary and expenses), they will be much happier when the salesperson's sales increase over that figure.

Sales managers will be responsible for so motivating the sales force that each individual will sell more than their lower limit. The degree of motivation required by salespeople can be measured in terms of the difference between present attitudes and those needed to perform more effectively and reach the full potential of the territory.

12. Getting rid of an outworn attitude to control

There has, traditionally, been a 'carrot and stick' approach to the sales force; you either paid them poorly and offered monetary inducements to achieve better efforts or you threatened them. These methods are inefficient and, if they prove necessary, probably reflect a poor standard of recruitment and training by the management.

An understanding of the need to motivate people by instilling the right attitude to their work obviates any need for the 'stick' attitude of many employers. Sales managers who periodically confront their sales force and admonish them with threats of dismissal as a means of improving performance probably need motivating more than they do.

13. Motivating the sales force

Motivation is not something that is done *to us*, it is something we do for ourselves. This means that, despite the common use of the term, management cannot actually motivate people to greater effort, but it can create circumstances in which workers *become* motivated. If you train a sales force, provide them with the proper equipment and recognise their value to the company, the attitude of the individual members of the sales team will be more positive and more favourable towards their job.

Professor Frederick Hertzberg summed up his view of motivation when he suggested that, 'Money doesn't make people happy, it stops them being unhappy; what they do is what makes people happy.'

14. Hierarchy of needs

People differ in their physical and mental make-up and their personal ambitions and expectations — management must never lose sight of this. It is almost impossible to devise a system that will work for everyone, but, by understanding something of the general characteristics of workers, it makes it possible to determine the way in which motivation might apply.

The hierarchy of needs lists the needs of people in an ascending scale of importance. As one need is fulfilled, so the next becomes more important to the person:

5 self-fulfilment needs
4 egoistical needs
3 status needs
2 security needs
1 physiological needs

A person who has been unemployed for a long time will begin at the lower end of the scale. Unfortunately there are individuals who suffer from physiological deprivation — lack of shelter, warmth etc. — although the objective of the welfare state is to eliminate the worst deprivations.

Assuming that a person obtains a job after being unemployed for a while, he or she may be satisfied with low pay. However, as this person begins to earn and feel greater security (fulfilment of needs 1 and 2), he or she may well begin to want more money — as tangible evidence of status — and so on up the scale. People are generally ambitious and, in modern society, where possessions (cars, houses, holidays etc.) are frequently evidence of status, salespeople, like others, will feel the need for increased status. People appealing to their managers for pay rises have been known to go away quite happily with a title — it has satisfied a need for status that more money alone would not necessarily have done. Often people don't recognise their real needs and, in answering demand for money, management may be satisfying *symptoms* rather than *causes* of unhappiness. Careful sales management and progressive training can channel these natural needs into personal development and advancement within the company. Egoistical needs are those related to people's feelings about themselves and will manifest themselves at work in the way they believe their companies regard them. Finally, when their other needs have been satisfied, people will seek self-fulfilment, often outside the workplace entirely, in, say, gardening, painting, writing or making furniture.

15. Need for recognition

The nature of the hierarchy is such that sales managers should be capable of recognising the reasons for discontent in their staff. People who feel they are not appreciated may have general feelings of discontent that manifest themselves in gossiping, rumour-spreading or a vague 'chip on the shoulder' attitude. Sales managers may interpret this behaviour as the result of dissatisfaction and genuinely seek to alleviate it. Increases in salary, a company car and other fringe benefits may be tried, and work for a while, but, each time, the general feelings of discontent will re-surface. In these circumstances it may be that communications between management and the sales force (or other employees) are inadequate, that people do not understand the company's objectives or their own roles, which is bad for morale generally.

16. Understanding the need for motivation

It is important to the success of the sales force that sales managers should recognise that the old 'carrot and stick' methods are no longer appropriate. Even if we consider the older concepts of the nature of work in the context of their historical and social environment, they may have been incorrect. The following points are worth bearing in mind:

(a) *work is an indispensable part of people's lives* and is the part that endows status and provides links with the community;

(b) *generally people like their work* and those instances when they do not are frequently attributable to the conditions of the job in terms of the prevailing psychological and social attitudes in the firm;

(c) *the workers' morale does not, of necessity, have a positive relationship with the physical conditions of the job* and so, although poor physical conditions may have an adverse effect on health and well-being, if workers are sufficiently motivated, their morale will not be affected;

(d) *money is not necessarily the most important incentive in motivating workers*: research has shown that job satisfaction and job security are regarded as more important than remuneration and unemployment is regarded as a strong negative incentive as it removes workers from their particular social world.

If sales management is to fulfill its essential responsibility of seeing that work gets done and, more importantly, that salespeople do their best over and above the minimum requirements, it must understand the problems of motivation and the needs of people to realise personal goals.

17. Management and objectives

If salespeople are ignorant of the objectives of the company, they cannot be expected to exert themselves to attain them. It has been repeatedly shown in industry generally that employees make more effort when they know and understand the objectives of the firm and their role in their achievement.

The corporate strategy of the company will provide the overall objectives of the company that, in turn, decide individuals' goals. A company seeking a 10 per cent increase in sales will be more likely to achieve its objective if it tells its sales force *what* it wants and *why*. Generally, employees like to play an important role in the business and feel that their efforts are worthwhile, effective and valued. It is for management to state the objectives, make sure that the sales force is aware of them and ensure that the employees' working conditions will encourage their accomplishment.

Application of the elements of sales management

18. Leadership

The whole concept of leadership is complicated and subject to wide differences of opinion among industrial psychologists. The important point about leadership here, however, is its practical application in sales management.

It does not necessarily follow that when we talk of the 'leader' of a group we are referring to the formally appointed 'head' of the group. A sales manager is undisputed head of the sales force and, because of this formal position will be accepted as the person in charge who must be obeyed; failure to obey could mean dismissal. The manager's ability to 'lead' the group will, however, depend on qualities that are independent of this formal appointment, more related to personal qualities of leadership and authoritativeness than to mere title. This is often seen in informal groups where one person assumes leadership and is looked to for direction by the rest of the group.

19. Types of leader

It is recognised that three basic types of leader exist:

(a) *autocratic leaders*:
    (i) strict autocrats;
   (ii) benevolent autocrats; and
  (iii) incompetent autocrats;

(b) *democratic leaders*:
  (i) genuine democrats; and
  (ii) pseudo-democrats;
(c) laissez-faire *leaders*.

Autocratic leaders give orders they expect to be instantly obeyed. Their attitude is that orders should go down the structure and reports come back to them. Policies are determined without consulting the group and such managers give no information about future plans. These managers remain outside the group and give praise or criticism based on their own judgement only. The distinctions between types of autocrats are only in the way they pursue their beliefs: benevolent autocrats will have a conviction that they know better than anyone else in the group and have a duty to 'lead'; incompetent autocrats frequently occupy the position by virtue of influence rather than ability and their autocracy derives from sheer incompetence and lack of knowledge.

Democratic leaders are those who will consult their group, solicit their views and opinions and will, where possible, act accordingly. It is important that democrats retain their responsibility for decision making and do not relinquish it to 'the vote'. Pseudo-democrats, on the other hand, will often make a pretence of sounding out opinions but will have already determined what will be done anyway.

Laissez-faire leaders simply let the group carry on without attempting to coordinate or control it. They are frequently found on the golf course, with clients who happen to be friends or some other such pleasant environment.

20. Importance of leadership in selling

Salespeople are frequently lonely people, in the sense that they work away from the company and home. It is important for them to feel trusted and not to feel neglected. Salespeople are often 'characters' and have their own ways of working. Good leaders blend these distinctive personalities into efficient teams. While the company must ensure that they comply with its policies and provide evidence of their efforts in terms of required levels of business, meeting their goals and supplying a steady flow of information, too much rigid control will frustrate and reduce their efficiency. Leadership, by inspiring confidence in the company, the sales manager, the management team, the sales force and the individual salespeople, will ensure that the whole team is well coordinated and the team well motivated.

Sales managers should have imagination in determining objectives and frequently can inspire teams to greater effort by projecting a vision of achievement expressed in their leadership and enthusiasm.

Sales management's tasks

21. Sales meetings

It is usual for companies to organise regular sales meetings, which will vary in their nature from a yearly, or twice-yearly, sales conference to periodical sales meetings.

22. Sales conferences

Sales conferences, often the big events of the sales year, are occasions of intensive activity. Their main objective is to bring together the two essential parts of the selling function — the sales manager, area managers, group leaders and salespeople and the administrative executives and staff. A sales conference will allow salespeople to meet and talk over problems with staff and executives who they might otherwise only contact by telephone or letter. It will also provide an occasion for new products to be introduced and explained by all concerned — designers, production manager etc. Existing products may also be discussed and complaints about any feature or delivery hold-ups dealt with.

It is usual on these occasions to invite staff that are ancillary to selling, such as the despatch manager, the office manager, the buyers, the production manager and the designers, so that there can be complete interchange of ideas during the informal gatherings between the formal events. The managing director and the chairperson usually also take part at some point.

Sales conferences are usually held during a period of low sales activity or just before the main selling period. In the latter case, the conference becomes a forum when new products can be introduced or new sales strategies explained. The conference might be held in conjunction with a major trade event, such as an annual fair or exhibition. As a general rule, a conference lasts two or three days, but the duration will depend on several factors:

(a) how much time can spared from selling;
(b) how much formal work has to be done.
(c) how much it will cost to bring together sales teams and management from around the country and, in some cases, from around the world.

Conferences usually extend from nine in the morning until seven in the evening, sometimes with the addition of a special event such as a staff dinner. Whatever the format, they can be quite strenuous exercises and sales managers, who bear a major responsibility for their success, will need to pace themselves with care.

23. Periodic sales meeting

These might be held on a monthly, three-monthly or even six-monthly basis, depending on the needs they have to fulfil. If conducted correctly, they can have a beneficial effect because of the motivation they generate. It is a well-known phenomenon that sales tend to rise sharply after such meetings because the salespeople have been energised by meeting their peers and the opportunity to exchange views.

If such meetings are to be held, however, they must have a purpose and it may be useful to ask individuals to read a short paper on some relevant aspect of their work. It should be clear, however, that the sales staff understand the purpose of the paper and how to present it to avoid disaster, e.g. like the man who, when asked to talk about finding customers, read from sections of the *Yellow Pages*, or the area manager who bored his sales team to sleep by taking three hours to read a very technical, and mostly incomprehensible, report on shot-blasting.

Regular sales meetings are an excellent and worthwhile idea provided they do not take salespeople away from selling without any real purpose. They are occasions when salespeople can discuss common problems, offer advice, especially to less experienced people and exchange ideas. Used in this way they are a real motivation to salespeople and all will benefit.

24. Improved sales techniques

Sales managers have a responsibility to see that their sales force use the best possible selling techniques and that their equipment is in excellent condition. The essence of good selling is to develop a technique that will convey to buyers an immediate message of what the product is about.

If possible, techniques should be capable of demonstration within buyers' offices or at a suitable site close by, depending on the product being sold. Sales managers can profitably spend time experimenting with new ways of presenting and explaining company products and their benefits, passing any new ideas on more convincing display methods to the sales force.

25. The sales office

Sales managers are responsible for the running of the sales office, generally delegating the day-to-day control to their sales office manager. While the routine work can be delegated, sales managers must ensure that the work of the department is related to the needs of the sales force and the customer and does not become an end in itself.

The sales office will receive incoming orders, check them for accuracy of price, detail and delivery instructions, record them on the appropriate system (computer, record card or whatever), translate them onto standard forms and pass them to the production department or to the stores for dispatch from stock. The methods employed will vary according to the systems different companies operate, but, generally, notice of items not available from stock will be passed on to the customer and arrangements made to buy in, or make, depending on the nature of the firm.

Progress test 15

1. What considerations should be taken into account when selecting a person for the position of sales manager? (**2**)

2. What are the four essential elements of management? (**3**)

3. What are the two ways in which the responsibility of sales managers for motivation may be summarised? (**7**)

4. What are the three basic types of leader? (**19**)

16

Training

Sales training

1. Types of training

How much training a sales force will need depends a great deal on the type of selling they are called upon to do. However, the training will be based on two areas, which are:

(a) selling techniques; and
(b) technical knowledge.

Skilled salespeople are those who are accomplished in both these areas.

2. Product knowledge

Product knowledge is of the greatest importance, no matter where the selling process occurs — in a shop or store, a buyer's office or in an industrial plant. The only differences in knowledge will be in the degree, depth and length of time taken to acquire it. Any training programme therefore must begin with an understanding of two essential points:

(a) How much will the customers need to know about the products?
(b) How do we ensure that our sales personnel have sufficient knowledge to inform them:
 (i) about the product; and
 (ii) about the company's policies of selling, administration and distribution?

Before sales personnel can be entrusted with direct responsibility for their territory or department, it is necessary to make sure that they fully understand the company's corporate policy, the sales function's operating policy and the company's administrative policy.

3. The basis of training

The quality of training given varies enormously from company to company. At one end of the scale are firms that recognise that sales training must encompass every aspect of the job — product knowledge, understanding of the buyers' motivations, awareness of competitive products, an ability to use and to demonstrate the products, the ability to handle complaints and faults etc. and, at the other extreme, are firms that still believe sales training can be accomplished within the salesperson's first morning with the firm.

The point is that, although proper sales training is expensive, it costs a lot less in the long run than losing business due to inadequately trained sales staff, whose ignorance may even be dangerous. 'Inadequate training can cause havoc' is not an over-statement, as shown by the example below.

Example

A company manufacturing specialist floor coatings often encountered extremely hard concrete floors, known as granolithic. To ensure their coats adhered to the floor, they would instruct their contractors to use a weak dilution of hydrochloric acid to 'key' the floor. A new salesman 'hit the big time' when he was asked to treat the brand new floor of a huge warehouse, the walls of which were almost entirely of glass. He remembered the floor should be 'keyed' but unfortunately recommended *hydrofluoric* acid instead of weak hydrochloric acid and the result was that all the glass was attacked by the fumes and became, literally, 'frosted'.

As products, processes and customers become more sophisticated, so too, must the sales force. It is no good producing hi-tech products if the sales force is inadequately trained to explain their technical advances and, therefore, to sell them. Equally, the sales force must be capable of understanding the customers' needs and of acting in an advisory role, often working closely with customers. Of course, not all selling is highly technical, but it is increasingly competitive, especially now that the British market is a part of the much larger and infinitely more aggressive European market.

Psychological bases of training

4.   Understanding the recruit

In the training of sales personnel it is necessary to emphasise *why* a job should be learned and to see the job from the recruit's viewpoint as far as possible. Few people learn well if they can see no cause to do so.

To help recruits and so make the training relevant to them, it is possible to hypothesise about their reasons for becoming salespeople. They may:

(a) regard the job merely as a means of making money;

(b) like a job where the standards to which they should work are familiar;
(c) see the job as a stepping stone to further development; or
(d) have no other options for making a living.

It is easy to oversimplify their reasons, however; they are likely to be a lot more complicated than those just suggested. For example:

(a) salespeople are unlikely to devote *all* their time to considerations of expected income as the only reason for their working;
(b) the standards of performance expected by the company may not be known to salespeople as many of them are allowed to develop their own level of performance;
(c) they may contemplate many other forms of employment; indeed it is likely that they will have already done other kinds of work before taking up selling, and
(d) there are now many younger people who have been trained on business studies courses and come to selling as a first step into the wider field of marketing and business; they may have a sound background of marketing training without having a clear understanding of what 'selling' entails, the correct temperament or good specialised training; they increasingly have a qualification in some specialism, such as electronics.

When recruits' reasons for becoming salespeople have been determined, it is then possible to ensure that the training is presented from their viewpoint to maximum effect.

In training salespeople we are concerned with learning and, in particular, how to develop motivation of the sales force, both during and, more importantly, after their training period. In the case of people who have already received what they consider to be a sound marketing education, post-training motivation may be even more important if they are to succeed in the long term as few educational establishments have a real appreciation of the *practical* selling task.

5. Motivation in training

New salespeople can be expected to start the job with enthusiasm. They will probably have been through the recruitment process, the interview and selection, and will be pleased to have been chosen from many. Enthusiasm may also spring from a number of expectations that they have of the job, such as:

(a) new job status;
(b) new products to learn about;
(c) new company car; and
(d) a new working environment.

People new to selling, perhaps from an educational, commercial or industrial background, will expect to find a new degree of freedom in their work, as they will be largely working on their own and without constant supervision. All these factors combine to induce the individual to create a new personal image, perhaps as a 'top salesperson', eventually sales manager or even a tycoon of industry, negotiating huge and important contracts. These images, the different roles in which the recruits see themselves, are all self-motivators, helped by an expectation of prestige, security of employment, enhanced status and income.

During the first weeks, they will be motivated by these various and shadowy goals — prestige, security, income and status all buoyed up by expectation. It is only later, when, as a small part of a much bigger organisation, that the new salespeople, obliged to conform and perhaps finding difficulty in producing business, feel their motivation begin to decline.

How long will new salespeople work enthusiastically and conscientiously towards goals that have become remote and indistinct? Before long they will find customers increasingly difficult and the work a task rather than a challenge. They will begin to avoid work, take days off or otherwise seek to escape supervision.

To keep salespeople enthusiastic over long periods, especially when they may be breaking into a new territory, ways have to be found of reinforcing their own original motivation.

6. How to augment motivation

With the realisation that the enthusiasm of new salespeople will begin to weaken once the initial expectations are not realised, it becomes vital to augment that motivation and sustain their effort. This will depend on:

(a) the type of selling, status of the salespeople and their degree of remoteness from the firm;
(b) salespeople's own concepts of the job and individual goals being replaced by a precise valuation of the knowledge and skills they need to acquire; and by
(c) the provision of precise, attainable goals to replace their own shadowy expectations of becoming 'top salesperson'.

Precise, realistic goals are important for they are within salespeople's abilities and will be reached fairly easily and quickly instead of being too remote. They will also be personal and related exactly to their job and role within the organisation.

Therefore, one purpose of training is to augment motivation by a process of replacing remote ideas with precise goals and supplying precise performance standards instead of indeterminate levels of achievement.

7.   Skill

All training programmes must be based on an appreciation of two distinct kinds of learning process. These are:

(a) *gradual development of skill* in a simple operation, which is characterised by a slow but steady improvement in performance; and
(b) *rapid intellectual understanding* of a problem, which allows swift advance in performance after a few attempts.

Any training programme will include situations in which both these forms of learning will be apparent so that salespeople's performances will be characterised by periods of rapid improvement as well as other periods when performance improvement happens more slowly.

The development of salespeople's skills, either in total or in part, for example in demonstrations, will result from practising the same actions many times. This practice integrates the habit patterns formed for each part of the selling process. With different customers, different parts of the selling process will be accentuated and the whole will become clearer. Eventually, after repeating a particular pattern of selling with many customers, salespeople will become adept in all areas. The presentations will become smoother when all the parts are integrated into the selling process and, as the understanding between the salespeople and their customers increases, they will feel more confident.

8.   Providing an opportunity for practice

A successful training programme must allow for adequate practice. This can be accomplished by sending new salespeople out with skilful members of the sales force experienced in training. Sometimes it can be accomplished by providing facilities for salespeople to practise in a controlled situation.

There are now a number of ways in which new salespeople may be trained in a controlled situation. This may be done by getting them to practice with tape and/or video recorders. The trainees may be given a sales task (to sell a particular product) and will then be allowed time to think out the correct presentation, rehearse it and refine it until they are ready to present it to their fellow trainees. The presentation may be recorded by either audio or video equipment and re-run so that each trainee's presentation may be examined in turn. This can be a traumatic, but nevertheless, useful experience, if the trainees are robust enough to survive it!

9.   On-the-job training

Providing salespeople with chances to learn is difficult in selling as there is always the danger of upsetting established customers. Many customers will be sympathetic to new salespeople and not put too much pressure on them, but not all will and even the best customers, when busy, cannot be expected to provide training facilities for other companies. A means has to be devised of overcoming this difficulty for, without practice, skills cannot be acquired. Often salespeople can spend the first few weeks going to see firms that are unlikely to become customers. This has several points to commend it. First, if the firm is unlikely to become a customer, for whatever reason, it is not so important to avoid upsetting them. Second, they will probably throw more adverse comments and objections against the products than established customers and this is good practise, developing the mental agility to make a quick response. On the debit side, though, it can be depressing for new salespeople to have so many refusals and can even lead to disillusionment with the job and lack of confidence in the products.

10. Training salespeople

The objective of sensible training will be to:

(a) achieve greater efficiency of performance;
(b) promote conformity to company regulations and reduce errors that might lead to customer complaints;
(c) create better job performance, increased earnings and more job satisfaction;
(d) develop a more stable sales force with less turnover in manpower; and
(e) reduce the amount of supervision required.

11. Training and company attitude towards sales

The quality of training will depend on the extent to which the company is anxious to protect its position in the trade.

Some firms provide little or no training and expect a high turnover from the sales force. In turn, they offer high remuneration to those who can achieve it. If a company has a low regard for training and cannot see any profitable result from it, little training will be given.

Companies with a reputation to defend will usually have a high regard for training and this will often be reflected in the care given to their selection of personnel. This attitude towards training will often be a reflection of how the organisation regards sales in general. Some firms do not see sales as an important aspect of the company when compared to production and, therefore, see no purpose in extensive and professional sales training. On the other hand, companies that recognise the importance of marketing generally and the key role in customer creation played by the sales function, will invest in sensible and adequate training programmes.

Organised training

12. Centralised and decentralised training

Centralised training is carried out solely by the department responsible for training. It does not always follow that personnel are sent to a single centre for training, although this often happens, but, often, that a central department devises the training programme. Some companies engaged in industrial selling will recruit salespeople at various times through the year and provide on-the-job training to begin with. Later all the new salespeople will be sent to head office or some other centre for formal training.

Decentralised training is often favoured over centralised training. It relies on new salespeople learning their jobs by performing them under operational conditions and the care of some responsible person with a knowledge of local conditions. The system has much to commend it, so long as the essential training in the products' performance, methods of manufacture and matters relating to company policy can also be given on a decentralised basis. Where it can be linked to some organised training programme ensuring standard training practices as well, it is probably the most suitable form for most technical salespeople.

13. Training programmes

Most companies have formal training programmes and, although they vary in intensity, generally they consist of:

(a) *initial* training; and
(b) *continuous* training.

Often the sales trainees will receive a simple initial training session amounting to little more than an introduction to the firm, for example:

(a) a visit to head office;
(b) an interview/discussion with the sales manager;
(c) a tour of the production facilities;
(d) a brief introduction to the manufacturing process;
(e) a brief demonstration of the products/how to use them; and
(f) a meeting with the head office staff with whom they will liaise.

Trainees then return to their territory and receive on-the-job training with an area manager or another salesperson. Later, when the trainees have learnt some of the problems and the basic needs of the job, intensive training in all facets of the job will be given at a training centre, probably with other trainees. This will last for a week or two, depending on the complexities of the products and the job, continuous training on a periodic basis beginning after they return to their territory.

14. Preparing a training programme

Although the methods of presentation and the need for product knowledge are common to all selling, nevertheless, distinct kinds of selling do need different training approaches. The basic distinction is between:

(a) selling products or services to the *final consumer*; and
(b) selling products or services to the *user*, that is, an organisation that will use the products as a part of its own production processes.

The distinction is that of satisfying *personal* demand and satisfying (or creating) a *derived* demand. In very general terms, these two classes can be reduced to:

(a) selling consumer products; and
(b) selling industrial or technical products.

However, the distinction is not really that simple to express. For example, an ice-cream salesperson is undoubtedly satisfying consumer demand, but so too is a sales representative selling biscuits to a supermarket. In Chapter 3, the different forms that distribution takes were explained and it is these distinctions — why people buy — that we are concerned with here.

15. Training to sell consumer products

Selling consumer products is generally related to advertising or other forms of promotion, where demand has been created through the media and the selling task is one of persuading customers that your products can satisfy this created demand. A typical programme for a company selling consumer products would be as follows:

(a) *Initial induction training.* Trainers must first identify the duties of the salespeople, that is, will they be selling to organisational buyers or to the final consumer, for example selling double glazing direct to householders? Trainers must be aware of the necessary knowledge and skills to be acquired and the level of knowledge the salespeople will need to be able to begin working until the next training seminar. They will learn about:

(i) the company's organisation structure, sales and product policies;

(ii) the products themselves;

(iii) documentation;

(iv) use and care of samples;

(v) selling techniques, especially types of customer, methods of contact, presentations, closing a sale and company policy on payments and credit.

(b) *Continuous training.* Following the initial training, the salespeople would receive regular additional training as part of an ongoing programme throughout their career with the company. This would include:

(i) operational training;

(ii) motivating sessions;

(iii) training seminars.

The objective of all the training would be the continual upgrading of the salespeople's knowledge and the creation of a strongly motivated sales force.

16. Training to sell 'user' products

These are the industrial, commercial, medical and other such products. This kind of selling requires a comprehensive knowledge of the particular market, as well as a sound knowledge of the company's own products. It will also be necessary to know about competitors' products and those products that might be used as substitutes. The training programme, therefore, will be comprehensive, including:

(a) the company's policies;
(b) the use and applications of the products;
(c) the manufacturing methods;
(d) administrative procedures;
(e) an outline of the industry in which the company operates; and
(f) competitive and substitute products.

17. Training seminars

A typical training seminar might be along these lines:

(a) Day 1:

(i) welcome to the seminar;

(ii) introduction to senior executives and functional heads;

(iii) tour of works and production facilities;

(iv) discussion on the aims of the company, its policies and plans;

(v) introduction to the product range;

(vi) syndicate discussions on the products.

(b) Day 2:

(i) lecture on the problems of the industry and its environment;

(ii) detailed lecture on the construction or composition of the products;

(iii) trainees practising using the products — a 'hands-on' exercise;

(iv) group exercises about the products, followed by discussion.

(c) Day 3:

(i) introduction to selling techniques;

(ii) lectures by sales manager and senior salespeople on their particular techniques;

(iii) trainees practise selling techniques with audio or video equipment, followed by discussions and critique;

(iv) test questions set for trainees on product knowledge, use and selling techniques.

(d) Day 4:

(i) introduction to main competitive products, their use and their prices;

(ii) methods of combating competition;

(iii) remuneration structures, perhaps including commissions and bonuses;

(iv) distribution, ordering and accounting procedures;

(v) issue of stationery, sales manuals, literature and samples;

(vi) review and winding up by sales manager.

Progress test 16

1. On which two areas should sales training be based? **(1)**

2. What expectations may new salespeople have of the job? **(5)**

3. What are the five objectives of sales training? **(10)**

4. What distinctions are there between sales training for selling consumer products and selling user products? **(14)**

17

Organising the sales function

Fundamentals of organisation

1. Introduction

Effective organisation is fundamental to good management. In any business there must exist some form of organisation structure to carry out the company's policies. In sales organisations, like any other, the structure will vary according to the size of the firm, type of product or service and according to the wishes of the owners or directors.

In many firms the organisation structure will have evolved over long periods of time and will have developed in response to the needs of the time and reorganisation is often necessary. A consultant or manager assigned the task of assessing the logic of a firm's existing organisational structure is usually concerned with reorganising the firm's current structure and not with creating a completely new structure. This situation often makes it difficult to draw up an ideal structure, though it should be stressed that organisation structures are frameworks on which to construct a sensible and efficient management organisation and not ends in themselves.

2. Organisation and the sales function

Firms exist to satisfy the needs of their customers and operate within the existing structure of a market or markets. There are a number of factors that form a containing structure dictating, to some extent, the possible shape of organisations, such as:

(a) the market(s);
(b) the products; and
(c) the needs of the organisation itself.

For example, a firm selling pharmaceuticals will have to operate within the practices, even the ethics, of that particular industry. There will be a basic range of pharmaceutical products that the company produces and its operations will have to conform to the way customers operate their purchasing methods. Similar conformities will exist in the sales of other products and all will, generally, be subject to the sorts of environmental factors explained in Chapter 1, including:

(a) technological;
(b) cultural;
(c) administrative;
(d) educational;
(e) legal; and, as in this example,
(f) medical.

3. Need for flexibility

The needs of efficient marketing and selling lay great stress on the need for flexibility in production and selling, although modern production methods often encourage greater rigidity through increasingly automated mass production techniques. This rigidity can easily be carried through to the organisation as well, especially in very large organisations where local needs may be overruled by the constraints of centralised control and by the demands for greater standardisation.

A major problem of sales organisations is that, while centralised control and automated production favours standardisation, customers are diverse and need specialist attention. This is especially true in export markets.

Creativity is necessary to obtain the flexibility in sales organisation that reflects the needs of both sides of this dichotomy.

4. The importance of organisation to the sales function

In striving to understand this point the aims must be threefold:

(a) to define what is meant by 'organisation';
(b) to examine the structures that different kinds of sales organisations have developed to meet their specific needs;
(c) to note the major prevailing trends in sales organisations.

In any selling organisation, the structure must be based on the specific needs and objectives that form the strategy of the firm. The structure must also have built-in flexibility to meet changes in the environment as they occur.

5. The nature of organisation

Definitions of organisation are numerous and vary in their scope. Essentially, however, organisation is:

A practice of dividing work into convenient tasks, of grouping such tasks into posts and delegating authority to each post, and appointing qualified and authoritative staff to be responsible so that the work is satisfactorily carried out in accordance with plans.

Organisation structures, then, define the responsibilities and the formal relationships throughout the enterprise. Furthermore, these responsibilities must be clearly and formally stated as a schedule of responsibility.

In drawing up such schedules for sales personnel, however, one should avoid turning a clear and decisive contract of responsibility into a straitjacket that limits individual flexibility of action. For example, one of the identified problems of British export salespeople for many years has been the limitation on decision making placed on them compared to that given to foreign competitors. It has often been remarked that while a German, French or Japanese salesperson can take on-the-spot decisions, the British salesperson all too often has to refer back to a higher authority. Clear and decisive schedules should be tempered by better training to permit flexibility in decision making as salespeople are often in positions where quick, but sound decisions are necessary. In this respect, one can refer to MacGregor: 'The personalities of the men (and women) who control enterprises have a profound effect upon the efficient operation of it.'

Inflexible attitudes of mind can have a disastrous effect if applied rigidly in today's global and highly competitive business environment.

6.   Planning organisation structure is vital

Between similar enterprises there may be some comparison in the pattern of delegation in certain appointments. There is not, however, a typical model for schedules of responsibility and each enterprise is inevitably unique. Appreciating the essentially unique nature of each enterprise is helpful in overcoming the desire for standardisation in organisation structures, a desire that is especially strong in the rigidly trained managerial mind. If managers recognise this individuality of firms, they can endeavour to solve their problems by bending the principles to fit their own firms.

Organisation problems may be overcome by compromise solutions but any such modifications forced on management to satisfy the existing personnel should be regarded as transient. There is no excuse for neglecting to plan a structure.

One of the biggest problems small firms have is coping with growth. The small successful firm can easily become the middle-sized firm with cash-flow problems if it has grown simply by demand and not design. It is too late when the firm is in difficulties to begin sorting out who is responsible for the mess. Planned growth must include planned organisation.

Each organisation structure has to be adapted to the individual needs of unique companies and must be developed to meet the needs of the enterprise it serves. Many years ago P. F. Drucker wrote, 'Good organisation structure does not by itself produce good performance … but a poor organisation structure makes good performance impossible, no matter how good the individual managers may be'. This is still very true today, but, in the euphoria of a successful new enterprise, organisation structure often gets neglected until it is too late. Bad, or simply non-existent, organisation structure can be a time-bomb, ticking away under any growing company.

7. Common functions

There are certain functions that are common to all business enterprises, irrespective of their size or purpose. All business enterprises will have some form of policy-making body and an executive that will be responsible for translating that policy into operational form and seeing that it is carried out.

The policy-making and policy-translating functions are innate. In a single proprietor business the owner will be responsible for both functions, while in a large public company it is generally for the board of directors to formulate company policy and a managing director to translate it and ensure its implementation.

So in all companies we have:

(a) the policy-making function (e.g. board of directors or owner);
(b) the policy-translating function (e.g. managing director).

In addition there are other functions that are fundamental to all business, although they may be called different names. They are:

(a) sales (or marketing);
(b) finance; and
(c) production (in some form).

As a company grows it may add another basic function — personnel. Other functions may be incorporated into some firms but are not fundamental to all enterprises. In small companies, one person may be responsible for some or even all the functions while, in larger companies, separate people will be responsible for individual functions.

8. Organisational development

As a small business grows into a more complex organisation, the workload related to each of the basic functions increases to the point where a single person can no longer carry out the work efficiently. At this point, functions will be physically separated. The responsibility for one or more functions will be allocated to a specific person who will become a specialist in that function and be responsible to a superior for its efficient undertaking. These are the beginnings of delegation of responsibility.

Assuming the business continues to grow, the organisation will develop along recognisable lines:

(a) functions will be physically separated requiring people with specialist functional responsibility, such as product development being separated from sales management;

(b) additional functions will be established, creating a need for more specialists with functional responsibility, for example a specialist sales promotion department is created and an experienced promotions manager is appointed;

(c) the tasks within the function will become greater and, eventually, it will be necessary to separate activities making up the function and to delegate responsibility for these newly separated activities to individuals; the delegation will be by the functional head to whom the people responsible for the activities will report direct — a developing sales force, for example, may specialise by distinguishing between different kinds of customer or by separating territories, so, say, a specialist salesman might be appointed with sole responsibility for sales to government departments.

Development is both vertical into levels of responsibility and lateral as more activities are added.

Example
A firm selling animal feeds to pet shops developed both vertically and laterally in order to allow for growth. The overall sales area was divided into two territories with a salesperson responsible for each. As sales and production developed further, a specialist salesperson with expert knowledge of horses was appointed to develop sales to horse yards and stables and another specialist appointed to develop sales of cattle and sheep feeds to farms. In due course, the first two salespeople were appointed area managers and the whole sales area expanded into four territories, producing vertical growth in the organisation. (Figure 17.1 explains this development).

9.   Delegation and responsibility

The provision for growth of an organisation structure is a planning activity and a basic management task. It should include:

(a) the delegation of responsibility and authority to cover the total activities of the enterprise; and

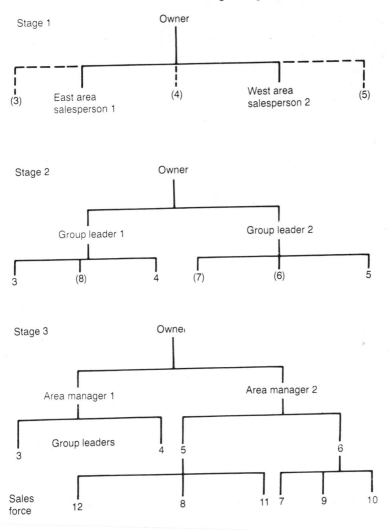

Figure 17.1 *The development of a sales force*

(b) the determination of formal relationships within the enterprise.

10. Types of organisation
Organisation structures must be created to fulfil the needs of the enterprise.

(a) *line organisation* — responsibility and authority are passed directly from superiors to subordinates and are reciprocal;

(b) *functional organisation* — each specialist activity has a direct line of responsibility and authority to the point of application;

(c) *line and staff organisation* — line and functional organisations are employed together, having lines of direct executive responsibility and specialist services.

Types (a) and (b) are illustrated in Figures 17.2 and 17.3.

11. Requirements of an organisation structure

As an organisation structure defines the responsibilities and formal relationships in an enterprise, it is important that they should be formally stated in the form of a schedule of responsibility. This should provide:

(a) *a chief executive* who will be responsible to the policy-making body for the manner in which the entire enterprise accomplishes its objectives;

(b) *an adequate and logical delegation of responsibility* allowing a decentralisation of decisions;

(c) *clear channels of communication and lines of responsibility* linking the chief executive to all the operations of the enterprise; and

(d) *rational spans of control.*

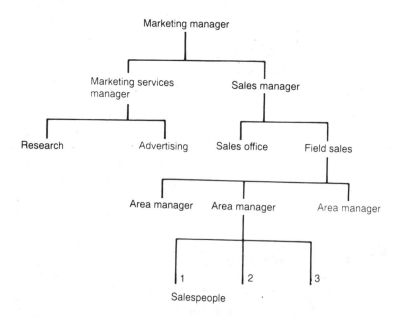

Figure 17.2 *Line organisation*

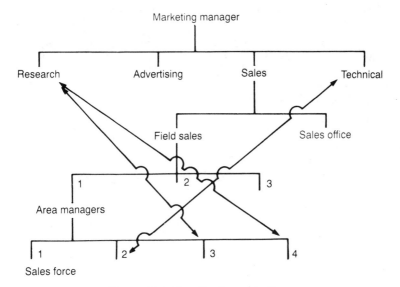

Figure 17.3 *Functional organisation*

12. Schedules of responsibility

The implications of defining schedules of responsibility for sales personnel need further elaboration. It is important to distinguish between formal organisation structures in which rigid 'ranks' are established, such as in the armed services, education and hospitals, and the less formal 'ranking' of most dynamic business enterprises.

Personnel in teaching, the military or nursing join an institutionalised structure in which promotion is won by fulfilling the needs of the organisation. Teachers' schedules of responsibility limit their horizons to a specific task. Innovation is not seen as a benefit because the system rarely permits it. Advancement is possible only by moving along predictable lines of promotion within the framework of that organisation or a similar institutional organisation.

Business people or salespeople within their chosen careers may move from one organisation to another and are able to advance by personality and ability and by the willingness to show initiative, to innovate and to shoulder additional responsibility. Nothing so encourages promotion as a person's willingness to take on extra work. The limitations to this 'empire-building' will be:

(a) the diminishing effectiveness of the individual; and
(b) the ability of colleagues to influence or resist this empire-building.

In the institutionalised organisation structure, the structure is designed to limit movement of individuals according to the precise needs of the organisation. For the dynamic business organisation, this rigidity may be the death-knell of profit. The dynamic organisation needs to allow for individual flair, which is a necessary stimulus for business. The institution, with its non-profit goals, has no need for the individual's flair and personal ambition may be 'harmful' to the organisational goals.

13. Organisation and goals

Organisation must be related to goals. If the purpose is profit, the structure must allow individuals to develop ideas and abilities that will favour the firm. If the purpose is some non-profit objective, the system may be mechanistic, in which case personal limits may lead to frustration if individual goals and ambitions cannot be realised. There are two organisation structure types:

(a) *profit-centred organisations*:

(i) the business organisation's survival is directly related to profitability;

(ii) the organisation must be adaptable to the changing needs of the environment and have no commitment to one purpose;

(iii) the people who make up the organisation are motivated by job satisfaction and financial reward for which they are prepared to accept a degree of insecurity;

(iv) they will be adaptable people and tend to enlarge their personal parameters of responsibility up to the point where they are limited by the ambitions of their colleagues;

(b) *Community-centred organisations*:

(i) typified by the institutional organisation, it is totally related to the needs of the community, has no need of adaptability, and is wholly committed to one purpose;

(ii) the people who form the organisation are more motivated by job security for which they are prepared to accept a lower degree of job satisfaction and financial reward;

(iii) the people tend to be less adaptable and work within narrow, well-determined parameters and schedules of responsibility.

We have become accustomed to job satisfaction and job evaluation in production units and the sales manager must apply the same concept to sales forces and design the organisation to permit it.

Characteristics of organisation structures

14. Organisation structures

As an organisation grows, it will become more complicated and managers of expanding sales organisations will be faced with both vertical and lateral growth. The characteristics of organisation structures are that:

(a) the work to be accomplished is divided; and
(b) it is arranged into manageable portions.

Sales managers faced with the task of arranging the work into manageable portions will, by a process of analysing, dividing and arranging, undertake a system of *departmentalisation*.

By creating such an organisation, the manager of each department will carry out his or her tasks in accord with a senior manager so that each department may be coordinated. The number of departments reporting to the senior manager is a structural characteristic, depending on the manner in which the work is organised. In the case, for example, of a sales manager, these will be the number of departments that must be coordinated and this is termed the *span of management* (*see* Figure 17.4 and 17.**22–28**)

15. Bases of departmentalisation

The creation of manageable departments is not an end in itself but a means of achieving objectives. As noted above (*see* 17:**1**), few organisational structures are created anew, but are usually the result of the reorganisation of existing structures. As all businesses are different, the selection of a basis for departmentalisation will be

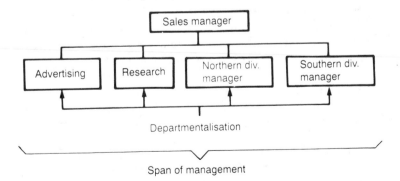

Figure 17.4 *Span of management*

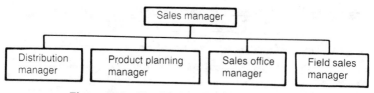

Figure 17.5 *Simplified marketing organisation plan*

dependent on particular needs and objectives. There are, however, a number of well-tried and accepted bases, including:

(a) function;
(b) product;
(c) customer;
(d) geographical;
(e) process;
(f) sequence.

16. Function

Function describes activities that can be related because of the similarity of the skills required in their performance, e.g. those activities associated with marketing - advertising, sales, market research, product planning, sales office, credit control, etc. A simple example is shown in Figure 17.5.

17. Product

Organisation by product is a familiar system when growth is accompanied by diversification of products. Initially all a firm's products will probably go to the same type of customer but, as the firm grows, different products may be produced for a wide range of customers. Some companies, such as the 3M Company, organise their sales force under product managers for different products. Selling to other organisations, it will frequently encounter buyers organised by product type, for example, as shown in Figure 17.6.

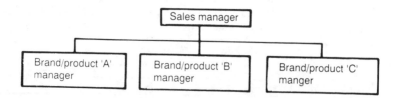

Figure 17.6 *Organisation by production*

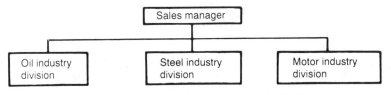

Figure 17.7 *Customer-orientated organisation*

18. Customer

Just as product diversification may be a basis for organisation, so growth of customers may produce a logical basis. Firms selling to both trade and retail, local authorities and heavy industry, the motor trade and the oil industry will all distinguish the fundamentally different needs of each customer and employ specialist salespeople to deal with them, as shown in Figure 17.7.

19. Geographical

Geographical organisation is logical where the area of sales coverage is too large for a single sales manager to be able to adequately administer it or where regional differences in the market dictate a more specialist organisation. Such an organisation is often found in companies with a high- density sales coverage, such as supermarkets, breweries and direct selling companies. Firms that export will usually break down their markets into logical groups on the basis of geographical location, while on a smaller scale any company selling nationally will divide the country into manageable regions. Figure 17.8 illustrates a geographical organisation of export marketing.

20. Process

The degree to which departmentalisation may be based on a manufacturing process may depend on its divisibility.

It is rarely practicable to arrange a sales organisation in this way, but many of its customers will be organised according to production processes. For example, a steel works will be organised into raw

Figure 17.8 *Geographical organisation*

materials, smelting, rolling, tinplating etc., while the oil industry is so complex as to be organised into many departments from exploration to retail outlets and publicity.

21. Sequence

Some departments may be organised on an alpha-numerical basis of sequence. With the spread of computerised filing systems a sequential system of departmentalisation is almost inevitable.

Span of management

22. What is a span of management?

Once the basis of departmentalisation has been settled, another problem arises - how many departments can one person manage?

The problem is known as the span of control, but the term span of management is a more accurate description. The span of management is related to the number of hierarchical levels in an organisation, and this, in turn, determines the length of the *lines of communication*.

It is a fundamental of organisation structures that if the span of management is increased, the lines of communication are shortened and vice versa.

23. How wide can a span of management be?

There are limits on the extent of the span of management, which prevents unlimited development. For example, it would be virtually impossible for one manager to have 50 subordinates reporting to him or her. There are four broadly accepted explanations as to why the span is limited:

(a) the limitations of the human brain (General Sir Ian Hamilton);
(b) the number of possible interactions (A. V. Graicunas);
(c) man's limited span of attention (Lyndall F. Urwick); and
(d) diminishing marginal effectiveness (P. Allen).

24. Hamilton's recommendations

… The average human brain finds its optimum work level when handling three to six other brains.' Hamilton's hypothesis was based on military experience and he suggested that the number of people under one supervisor should be greater at the lower levels of the organisation than the number supervised at the top. This was

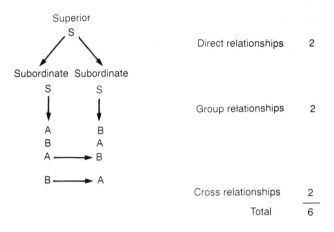

Figure 17.9 *Graicunas' relationships in an organisation*

proposed because, at the bottom, the decision making would be less challenging and more predictable than at the top.

25. Graicunas' theory

Graicunas perceived that, in establishing a satisfactory span of management, a number of possible interactions could occur between a manager and the subordinates (*see* Figure 17.9).

When a third subordinate, C, reports to S, one additional direct relationship is established between S and C; but seven additional group relationships are possible (AC, CA, BC, CB, ABC, CBA, BAC). Also, 4 more cross relationships bring the total possible interactions to 18 (A → C, B → C, C → A, C → B).

Subordinate	4 possible interactions	44
..	5	100
..	6	1080

The mathematical analysis of all possible relationships according to Graicunas is significant because:

(a) *it underlines the intricate social interactions* between a superior and the subordinates;
(b) understanding of the theory enables *the rate at which the interactions increase to be appreciated.*

Graicunas' theory did not envisage such complicated interactions occurring generally. Rather it suggested that if spans were allowed to grow uncontrolledly, then, eventually, there would be one extra inter-action too many, which would 'break the camel's back'. While that is undoubtedly true, the theory ignores the likelihood that, before that point is reached, the manager's effectiveness would have deteriorated.

26. Urwick's principle

Urwick offered as reason for limiting spans of management the recognised psychological pattern that man has a limited span of attention. This concept limits the number of items that can be attended to by a person at any particular time. There will be other limiting factors, such as the amount of energy or the extent of time available. Essentially, Urwick recognised the variable complexity of the supervisor's job.

27. Allen's diminishing marginal effectiveness

Economists have long recognised that the law of diminishing returns can, and does, apply to personnel. Adapting this concept to the span of management (*see* Figure 17.10) it can be seen that while it is the extra unit in the span that will diminish the effectiveness, the marginal unit will be indistinguishable from all the other units: 'Successive additions to a manager's span of control will, other things being equal, produce a diminished marginal effectiveness.'

Diminishing marginal effectiveness is a physical limitation that must eventually apply in all situations, otherwise 'one person could control all'. It also explains the gradual limitations on effectiveness, which Graicunas's hypothesis is unable to do.

28. Importance to sales management

That sales management pays too little attention to rational spans of management is manifest in the many examples of firms with unwieldy spans. The existence of these organisations often arises due to uncontrolled growth. The early successes of the company are naturally attributed to personalities in control at the outset, but, as the organisation grows, these people increase their subordinates until the span of management is unwieldly and frequently uncontrollable. Then, when the lack of control begins to affect sales performance, it is the salespeople who are dismissed for poor results when the blame may well lie in management's lack of control and guidance and poor communications in general. The span of management should:

(a) enable sales management to enjoy face-to-face relationships with its immediate subordinates;

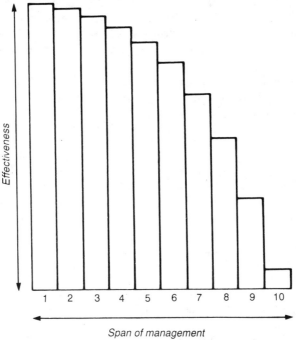

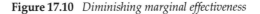

Span of management
(number of subordinates)

Figure 17.10   *Diminishing marginal effectiveness*

(b) allow adequate attention to be given to training and guidance to individual salespeople; and
(c) permit optimum two-way communications to develop and be maintained.

Organisation structures

29. Organisation charts

The purpose of an organisation chart is to illustrate how work is divided into manageable portions and allocated to people in the enterprise. It can serve both as a blueprint of a proposed structure or reorganisation structure or a record of the way in which an enterprise grows. The chart has five main uses:

(a) it is an aid to management in considering the way in which *duties are distributed* within the enterprise;

(b) during periods of changing conditions, it enables *rapid identification* of those jobs or personalities needing *modification*;

(c) it serves as a general guide to the way in which *duties are distributed* and assists the staff in their contacts with other parts of the organisation;

(d) at the induction of new staff, it is a *valuable training document* to explain the organisation;

(e) it enables the *delegation of authority* to be recorded and responsibilities to be clarified and is a guide in any reappraisal of the existing structure.

An organisation chart is an important factor in planning the organisation structure.

30. What kind of structure?

There are various forms an organisation structure will take, but three broad forms are generally recognised:

(a) production-orientated;

(b) sales-orientated; and

(c) marketing-orientated.

In the 1960s, when there was euphoria about all things 'marketing', (c), the marketing-orientated organisation structure was held to be the ultimate form. However, events in the 1970s have shown that there is justification for all three and the 'best' organisation structure is the one most suited to the survival of the firm. Whatever form the structure takes, it is the attitude of the individuals, especially those who control the organisation, that determines its character. Broadly speaking, the choice is probably between the technocrats and the hidden persuaders.

31. Production-orientated structures

In this form of organisation, selling and marketing are subordinate to the objective of optimising production. Product development will be related to the firm's experience and skill rather than to customers' needs. *Technical* research will be more important than *market* research and advantages will be derived from cost savings rather than by applying marketing ideas and innovations.

Personnel will tend to be orientated towards technical and production abilities, with marketing and selling skills seen to be of less value. Generally the senior managers will be drawn from the production function and technical people are likely to be favoured in promotion.

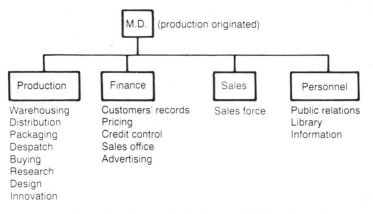

Figure 17.11 *Sales and marketing activities in a production-orientated structure*

Selling in such an organisation is often regarded as a low-priority necessity and little more than order taking, the belief being that the technical quality of the product is sufficient inducement to people to buy. An example of such an organisation is a well-known multinational electronics firm that manufactures telephone exchanges. When demand for that product was satisfied, the company literally did not know what to make. After substantial job losses and a traumatic period of struggling to survive, they used their technical expertise to develop a new mini-telephone exchange. However, they displayed little creativity in their marketing plans and relied on their technical reputation to encourage customers to buy from retail outlets.

In the production-orientated structure, many sales/marketing activities will be handled by non-marketing departments, for example, credit control and company records by finance, and dispatch and packaging by production.

This form of organisation should not be dismissed entirely, however, because there are firms in which it is still sufficient. Firms that make components for other companies may not need to market or sell their own products but only produce at a low unit cost to satisfy a small number of large customers. Such firms, however, can be dangerously exposed if their main customers, perhaps in the motor trade, suffer a major decline for example, Leyland DAF. They may not have the selling skills available to compete on their own. Figure 17.11 shows a typical production-orientated structure.

32. Sales-orientated structures
When the importance of the customer is appreciated in the con-

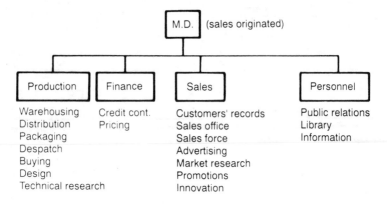

Figure 17.12 *A sales-orientated structure*

text of maintaining full production, the organisation tends towards a sales-orientated structure, as illustrated in Figure 17.12.

The abilities of the sales force receive wider appreciation and sales personnel will have a strong voice in policy-making decisions. More activities will be controlled by the sales function and there is greater emphasis on market research. Advertising and promotion will be less information-based and will adopt a more dynamic note, often being used directly in support of the sales effort.

Sales-orientated structures are very well suited to selling industrial and specialist products where technical information and demonstration are important. They are also vital to successful export selling.

33. Marketing-orientated structures

It was the vogue some years ago to regard marketing-orientated structures as the final development, but, with the realisation that the best form of organisation is the one that gives the company the most competitive edge, this is no longer widely held. For a wide range of consumer goods, especially fast-moving products, marketing is necessary. The products are carefully researched to make sure that they are what consumers want, heavily promoted to ensure that they are widely known and then merchandised into the retail stores. In the marketing-orientated structure, as shown in Figure 17.13, the entire policy of the company undergoes a change inasmuch as all strategy begins with consideration of customers and their needs.

Senior management will be drawn from marketing personnel and promotion will tend to favour marketing personnel. Practically all

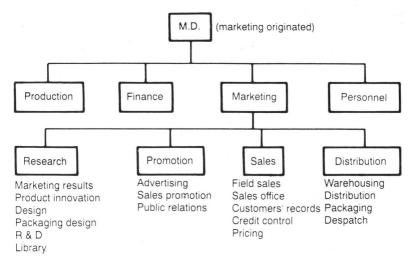

Figure 17.13   *Marketing activities in a marketing-orientated organisation*

innovation will stem from marketing and consumer research and innovation will frequently be in anticipation of consumers' needs.

In adopting a marketing-orientated structure, a company is by means of an influential marketing function, ensuring a consistent, or even enlarged, share of their market. The organisation structure will:

(a) enable production of products of a design and performance *in accord with customers' demands*;

(b) it will promote and distribute its production by *methods most suitable to dynamic markets*; and

(c) production, promotion and distribution will be based on *continuous marketing research*.

34. Marketing orientation is not a marketing concept

Many students and others confuse being marketing orientated with a company adopting a marketing concept (*see* 1:**6**). They are not the same. In the former case it implies that the function concerned with the customer realises the need to direct its efforts towards customer satisfaction, but that does not necessarily mean that *the firm as a whole* sees that necessity or is prepared to modify products or take customer needs into account in new designs, or have flexible accounting and credit and so on. It is only when the whole business operation is integrated towards the prime objective of customer satisfaction that a firm can be said to have embraced the marketing concept.

Progress test 17

1. There are a number of factors that form a containing structure dictating the possible shape of an organisation; what are they? **(2)**

2. Why is organisation important to the sales function? **(4)**

3. What are the three types of organisation structure? **(10)**

4. Do you know the four requirements of an organisation structure? **(11)**

5. List the bases of departmentalisation. **(15)**

6. Can you describe the differences between sales-orientated and marketing-orientated structures? **(32, 33)**

Business planning and sales forecasting

Planning and objectives

1. Importance of planning

Planning is one of the basic elements of management and has a prime position inasmuch as it is the start of any sequence of management functions. Planning also has a profound effect on other management and organisational activities.

Planning is unique among the elements of management as it may warrant no further action. A company may, as a result of the investigation required prior to planning, decide not to pursue the project further.

Implementing the results of planning is fundamental to the functions of organising, motivating and controlling. Planning activity is essential to effective sales management in several ways, such as the planning of:

(a) product mix;
(b) distribution channels;
(c) physical distribution and the location of distribution points;
(d) promotional activities;
(e) control activities; and
(f) financial resources and allocations.

In addition to planning the operational needs listed above, sales management must also determine objectives for the organisation, in accordance with the stated company policy:

(a) corporate policy;
(b) company objectives;
(c) departmental objectives;
(d) management objectives;
(e) individual goals.

2. Objectives

Objectives may be defined as the recognisable and predetermined goals to which the efforts of the organisation are directed.

Any organisation must have clearly defined objectives to which it directs its efforts if it is to avoid a meaningless progression of ideas. The statement of an objective is a recognition of a purpose and, when applied to sales management, it becomes the *raison d'être* of the function. Objectives must be clearly stated in writing and made known to those who will be involved in their accomplishment.

3.   Characteristics of objectives

The main points are that:

(a) the essential characteristic is that an objective is *predetermined*, a fact that isolates it from the process of accomplishing the objective;
(b) it has to be *clearly stated*, generally in written form, to assist in clarifying the objective and commit personnel to its accomplishment;
(c) it should be *logical and attainable*, but should serve to encourage the organisation to greater effort to ensure its accomplishment.

Objectives have four benefits to the organisation, resulting directly from their statement:

(a) *direction*: objectives, by definition, provide a goal to which management and sales force will direct their efforts and also serve to coordinate the efforts of the entire organisation towards common goals;
(b) *motivation*: once an objective has been defined and clearly stated, it serves to motivate sales personnel and incentives in the form of extra commission, bonus or promotion may be used in conjunction with functional and personal targets;
(c) clearly defined and realistic objectives form a basis for the *control process* — plans are made to achieve particular goals and the control element monitors the results to see whether they are achieved and if any modification to plans is needed;
(d) objectives provide a basis for the *style of management* — management by objectives avoids the alternatives of 'management by reaction', reaction to unforeseen problems and, applied to sales management, management by objectives provides the essential continuity and also flexibility, which is both responsive to, and in anticipation of, consumer trends.

4.   Control

Business organisations take many forms, with the recent resurgence of small companies, including single-person businesses, partnerships, limited companies, corporations and nationalised concerns.

Whatever form is taken, however, control will be vested in some authoritative person. The person in command will have the task of ensuring the accomplishment of the general business objective.

A manager's ability to ensure the success of the business, however, may be restricted by factors outside the company's control in the short term. These are:

(a) size and efficiency of the plant;
(b) amount of working capital;
(c) efficiency and skill of management and staff;
(d) the firm's reputation; and
(e) quality and variety of its products.

There are factors in the business environment that management may not be able to remedy in the short term. As technology increasingly plays a bigger role in production and control, it may take several years for a large business to change, as has been seen in shipbuilding and motor car production. Even smaller firms that are inherently flexible may find changing products difficult if their suppliers cannot obtain or produce components. There will be physical factors, too, such as plant size or capital resources, that can only be gradually changed and, because of them, management planning has to be precise but also have a built-in flexibility to deal with a rapidly changing business world.

Management is better placed to take remedial action, though, if it has established the correct organisational structure to ensure that the element of control is effectively fulfilled and that profitability is measured as a means of telling what is happening.

5. Determining objectives

The determination of objectives is a management planning task and, like all management decisions, must be based on reliable information.

Sales management's task in determining its objectives is often a difficult one because it is dealing with factors largely outside its control:

(a) consumer trends;
(b) economic trends;
(c) the results of political and legal decisions;
(d) general level of investment;
(e) social influence; and, increasingly,
(f) environmental pressures.

It is a field in which change may be brought about very swiftly, by exploiting new resources, technological discoveries, technical innovation, environmental planning, development of new distribution systems etc. Even the largest organisations may get caught out by the technology trap. For example, a college that set up a distance learning programme using computers and video tapes found that, even before it had completed its production, the computer equipment they used was passé and the simple video tape had been overtaken by the interactive disc.

The increasing technical complexity of many products means that the development period is both long and costly, while the rapid increase in knowledge will, by advancing more rapidly, overtake the development time and cause early obsolescence. This has been clearly discernable in aircraft development for many years, but is now increasingly evident in a range of products from pharmaceuticals to video games and computers to domestic appliances. In these circumstances, one may question whether simple 'product research' is any longer viable or whether it is now a matter of continuous technological research into every aspect of a firm's product range in the hope that, from the plethora of new discoveries, something practical and marketable will emerge. That being so, it is only the very largest corporations that will produce the bulk of the new developments; in fact this is already happening in Japanese electronics technology.

However, for sales managers faced with these problems, it is no longer sufficient to simply ask the 'seventies' question, 'What will consumers want in X years that they don't have now, can we profitably make and market it and for how long will they want it?' Technology and development is moving at such a pace that, as consumers, we can no longer anticipate what might become available in five years! This can be easily seen in the increasing rapidity of electronics developments. For example, the introduction of the CD player has made records virtually obsolescent in just two short years.

6. The effect of rapidly increasing technology on product planning

Before a company commits itself to producing a product involving prolonged research, high development cost and, perhaps, a limited life, it must try to predict the level of sales and the length of time in which the product might be sold. Figure 18.1 shows possible patterns. The product life cycle (explained in Chapter 1 and shown in Figure 18.2), becomes relevant in this situation, too, because it helps predict, and therefore plan, future events. In this situation, however,

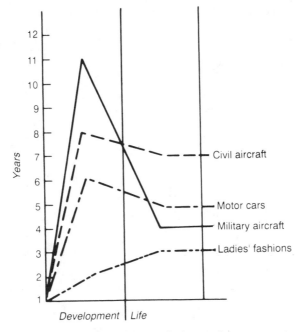

Figure 18.1 *Sales prediction graph*

it becomes useful to extend the cycle forwards to include the re-development period and perhaps even to attempt to track the effects of competition on a newly developed product; such competition will include:

(a) product competition;
(b) similar technology competition; and
(c) new technology competition.

7. Setting the objectives
Planning must involve doing everything possible to ensure that, once objectives have been determined, everything that is done assists in their realisation. In the small manufacturing company, objectives are likely to be simple and capable of easy communication to small numbers of staff. In larger companies, the organisation structures will be complicated and communications to the many activities contributing to the objective will involve management coordination and control. If the central objective is greater profit, other lesser goals may also be involved, including:

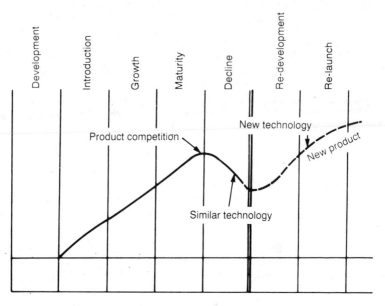

Figure 18.2 *The product life cycle and planning*

(a) corporate growth;
(b) diversification of business;
(c) new product innovation;
(d) entry into new markets;
(e) increasing the share of existing markets; or
(f) economic integration by merger or acquisition.

8. The role of planning

Having set objectives, the role of planning is to decide how far they can be realised with existing resources. A sales manager's decision to enter a new market, to export or to introduce a new product, will need to be based on an examination of:

(a) the existing sales force;
(b) manufacturing capacity;
(c) financial resources; and
(d) the level of promotional expenditure.

Sales management bears a large responsibility for planning, whether or not the objective is purely a 'sales' objective as the company's revenue is ultimately derived from some form of sales. The anticipated volume of sales, therefore, is all important in judging the practicality of the objective.

A company has certain fixed costs that will be incurred whether the company sells or not and they will not rise with increased sales. Other costs, such as packaging, production and distribution, will be variable and will increase in line with the amount of sales and production activity going on. This is illustrated in the break-even chart (*see* Figure 18.3).

The fixed costs (A-A^1) will remain constant and start well above the point at which sales commence. The variable costs (B-B^1) start from the line of the fixed costs and increase in proportion to sales (C-C^1). As sales increase, the line crosses the fixed costs and variable costs and this juncture, where variable cost and sales intersect, is the break-even point, at which costs and revenue are equal. Beyond break-even point, profits increase rapidly as the fixed costs are spread over a larger number of units of production.

Sales planning will endeavour to predict sales so that the level of profitability can be forecast. It will also predict the life of the product as, the longer a product can be sold, the greater the spread of the costs over its production life and the better the return on the money invested in equipment to produce it. The prediction of sales by volume, price and time scale, is essential to realistic objectives and fundamental to good planning.

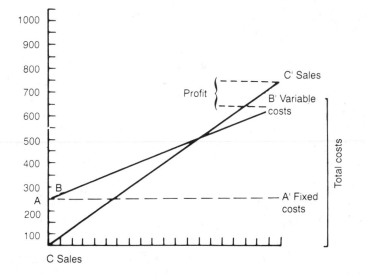

Figure 18.3 *Break-even chart*

Forecasting

9.   Understanding a changing world

All business takes place within the world about us and we, as individuals and companies, really have very little control over global events. For example, in October 1987 there was a sudden and dramatic fall in share prices in the United States. Within a few days, the effect of that fall on Wall Street in New York was reverberating around the world, bringing share prices down in each financial market in turn, like dominoes.

The fall in share prices had a cataclysmic effect on the fortunes of many companies and not only the major companies whose shares were quoted, but also hundreds of smaller firms that looked to them for supplies and orders. Companies that had intended to place orders, suddenly found themselves in unexpected financial difficulty and many therefore had to cancel orders.

At a different level, in early 1988, there was a rise in the value of the pound sterling, which made British exports more expensive abroad. For example, my own company makes exhibition trailers that we sell in several European countries. A £1900 trailer that sold in Holland for 5510 guilders when there were 2.9 guilders to the pound, rose to 5700 guilders when the pound rose to 3 guilders.

Many such currency movements are only temporary and may, anyway, seem insignificant but, for a company selling a major machine costing £100 000, such a movement would result in a rise in the cost of the machine in Holland of 10 000 guilders!

10.   The need to predict the future

The problem many companies face is to try and predict what might happen in a market in the future. For companies making complicated products it may be necessary to try to predict a long way ahead. Some years ago, there was a shortage in the UK of certain petrochemicals and thousands of tons were imported. Some companies saw a profitable opportunity in the situation and planned to move into the market. Unfortunately, the plants needed to produce these chemicals took several years to build and, by the time they were ready, there was a glut in the supply of petrochemicals. The situation of excess supply resulted in a sharp fall in price, to a point where it had fallen too low for newcomers to make a profit.

It isn't only hi-tech products that suffer from rapid changes. The fashion industry is an example where the need to try and predict future trends is also strong.

11. Sales forecasting

The central problem of forecasting sales arises from the need to predict customer actions in buying goods at particular prices. A simple answer is that forecasting cannot do this accurately, but it can, by means of forecasting techniques, provide an indication of results.

Forecasting can be used for predicting both consumer trends and industrial demand for the goods needed to make other manufacturers' goods. Obviously there is a connection between consumer and industrial demand for related goods. If there is a fall in the demand for consumer goods, such as washing machines, then there will be a corresponding fall in the demand for the machinery, spares, supplies etc. used by the washing machine manufacturer.

12. Consumers and trade

Marketing depends on maintaining consumer demand at a level that can continually absorb expanding output. In the marketing-orientated economy, the motivation of individuals towards mass consumption ensures not only a continuing reason to produce consumer goods, but also provides a reason for making capital, or producers', goods. As more people are employed and demand is levered up, so more labour and raw materials will be needed. A good example of a cycle of rising demand is a rise in the sales of new houses. As people buy houses, they create a demand for a whole range of other goods, from bricks and timber to furniture, carpets and household goods. Of course, the opposite is also true and, in the 1970s, 1980s and 1990s, unemployment was caused by falling demand, which in turn created more unemployment, reducing demand further — a cycle of falling demand.

From the viewpoint of predicting change, there are a variety of general indicators that give a rough guide to what is likely to happen. For example:

(a) demand for houses;
(b) demand for cars;
(c) demand for household appliances;
(d) changes in levels of employment;
(e) changes in values of currencies.

13. Differences between consumers' goods and producers' goods

The differences are that:

(a) consumers' goods provide satisfaction in themselves, e.g. a television, a car, a washing machine, food or furniture;

(b) producers' goods are a derived demand and are not wanted themselves but for the use they have in making something else, ultimately consumer goods — a lorry is wanted only as a means of transporting other goods or materials; a lathe, to produce tools or other articles.

The essential point is that the strength of the economy and, therefore, the likely trend in purchasing, is most clearly and readily indicated by consumer trends. If consumer spending on washing machines is rapidly declining, manufacturers of washing machines will need less of the materials and tools they use to make them. An understanding of this relationship between consumer goods and producers' goods is important to every sales manager and salesperson and would save the latter, especially, a great deal of wasted effort in trying to persuade buyers using the wrong reasons. Figure 18.4 is a simplified model showing the relationships between consumption and production.

14. The time period of the forecast
Sales management's decisions as to what can be sold, in what quantities, where, how and when, have to be quantified in terms of time if they are to be of practical, operational value. One may ask,

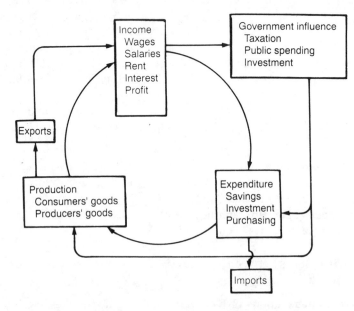

Figure 18.4 *Simplified economic cycle*

'During what period of time will quantities of particular goods be sold in particular areas at particular costs?' This should include:

(a) costs of promotion;
(b) costs of sales; at
(c) predetermined prices.

Once these answers have been determined, a projection of costs and income can be made. This, predicted as a break-even chart, will be essential for a valid control system. As all answers depend on being able to predict the quantity of goods to be sold, the first step in the process is to determine this.

15. As far as can be seen

The object of the forecast is to predict future trends and the further into the future the forecast can be made, the more helpful it will be in planning the general and specific direction of the business. This is especially true in new or small businesses where the cash flow needs to be estimated to some extent so that management can have some idea of what resources it will have available at particular times and, therefore, what it can and must do to survive.

Nevertheless, there are inherent dangers in this type of prediction if the forecaster fails to foresee some significant event. A recent example of such an unexpected event was the sudden fall in share prices in October 1987 (*see* 18:**9**). Looking back a little further, the unprecedented rise in oil prices after the Arab-Israeli war of 1973 caught most economists and politicians by surprise and had dramatic effects, all but wrecking many Western economies.

16. Three forecasting areas

The purpose of the forecast is to predict the future trends, but it should not be a static period. Forecasts should continually search ahead, like radar, but resembling the probing radar on a moving ship rather than static ground radar monitoring its surroundings. The scanner must move ahead and not passively wait for events to reach it (*see* Figure 18.5). In order of time, the forecasting areas are:

(a) long-term objective forecast;
(b) long-term operational forecast; and
(c) immediate forecast.

17. Long-term objective forecast

This forecast may form the basis of the company's long-term

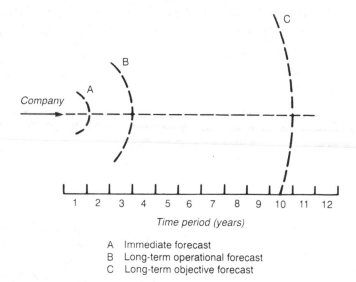

A   Immediate forecast
B   Long-term operational forecast
C   Long-term objective forecast

Figure 18.5 *Three forecasting areas*

marketing strategy if, for example, it identifies a significant change in the company's marketing environment that will necessitate an important change in the company's course. Changes in legislation affecting motor car safety, smoking and drinking habits or changes in leisure activities, for example, may suggest that a company's long-term strategy should change. Many tobacco companies saw that increasing public concern with the effects of smoking on health would reduce the size of the cigarette market and moved into other areas, such as supermarket ownership, leisure and fast foods.

Two important aspects underlie this forecast:

(a) that it makes no pretensions to accuracy; and
(b) that it seeks to indicate the general changes that are likely to occur in the future which could have a fundamental effect on the company's operations.

To understand fully the company's objective, it is necessary for the company to examine critically and systematically its capabilities, experience and marketing skills. For the factors that may influence a company's operations, see 1:3, but, just to recap, the most important in relation to forecasting are:

(a) population changes,

(b) economic trends, and

(c) technical innovation.

The main reason for the long-term objective forecast is to remind the company's executives of the purpose for which they are in business and it should alert them at the earliest moments to forces that may cause changes to be made to their declared objectives.

18. Long-term operational forecast

How much the time scale may be shortened is limited by the ability of executives to act on information and this determines how far ahead the operational forecast should scan. The manner in which industry has evolved, becoming increasingly more complicated, has necessitated that operational forecasts become longer. For example, my own company decided to market a lifting mechanism for chairs for the disabled and, not having the necessary skills, we decided to go to a small engineering firm that frequently manufactured various one-off items for us. We anticipated that they would be able to respond quickly, being small and flexible. However, modern technology dictated that they use a specialist folding machine to make our product at a competitive price and it took them several months to get the machine installed and running. Our sales forecast, therefore, had to take account of an operational forecast of three months, that is, the

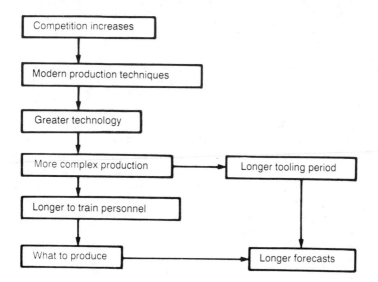

Figure 18.6 *Development of longer operational forecasts*

time taken to change production. In industries such as chemicals and aircraft, such changes may take several years. Figure 18.6 illustrates this process.

The stringent regulations surrounding the automobile industry make forecasting very difficult. An example of the problem of forecasting demand is the way in which many millions of pounds may be spent over a period of several years in the development, pre-production engineering and promotion of a new model. Successful automobile marketing must look far ahead if it is to avoid setting up production lines for cars that will have a limited life, due to 'unforeseen' market or legislative changes.

Similar situations exist in the aircraft industry. A recent example has been the Nimrod airborne early warning radar aircraft. Production of the airframe and the electronics started together in the belief that eventually the finished aircraft would emerge. In fact, the difficulties in getting the super-sophisticated electronics to work to ever-higher operational standards meant that eventually, the project had to be cancelled — although ironically the airframes were then ready.

Modern industrial complexes have differing degrees of flexibility. At one end of the scale is the fashion industry, in which the high level of operative skill and low degree of specialist equipment allow easy changes, and, at the other end, are power generating plants, which have to be planned 20, or even 30, years ahead. Chemical production is another example of highly specialist and non-adaptive plants that have to be planned many years ahead. We can postulate a simple equation to explain the problem:

hi-tech industry = process production = growth in investment = less ability to reallocate resources.

19. Commitment to objectives

Under circumstances of rigid commitment to an objective, intuitive judgement has to be replaced by realistic appraisal of possible effects. The period of the operational forecast may be determined as the time required from the moment of decision to the time when the decision is finally implemented. Sales management must forecast objectives and the process is represented in Figure 18.7.

20. Bases of information

The amount of information needed to fulfil the task of forecasting objectives will vary according to the nature of the business, but can be broadly classified into two groups:

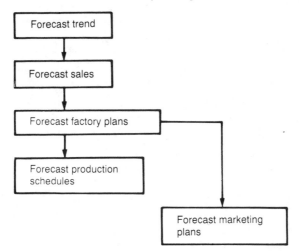

Figure 18.7 *Objectives forecast*

(a) *economic information*:
    (i) trading patterns;
    (ii) structure of the industry;
    (iii) use of resources;
    (iv) trends in population; and
    (v) level of income.
(b) *social information*:
    (i) consumer trends;
    (ii) buying habits; and
    (iii) distribution of income.

21. A determined time period

Any major sales plan must relate the forecast to a determined time period, say, five years, and will concentrate on those areas likely to affect the company. Thus, a company venturing into a new product area will seek information on that market, using market and marketing research, as well as knowledge of the environmental factors that have been discussed above (*see* 18:1). More specifically, it will want to know:

(a) How fast is this market growing?
(b) How much are consumers/users spending — is it rising, falling or stable?
(c) What is the level of competition?
(d) What is likely to happen in this market in the next n years?

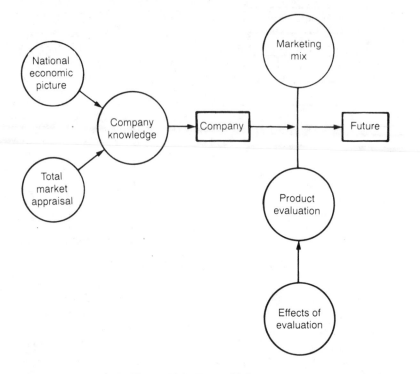

Figure 18.8   *Bases of information*

Only after careful collection of information, analysis and interpretation can predictions be made enabling the forecast to be prepared that will assist in management's decision making. Figure 18.8 shows the bases of information.

22. Short-term or immediate forecast

The immediate forecast is concerned with the period during which management will be taking decisions continuously, on a day-to-day basis. The control element will be most effective if the objectives have been clearly and precisely defined, even if they have to be flexible. An example of this might occur when a company asks its bank for a loan. The bank is likely to ask them for a cash flow prediction. This must show what sales and costs they anticipate incurring within a short period, 12 months for instance, and from these income and outlay predictions, cash flow can be anticipated. If nothing else, such an exercise helps management concentrate realistically on the short-term future and often enables them to take better decisions, about, for example, when to buy a new machine, or increase the staff. Such predictions at best can only be estimates because one can never be sure that specific orders will arrive, but it does enable a general picture to be formed. The short-term forecast is an important basis for the annual sales budget.

Information for the short-term forecast can be obtained from salespeople's reports, which will be useful both in compiling the forecast and in modifying it during the forecast period.

It is usual to consider a period of one year divided into quarters, or months, to be the logical length for the forecast. The forecast may be calculated in several ways but the following four are the most used:

(a) extrapolation;
(b) economic forecasting;
(c) market research; and
(d) sales-originated data.

23. Extrapolation

Extrapolation is a simple forecasting technique that relies on the projection of past trends, as in Figure 18.9. If a company examines its past sales and finds a yearly increase of ten per cent then it can reasonably predict that the next year is also likely to produce a ten per cent increase.

Extrapolation can be effective and reliable in those areas where changes take place slowly, such as population growth or anticipated

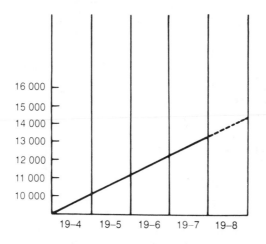

Figure 18.9 *Extrapolation of next year's sales at 10 per cent p.a.*

growth in demand for electricity. As a technique for forecasting sales, it has limitations. Competitive activity is unpredictable, as new products may influence market trends. It also has to be understood that wholly dissimilar products may influence each other's sales. As has been seen in recent years, a share offer in the government's privatisation schemes may attract consumers to buy shares and the money spent might have been used in other ways, to buy cars, holidays or domestic appliances or to increase savings. Unexpected hazards may also influence sales, favourably as well as unfavourably. The hurricane in the autumn of 1987 caused great damage to a variety of goods and properties, which led to increased sales of replacements of all types. Strikes, disasters, and political strife may all affect supplies and cut back output, thereby reducing sales.

24. Economic forecasting

For the immediate future, economic forecasting can be a guide to the expectancy of sale. However, it still cannot do more than indicate a trend and economic indicators are notoriously unreliable in the short term.

Nevertheless there are some areas that can give the alert salesperson an indication of likely trends. A salesperson selling in the building and construction industry may be alerted to a downward trend, if changes in the money supply lead to rising interest rates (making mortgages more expensive), and an exporter will view seriously an unprecedented rise in the international value of the pound. The converse also applies, of course, with a fall in interest rates and in the pound encouraging builder and exporter respectively.

25. Market research

As an aid to short-term forecasting, market research has to be directed accurately at selected areas. For example, a firm planning to launch a new product can use questionnaires to acquire relevant data that will help it calculate sales estimates.

26. Sales-originated information

The sales force is a valuable aid to forecasting short-term trends and the information can be kept up to date and revised quickly in response to change.

Salespeople are required to submit a monthly sales report giving information on actual sales achieved and this data will be collated and used for extrapolation. In addition, they can provide specific information, such as:

(a) What orders do you expect next month?
(b) What orders do you anticipate within the following two months?
(c) Information on competitive activity.

27. The year as a measurement

There are advantages to be gained from using the year as a period for the forecast. Most government reports, statistical surveys etc. normally extend over months and years. The government's Budget also uses a year as a base and affects many business decisions.

However, problems can arise from a commitment to the period of one year, especially in areas where the operation is known to extend more than a year and where there would be disadvantages in breaking these operations into single-year periods, for example:

(a) *New product launch.* The high investment in promotion at the launch of a product, to ensure an acceptance in the shortest possible time and to achieve maximum profitability, will almost certainly entail a loss for the first yearly period.
(b) *Forecasting the results of export marketing* will certainly need to extend over a period longer than one year. For example, my own company made a loss on exports to Holland in the first year, because we had to make a number of sales and promotional visits, and to deliver in uneconomic quantities, pay for the translation of literature and so on. In the second year, though, these initial extra costs paid off, producing much more substantial orders.

28. Using the forecasts

Obviously these forecasts have to be put to good use. Like so much in the management process, however, it is often difficult to define the precise starting point. Even if you have a brand new business, you will have researched, forecast and planned before setting out — or did you plan first and then make forecasts to confirm your ideas? It is really a continuous cycle of ideas, plans, research and forecasts and then detailed planning.

29. Elements of sales planning

Sales management's first responsibility is the planning and control of the selling effort. In order to achieve these targets, sales management:

(a) directs and controls *field selling activities*;
(b) determines the *distribution channels* that will be most suited to customers' needs;
(c) organises the *physical distribution* method; and

(d) ensures that these activities are carried out *within the agreed costs*.

30. The planning task

In any sales organisation, the sales force will be important in accomplishing objectives. A great deal of planning and control will be needed to ensure that individual salespeople carry out their tasks efficiently and at an acceptable cost. To do this sales management's planning task will include:

(a) setting up procedures for sales reporting;

(b) determining standards of performance for the sales force;

(c) evaluating sales results against planned performance;

(d) establishing a system of statistical analysis and evaluation of sales; and

(e) establishing an adequate feedback control system to alert management to any necessary change in plans to correct deficiencies.

31. Objectives of sales planning

We have seen how forecasting will endeavour to predict likely trends. Planning is concerned with analysing the forecast and interpreting the results into operational requirements. It will be concerned with information and communication needs as much as it will with financial and sales results, in order to provide the necessary controls. Its objectives are:

(a) sales communication;

(b) sales reporting;

(c) statistical control; and

(d) review of staff's performance.

Progress test 18

1. What has been the effect of rapidly increasing technology on product planning? **(6)**

2. What is a break-even chart? **(8)**

3. What future costs should be considered in making a forecast? **(14)**

4. What are the three forecasting areas? **(16)**

5. What is the relationship between the short-term forecast and the sales budget? **(22)**

Appraising performance

The need for appraisal

1. Introduction
Any sales force has to be subjected to a periodic appraisal to check if its performance meets whatever objective or standard was set. This needs arises out of:

(a) personality changes in individual sales people that may arise from overconfidence or complacency;
(b) changing industry and market conditions;
(c) new or improved selling techniques.

The purpose of an appraisal will be to satisfy management of the effectiveness of the overall sales force as well as being an appraisal of the individual's performance. Appraisals also have to be made when considering possible promotions, bonus incentives or salary increases.

2. Major considerations
Sales managers will want more specific information in certain areas of the operations. They will want to assess the abilities of salespeople in particular aspects that have a major effect on the efficiency of the sales function. Major consideration will be given to the following:

(a) Is the salesperson obtaining a *satisfactory volume of orders*?
(b) Is the salesperson providing a *satisfactory level of service* to maintain good customer relations?
(c) *If there are faults*, is the salesperson to blame or is management lacking?
(d) What *effective action* can be taken to help?

The answers to these questions will determine the manner in which management at all levels will perform in the aspects of leadership, motivation and control.

3. Aims of appraisal
Formal appraisals of performance are not intended to enable management to make categoric decisions, but to create conditions of

confidence between management and sales force that will allow maximum cooperation between the policy-making and operational bodies.

Formal appraisals were originally developed to assess the performance of workers in factories. Supervisors were asked to evaluate the abilities of subordinates on a form. This system, known as 'merit rating', was concerned with:

(a) quality and volume of work; and
(b) attitudes towards the firm and colleagues.

In making such judgements about others, managers and other supervisors have to beware of what is known as a 'halo effect'. This effect is seen when the appraiser, having judged a person to be good or bad at one aspect of the work, will tend to *believe* that he or she will be equally good or bad at all other aspects too. This tendency has been frequently noted in the appraisals of salespeople, when, for example, a person's ability to perform paperwork or reporting duties becomes a standard for their selling or vice versa.

The appreciation of this human tendency to be biased is generally countered by varying the categories down the form, making the assessor deliberate on each answer.

4.   Appraisal of performance

Having made allowances for the halo effect the form will request information on the way the salesperson carries out his or her duties. Normally, the sales manager will accompany each salesperson in turn and make an appraisal from observations, although other methods may be used. A number of reports will be made on each person in the course of a year, the exact number depending on the company's policy. Salespeople can be assessed in the following ways:

(a) a manager will accompany a salesperson on a day's work;
(b) a manager may make independent calls on customers with the purpose of checking the salesperson's efforts when he or she is alone;
(c) random checks on the accuracy of a salesperson's daily report may be made.

5.   Personal appraisal

When sales managers or other supervisors accompany salespeople on their daily work, they will be watching several aspects of their performance:

(a) their appearance and manner;
(b) attitudes;
(c) experience; and
(d) administration.

None of these factors are as intangible as they may appear. Sales records will reveal a great deal about the salespeople's attitudes, experience and administrative ability and sales managers will bear this in mind in the direct personal observation. At first, salespeople may be nervous when dealing with customers under their manager's scrutiny but experience usually overcomes this hesitancy. Good managers will make allowances for the artificial nature of the event and try to put salespeople at their ease and the success they achieve will also be indicative of managers' leadership abilities.

It is true, however, that buyers have a tendency to bypass a salesperson and talk directly to the manager on these occasions. Managers must try to discourage this without offending customers but, if the relationship between sales manager and sales team is good, they will play 'box and cox' with the conversation and let it flow naturally between them. The whole exercise is a valuable aid to a good assessment and will show salespeople's abilities in handling interviews and customers.

6. Two-way reports

Sales managers' appraisals are not limited to comments on salespeople, but should also be a part of their duties to coordinate and control those under them. Senior sales management, in assessing managers' appraisals, will have this in mind and will want to see just how much work managers or supervisors do with the salespeople and how well managers motivates their sales force. Most appraisal forms have a section dealing with 'managers' comments and recommendations' and senior management will want to know:

(a) what managers thinks of their sales force; and
(b) what action is being taken.

7. Statistical appraisal

Statistics are the lifeblood of the modern business environment and are essential for market research and planning, in addition to being used by many departments for their own purposes. Many of these statistics emanate directly from the sales force's results. They have to be collated and presented in an easily understood form in order to be useful to management.

Salespeople can, with some practice and experience, keep records of their own performance and details of their territories in this easily assimilated form and make their own self-appraisals.

8. Moving annual totals

Sales targets are normally set for a period of 12 months. At the end of the period, it can be seen whether or not salespeople achieved their targets. It is possible to break that yearly figure down into 12 monthly figures and check those as they occur but sales results are rarely accommodating enough to get a real picture of progress in that way. The need for immediate and up-to-date information demands something more effective than a simple month-by-month or yearly progress report. The moving annual total (MAT) shows, at any point, how salespeople's results compare with the previous 12 months. Here is a simple illustration of a MAT:

Year	Month	Actual sales £	MAT £
1991	January	3000	—
	February	3200	—
	March	2500	—
	April	2700	—
	May	3600	—
	June	3800	—
	July	4250	—
	August	4700	—
	September	4950	—
	October	5000	—
	November	4600	—
	December	3900	46 200
1992	January	2850	46 050
	February	3100	45 950
	March	2850	46 300
	April	2650	46 250
	May	3450	46 100
	June	3700	46 000

In this example, records extend only so far as June 1992, but already a trend can be seen. There can, of course, be no MAT for the first 12 months' operation, but, at the end of the year, a final figure is available — in this example, £46 200. Each successive month of the next year, however, provides a ready indication of how it compares with the previous year. This is quite simple to calculate. Subtract from the final previous year's figure (£46 200) the sales figure for the corresponding month, for example January 1991 (£3000), and add on the new sales figure, that is January 1992 (£2850). Although the year is not ended, it can be seen that sales are down and, if last year's figure is to be exceeded, a greater effort will be needed in the second half of 1992.

9. Moving average figures

The moving average is simply a refinement of the previous method, which is obtained by dividing the total figure by the number of months it represents. For example, the moving average for June 1991 in the previous example would be the total sales of January to June divided by the number of months:

$$= \frac{18\,800}{6} \text{ (number of months)}$$

giving a moving average of £3133. This, continued over a period, will enable a salesperson to see whether sales are falling or rising in relation to the previous year.

10. Use of graphs

Both sales force and sales management can make use of graphs to give a visual presentation of information. They can be both simple and clear. Two types of graph are most commonly used. They are Lorenz curves and Z charts.

11. Lorenz curves

Lorenz curves can be used to illustrate the disparity arising from a disproportionate spread of sales over a number of customers. Examination of sales results often indicate a dangerous situation if the largest share of the business comes from a small number of customers. Salespeople need to know if this situation is arising. A simple example illustrated in Figure 19.1, will illustrate the point:

Example

A firm manufacturing bath lifts for the disabled sold virtually all they produced through a single distributor situated in Liverpool but with a national sales force; their remaining sales were direct to individual users and were, therefore, one-off sales. After some months, the Liverpool distributor began to put pressure on the manufacturer to give them a bigger discount. The manufacturer could not afford to do so, but, as the distributor represented some 90 per cent of trade sales, there was no other option than to increase discounts.

A Lorenz curve doesn't identify the customers, but it will make clear where the sales are coming from and the number of customers making

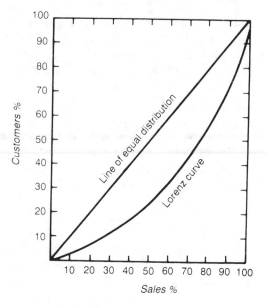

Figure 19.1 *Lorenz curve*

the bulk of sales. This enables further investigation and correction. Figure 19.1 shows that 70 per cent of sales are coming from only 40 per cent of accounts, a situation that could be improved.

12. Z charts

A Z chart extends over a single year and incorporates three types of information:

(a) individual monthly sales;
(b) cumulative sales for the year;
(c) moving annual total.

It is usual for a double scale to be used because the cumulative figure will be 12 times larger than the average and would result in the latter being too insignificant if drawn on the same scale (*see* Figure 19.2). The Z chart is useful to the salesperson for a continual check on performance against the previous year.

13. Motivation by appraisal

People like to see how well they are doing. Stimulation to self-analysis and self-appraisal will lead to well-motivated salespeople. It also encourages a spirit of self-competition and leads to analysis of

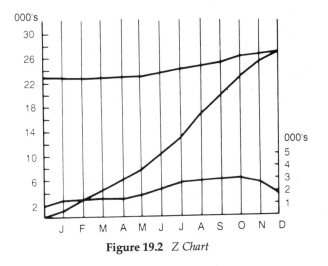

Figure 19.2 *Z Chart*

other factors by which sales and performance can be further improved.

Appraisal of the selling organisation

14. Analysing sales performance

The first stage in keeping control of the selling organisation is to understand what is happening. For example, the following are a few of the variables that might influence cost-effectiveness:

(a) How much do salespeople actually cost?
(b) Taken individually, do their sales results cover their costs?
(c) How do they actually perform, that is, how many calls do salespeople make before achieving orders?

The cost of sales personnel is not just their salaries, expenses, car etc., it is also the greater cost of their performance if it is found to be less than optimum. For example, supposing each salesperson costs the company £15 000 a year in total, including salary, expenses and car. The profit margin on sales is reckoned to be 10 per cent, therefore, each must sell £150 000 a year to cover the basic cost to the company of £15 000. If that figure is achieved, then it might be thought a satisfactory result. However, supposing the territory is capable of producing £200 000 a year? That means there is another 25 per cent potential business not being achieved and, presumably, going to the competition. It can be argued that the total cost of sales personnel must also include the opportunity cost of business not obtained. The salesperson just described might, if achieving maximum sales, subsidise another territory, which, for economic reasons, cannot provide sufficient business to cover its salesperson's total costs, but that, for reasons of prestige or because the sales are important even if they cannot quite provide the full economic return, should be maintained.

15. The sales force as a cost-centred unit

The sales force is a semi-autonomous unit within the larger sales organisation. Its costs, however, should be monitored and recorded separately. This is because sales force costs are:

(a) more variable than sales office costs and less predictable;
(b) more subject to outside influences, such as varying fuel costs;
(c) more likely to get out of control if not carefully monitored, for example salespeople may incur unacceptably high costs in pursuing particular sales objectives.

16. Measuring sales outputs effectively

The measurement of output is a basic need for all systems as it provides a means of control. Such measurements may be based on:

(a) the return on investment;
(b) the return on capital employed;
(c) contribution to company growth;
(d) level of profitability.

These criteria, while suitable for measuring the cost-effectiveness of the marketing organisation as a whole, tend to be too remote from the day-to-day running of the sales force and so other measures need to be used. There are five ways of doing this:

(a) contribution to profit;
(b) sales cost ratio;
(c) return on assets employed;
(d) achievement of sales/marketing objectives; and
(e) share of the market.

Let us look at each of these points in turn. First, the goods that are produced in the company are made over to the sales organisation at cost to which is added the selling and distribution costs and a margin for profit, resulting in a price commensurate with what the market will stand. The extra cost is the sales force's contribution to the total company profit. If sales costs are unnecessarily high, due, for example, to low call–sales ratios, the extra costs will reduce the overall profit. It may, of course, be possible to sell the product at a higher price by claiming some special benefits over the competition, but the question is whether this will allow for volume sales in line with production costs.

Second, as regards the sales cost ratio (sales expenses divided by sales volume) it gives a ratio for measuring performance against the cost involved in achieving it. However, it must be related to market size. For example, a company selling £100 000 at 7 per cent expense/volume ratio may not be as profitable as one selling £500 000 at 10 per cent ratio. This is especially true of firms selling competitive products in volume markets where the costs of production are optimised at certain high levels.

Third, return on assets employed. As was noted above (19:**13**), a sales force is an amalgam of many costs — cars, samples etc. Equally, money has to be invested in raw materials and finished goods stocks, distribution organisation and outstanding accounts. To obtain the return on the assets employed, the sales force's salaries and expenses must be subtracted from gross profit on the capital assets employed.

Depending on how the company is organised, the sales force will be given the task of meeting sales or marketing objectives — maybe even both. Such objectives will result from an analysis of the market, its potential and a determination of the particular segment or share of the market the company identifies as both desirable and attainable. A typical objective might be to obtain a particular measured share of the market or to sell the products into certain key customer companies. Such objectives are measurable by sales management and, therefore, are a means whereby sales performance can be gauged.

Market share and sales force performance do not relate directly in the sense that one is dependent on the other. Nevertheless, if the objective of sales management is to obtain a certain measured share of a specific market, 15 per cent for instance, then clearly the sales force will have a major role in achieving that objective. This is especially so if the products are being sold to markets in which the sales force will be the prime selling method, e.g. technical sales.

17. Seven stages in analysing the sales force

Analysing the sales force should follow a logical process, as follows:

(a) define the objectives of the sales force;
(b) quantify the relationships within the sales force/sales organisation, that is what inputs are needed;
(c) determine the measurable performance outputs;
(d) evaluate, in terms of cost–benefits, alternative solutions;
(e) define the efficiency of the sales force's output relative to its inputs; and
(f) implement the 'best' solution.

18. Improving performance

Sales management as a process comprises three sets of variables:

(a) management's control variables;
(b) sales force's inputs; and
(c) sales force's outputs.

Performance can be measured in five ways (*see* 19:**16**) and, in the event of performance not meeting the required standard, management should then analyse the variables that have influenced this result. For example, if the overall sales force's invoiced sales during a particular period did not meet the forecast targets, was there any specific variable that failed? Could the failure be attributed to poor deliveries of finished goods, for example, or perhaps the problem was more fundamental, such as the sales force not having the technical knowledge necessary to sell a new product.

The sales force's performance can be analysed in one of two ways:

(a) by sales volume; and
(b) by its cost ratio.

An improved cost ratio, for example, will result from increased sales volume without a proportional increase in costs; the increase might, however, derive from increased public relations activity, such as press releases. The combination of products sold by the sales force will contribute overall to both results as products will vary in their profitability, especially where accessories or extensions to the products or regular repeat orders from well-established customers are involved. There will be an optimum sales mix and product mix. This means that a good balance between repeat business from existing customers and new business from new customers is achieved. A good product mix likewise combines sales of the *whole* range of products in a *balanced* mix. How these optimum balances are achieved will result from sound sales analysis and sales training.

19. Effective selling is efficient selling

How much effort is expended to obtain sales indicates the quality of the sales presentation. If, for example, a salesperson is making ten calls a day and obtaining only one order, this may indicate poor presentation and lack of sales skill; perhaps more training is required. The effectiveness of individual sales presentations is measured by the calls–order ratio. This will inevitably vary according to:

(a) the experience of the salespeople;
(b) the quality of the products;
(c) whether the products are new or established; and
(d) the stage of development of the territory, whether it is new or well-established.

20. Maximising calls–orders ratios

Management can ensure that selling efforts are maximised by providing sound initial training, followed by continual on-the-job training programmes. Visits by sales managers should identify salespeople's problems or failings. Guidelines can be provided to help salespeople decide priorities, for example:

(a) which key activities will lead to increased selling success:
  (i) product story;
  (ii) follow-up enquiries;
  (iii) preparing specifications or special samples in advance;
(b) selling strategy:
  (i) emphasis on cost–benefits;
  (ii) stressing product reliability.

Determining some reliable measure of performance will depend greatly on the type of selling being done. For example, analysing performance is easier if the sales force is selling rapidly moving products, heavily supported by advertising and promotions, to grocers, where every call should produce an order, than if they are selling industrial goods where sales may depend on careful cultivation of a customer towards a specific order. Industrial selling frequently involves non-selling; these calls are more accurately expressed as *selling development* calls.

21. Productivity of calls

If salespeople allocate their time efficiently between different types of calls, then an optimum productivity should result. For example, a lot of industrial sales depend on certain types of customers specifying products, e.g. architects, designers, engineers and local authorities. These calls rarely produce immediate orders and, if sales-people spend too much time with this category of customer, the short-term sales volume will suffer. However, if they are ignored, the long-term sales volume will also suffer. It is a matter of balance.

Sales management can provide guidance in these areas as a result of analysing sales performance and directing and controlling the sales force's continuing sales effort. It does this by:

(a) determining which sales prospects deserve attention and indicating how time should be allocated in the most efficient and productive way;
(b) analysing territory and markets to determine potential and directing the sales effort accordingly; and
(c) evaluating selling requirements to ensure the development of existing and potential business.

Sales managers should be like conductors, orchestrating the combined efforts of the sales force towards specific goals.

Progress test 19

1. What are the major considerations in assessing the performances of salespeople? **(2)**

2. What personal aspects of salespeople's performance should sales managers watch for? **(5)**

3. How does a *moving annual total*, MAT, work? **(8)**

4. Can you name two commonly used types of graph? **(11, 12)**

Appendix

Case study 1: sales planning

XYZ is a small company that has been in existence for two years. Starting as a design company offering graphic services to industry generally, the partners (we'll call them Mr Brown and Mr Green) soon found themselves having to organise clients' exhibitions and purchase display systems on their behalf.

In 1986, they decided they could make equally good display systems at a much lower cost than those available and so began manufacturing them. Mr Brown then spent most of his time selling the new product, while Mr Green concentrated on its manufacture.

By the spring of 1988, sales of the new product had grown to the point where the partners could no longer cope with its manufacture by themselves, on top of the continuing graphics, design and mounting work they still undertook for clients. They decided to take on two people to help manufacture the systems while Mr Green concentrated on the specialist work and Mr Brown continued to sell. Within two months, they needed a third worker to enable them to keep up with the growing volume of orders for their increasingly popular product. They also rented additional office accommodation for use as a drawing and sales office and took on a full-time sales assistant/clerk.

In the autumn of 1987, however, XYZ realised that they were getting into trouble. They had a major cash flow problem, due not to lack of business, but quite the reverse. This arose because:

(a) the increasing volume of business meant increased purchases of raw materials;

(b) the increased number of customers meant more credit was being extended and money was slow in coming in;

(c) to cope with the ever-increasing flow of orders necessary to generate revenue to cover increased costs, more staff were necessary; and,

(d) they had increased their fixed costs due to the need for extra accommodation.

At this point their bank began to complain about their overdraft and insisted that they take immediate steps to reduce it.

XYZ were very successful — they had excellent products and a good reputation, they were receiving increasing orders for their systems, graphics and other display materials and they had a large number of orders in hand and invoices awaiting payment. So what had gone wrong? What steps should they have taken to rectify their problem?

XYZ's fundamental problems were that:

(a) they didn't really know how much each product or service cost them to produce;
(b) they were pursuing volume in the belief that this would produce the necessary cash flow; and,
(c) they were not keeping a tight enough rein on customers' payments.

Their remedy was two-fold:

(a) short term; and,
(b) medium term.

In the short term, they chased up all overdue accounts, which they had hitherto been reluctant to do in case they offended customers. In fact, when approached sensibly, with an explanation of *why* XYZ needed settlement by the due date, most customers were accommodating and understood the company's problem.

In the medium term, they carefully costed out all their products and services to discover:

(a) which were the most and least profitable;
(b) whether it was possible to drop the least profitable without upsetting customers or creating a situation in which customers would go elsewhere for all their needs; and
(c) they questioned whether they needed to sell as much volume per month in order to exist, that is the most profitable level of sales at which XYZ could operate (to find this optimum level, they created break-even graphs, each representing different levels of sales).

Conclusion

As a result of this analysis, XYZ decided that their optimum level was when they sold *x* numbers of systems per month, that figure being only two-thirds of the level for which they had been striving. At that level of sales, the cash flow generated was sufficient to cover all costs, fixed and variable, and did not over-extend the company in either debts for supplies it bought or excessive credit given to customers.

By recognising the optimum sales level, XYZ were able to plan their sales more effectively and concentrate efforts on those customers, or potential customers, that would offer the best return and the best possibility of repeat business (which would be at a reduced selling cost).

They identified graphics and design as being much less profitable than manufacturing the range of systems and decided that, in future, they would offer graphics and design as a service only to customers who either bought their systems or might do so as a result of providing this service to them. This last decision enabled them to get rid of office accommodation that was not being economically utilised.

Case study 2: the correct selling approach

Malvern Animal Feeds began as a shop retailing horse feed and pet foods in the West Country. During the bitter winter of 1981–2, a sudden cold spell caught out many horse owners as well as professional stables, who found that their feed supplies were short. Malvern had contacts with local farmers and was able to buy-in raw materials, such as grains, as well as the various mixers, to enable them to begin producing their own horse feeds. The acute shortages in supply at that time meant that they were very successful.

As a result, Malvern decided to go into the full-time manufacture of horse, and then other, animal feeds. They rented extensive accommodation on a farm and acquired second-hand milling and mixing machinery. Before long, they were producing several different kinds of horse feed, including specialist types for racing horses, as well as other pet foods.

For the first year, business was very good: the new brand was well-presented, competitively priced and many people who had been grateful to Malvern during the shortages proved to be loyal to the new brands. The company expanded, took on several salespeople and started selling regularly through local pet shops. As business grew, they added more product lines and ventured into selling to stables, kennels and so on.

Heartened by the response, Malvern expanded production further and took on more staff. However, the profitability of animal feeds that had occurred during the shortages of 1981–2 had also attracted other firms into making such products and this, in turn, was putting pressure on the long-established 'big names' in the market. These big companies had begun to feel the effects of so many small manufacturers and started to hit back with large discounts for quantity, special services and advice and long-term credit. In the face of such strong competition, many of the small producers went out of business. Malvern responded by taking on the big firms: they offered discounts and allowed credit to be extended. It wasn't long before they, too, began to feel the pinch and found themselves with an acute cash flow problem.

Their response to this situation was to lower their costs, which they did by reducing the quality of their feeds. This was achieved by increasing the percentage of cheaper grains, such as wheat, in the feeds and reducing the content of other ingredients, like molasses. The result was much cheaper feeds, but of considerably lower quality. Customers were not advised of the changes and soon began to complain about the standard of the products. As they began to lose ground in the horse feed market, Malvern switched their efforts to pet foods, such as dog and rabbit food. That market was dominated by major national producers, however, and competition was again so keen that profits were low.

Next, Malvern recognised their long connection with farming and began to produce sheep and cattle feeds. Thorough marketing and product research was carried out and, within a few months, the company was manufacturing several kinds of these foods. Then they encountered further problems:

(a) farmers were not impressed by salespeople they perceived as lacking farming experience;

(b) selling to farmers required quite a different approach than that used for previous customers — an ability to converse widely on farming topics to gain farmers' confidence, for example;

(c) farmers bought in bulk and often wanted long credit terms while their animals matured; and

(d) because of the nature of selling to farmers and the relative isolation of farms compared to business premises, the number of calls per day and week fell sharply, increasing selling costs.

The result of this new venture was disastrous. How should Malvern have responded to the combination of market and competitive pressures?

It should have recognised that the rapid increase in demand for horse and other animal feeds during 1981–2 was abnormal and artificially created by the unusually severe weather — that the market was therefore unnaturally inflated.

The rise in animal feeds prices during that winter meant that many people who kept horses for pleasure found the costs of keeping them rising too acutely and many sold their horses, thereby reducing demand for feeds.

It was inevitable that the big firms, which dominated the market, would respond by offering better prices and incentives to the markets, which generally lowered profits in the short term and removed many smaller firms from competition.

Malvern could not compete price-wise with these firms and would have been better advised to concentrate on small, specialised segments of the market, e.g. high-quality horse racing feeds and/or quality pet foods.

It should have recognised that the farming market was by far the most competitive of all, demanding:

(a) a highly specialised sales force with intensive training in farming and agricultural selling;
(b) an ability to offer longer credit and, therefore, the financial reserves to carry such credit;
(c) an ability to carry the much higher sales costs resulting from the reduced number of calls a representative could make during each day.

Conclusion

Although this case study is about selling animal and pet feeds, the underlying problems are common to any competitive market situation. A firm operating in such conditions must recognise its own strengths and weaknesses and plan accordingly. It is rarely a good idea to take on big companies on their own terms because, whether a firm makes animal feeds, groceries or machinery, there will be specialised segments of the larger market in which it can operate more successfully. This may be because that segment will demand modifications or special products that the larger firms can't or won't produce, because it will stand a higher price or because it will expect longer delivery periods or more specialised advice, all calling for a skilled sales force that larger firms cannot justify.

Index